Just the Usual Work

Just the Usual Work

The Social Worlds of Ida Martin,
Working-Class Diarist

Michael Boudreau
and
Bonnie Huskins

McGill-Queen's University Press
Montreal & Kingston • London • Chicago

ISBN 978-0-2280-0548-3 (cloth)
ISBN 978-0-2280-0549-0 (paper)
ISBN 978-0-2280-0691-6 (ePDF)
ISBN 978-0-2280-0692-3 (ePUB)

Legal deposit first quarter 2021
Bibliothèque nationale du Québec

Printed in Canada on acid-free paper that is 100% ancient forest
free (100% post-consumer recycled), processed chlorine free

This book has been published with the help of grants from
St Thomas University and the University of New Brunswick.

We acknowledge the support of the Canada Council for the Arts.

Nous remercions le Conseil des arts du Canada de son soutien.

Library and Archives Canada Cataloguing in Publication

Title: Just the usual work : the social worlds of Ida Martin,
    working-class diarist / Michael Boudreau and Bonnie Huskins.
Names: Boudreau, Michael, 1967- author. | Huskins, Bonnie, 1963-
    author. | Container of (work): Martin, Ida, 1907-2004. Diaries.
    Selections.
Description: Includes bibliographical references and index.
Identifiers: Canadiana (print) 20200361538 | Canadiana (ebook)
    20200366351 | ISBN 9780228005483 (cloth) | ISBN 9780228005490
    (paper) | ISBN 9780228006916 (ePDF) | ISBN 9780228006923
    (ePUB)
Subjects: LCSH: Martin, Ida, 1907-2004—Diaries. | LCSH: Working
    class women—New Brunswick—Saint John—Diaries. | LCSH:
    Housewives—New Brunswick—Saint John—Diaries. | LCSH:
    Diarists—New Brunswick—Saint John—Diaries. | LCSH:
    Saint John (N.B.)—Biography. | LCSH: Saint John (N.B.)—
    Social conditions—20th century.
Classification: LCC FC2497.26.M37 B68 2021 | DDC 971.5/32—dc23

This book was designed and typeset by studio oneonone
in 11/14 Minion

To Ida, AR, and Barbara

Contents

Figures

Acknowledgments

To say that this book has been a "labour of love" for us is indeed an understatement. In some ways the completion of this book is a sad occasion as it marks a formal end to our very close interaction with Ida Martin's diaries. But it is also a joyous occasion, for this book allows us to share Ida Martin's words, thoughts, and social worlds with a wider audience. We can only hope that she would be pleased with the outcome.

Like any labour of love, this book owes a debt of thanks and enduring gratitude to a plethora of family, friends, and colleagues. Barbara and Sterling Huskins have been steadfast advocates of this project for years. Their love and support have been immeasurable. Catherine Gidney read the manuscript and provided much-needed insight into the world of diaries. We are indebted to the two anonymous readers whose careful and incisive reading of the manuscript pushed us to clarify our arguments and sharpen the book's focus. Greg Marquis, Harold Wright, and David Goss lent us their encyclopedic knowledge of the history of Saint John. And thanks are also due to Harold for allowing us to use two images from his vast collection in the book. We also wish to thank Brunswick News, the Provincial Archives of New Brunswick, and Leah Grandy at the University of New Brunswick Libraries (UNB) for permitting us to use several images. Our sincere thanks as well to *Acadiensis* and *Labour/Le Travail* for granting us permission to reproduce previously published work in this book. The staff at the Provincial Archives of New Brunswick, the New Brunswick Museum, the UNB Libraries, especially Archives and Special Collections, and the Frank and Ella Hatheway Labour Exhibit Centre in Saint John, were extremely helpful in many facets of the research for this book.

Special thanks are due to McGill-Queen's University Press, in particular Kyla Madden our acquisitions editor, whose support for this project has been unwavering and heartfelt. Indeed, Kyla suggested the photo that graces the book's cover. This book would not have been published without her commitment to us and to Ida's diaries. Managing editor Kathleen Fraser answered our countless questions about formatting and editing with aplomb and worked closely with us on the design of the book. And copy editor James Leahy had a keen eye for detail. We are also extremely grateful to Susan Parker for compiling the index.

We wish to thank St Thomas University for providing funding for this project, notably the Office of Research Services and the Senate Research Committee, and a bevy of colleagues who have supported us and this project, notably Michael Dawson, Jane Jenkins, Jean Sauvageau, Peter Toner, and Tony Tremblay.

At the University of New Brunswick thanks are due to the Department of History, Elizabeth Mancke (CRC in Atlantic Canada Studies) and UNB's Atlantic Canada Studies Centre, and the office of the Vice-President (Academic) for helping to fund this project. Friends and colleagues at UNB also deserve our gratitude, especially Wendy Churchill, Margaret Conrad, Gwen Davies, Heidi MacDonald, Erin Morton, Sasha Mullally, Janet Mullin, and Gary Waite.

This book is dedicated to Ida Martin, her husband AR, and their daughter Barbara, whose photo adorns the cover. While Ida Martin and her diaries are the focus of this book, and deservedly so, family was tremendously and passionately important to Ida; it was at the centre of her social worlds, so we would have been remiss not to have made them a part of our dedication. Nevertheless, as we recount in the pages that follow, Ida Martin was, and remains, an (extra)ordinary person.

Just the Usual Work

Introduction

Ida Martin, Her Diaries, and Diary Conventions

Ida Louise Martin (1907–2004) was a working-class housewife who spent most of her adult life in postwar Saint John, New Brunswick. When she died, she left behind an assortment of personal artifacts, all of which provide a window into her life and legacy. One of the most well-used items, still in the possession of the authors, is a treadmill sewing machine, on which she mended her family's clothes and sewed for a local dry cleaner to contribute to the family economy. There is also a tin of recipe cards, which, as folklorist Diane Tye has shown in *Baking as Biography*, can be used to demonstrate the interplay between production and consumption in the postwar era.[1] A modest yet well-polished dining room table hosted many dinners and parties, a reminder of the importance of domestic sociability. Moreover, a wallet containing a social insurance card, Medicare, Old Age Security card, New Brunswick Prescription Drug Program card, and an International Longshoremen's Association (ILA) benefits card, reveals the centrality of unions and the welfare state for many working-class families. But most fascinating, and the foundation of this book, are the ten commercially produced five-year diaries which Ida Martin kept faithfully from 1945 to 1992.

These diaries were lovingly bequeathed to Bonnie Huskins, Ida Martin's maternal granddaughter. Ida did so in recognition of Bonnie's love of history and because of the close bond that she had with Bonnie.[2] It is through a careful and critical reading of these diaries, supplemented by archival documents and secondary sources, that this study will highlight the life of a female diarist, the family economy, working-class masculinity and sociability, and widowhood and aging, along with the social history of post-1945 Saint John. In so doing, we enhance the understanding of these key elements of

Figure i.1
A five-year diary

mid- to late twentieth-century Canadian history and deepen our knowledge of Saint John's rich history. Moreover, we hope to reinforce the importance of diaries, especially those written in the post–Second World War era, as valuable sources for unearthing the history of daily life and thereby encourage more scholars to utilize diaries to illustrate the "various venues of everyday life."[3]

Ida Martin's diaries are significant because they were penned by a working-class woman and cover the postwar period. According to Canadian social historian Bettina Bradbury, "few working-class women … appear to have kept diaries and few letters or other writing by such women have been preserved in archives."[4] Most of the working-class autobiographies still in existence were written by male labour organizers and activists. Female members of the working class have often lacked access to male organizational culture, and thus have not possessed the resources or "self-confidence" to pen their own life accounts.[5] If they did, it was usually in the form of unpublished informal diaries such as Ida's, rather than formal and published memoirs. Moreover, societal expectations dictated that women could write as long as they had "no ambition to make the contents public."[6]

Ida's diaries are also a rich lens into the nature of post–Second World War society, including insights into the construction of gender identities, informal family economies, religious and social life, and the process of aging. Most manuscript diaries and published diary collections in Canada date from the eighteenth and nineteenth centuries. Moreover, while similar studies on working-class culture and society focus on Ontario, this work is important because it illustrates the dynamics of working-class life in postwar Saint John. These dynamics include the persistence of the informal economy to the survival of many working-class households, the limited effects of modernity notably on consumerism and the social and economic lives of working-class residents of Saint John, the existence of nineteenth-century forms of working-class masculinity, the importance of religious faith and communication technology to social and political engagement, and ways of coping with and adjusting to aging and widowhood. All of this speaks to a central theme of this book, namely the tensions and interplay that existed between change and continuity, or the past and the present, in the postwar era.

This book joins a handful of other diary-based works that have been published in recent years. Many of these publications take the form of annotated diaries such as *Hector Maclean: The Writings of a Loyalist Era Military Settler*;

A Calendar of Life in a Narrow Valley: Jacobina Campbell's Diary, Taymouth, New Brunswick, 1825–1843; or *More of a Man: Diaries of a Scottish Craftsman in Mid-Nineteenth-Century North America.*[7] Other works are conventional monographs that use diaries and personal writings as primary sources, such as Gail G. Campbell's *'I wish to keep a record': Nineteenth-Century New Brunswick Women Diarists and Their World*; Joanne Findon's *Seeking Eden: The Dreams and Migrations of Sarah Jameson Craig*; and Robert M. Mennell's *Testimonies and Secrets: The Story of a Nova Scotia Family, 1844–1977.*[8] This study differs from these key works by taking the form of a series of critical essays based on the authors' interrogation of the diaries.

In her seminal work on religion, leisure, and identity in late nineteenth-century rural Ontario, Lynne Marks admonished researchers to "integrate fully the study of politics, work, religion, leisure, and home life."[9] This book is an attempt to accomplish this ambitious goal, however modestly, by exploring Ida Martin's social worlds through her diaries. These worlds included the daily rhythms of work and home life, her faith, her engagement with politics, and her limited leisure pursuits, all in the context of postwar Saint John. In so doing, this book will contribute to the rich literature of post-1945 Canada by providing a nuanced analysis of working-class life as articulated by Ida Martin. The popular historical understanding of postwar Canada has tended to focus on major socio-economic and cultural transformations that accompanied modernity, including the emergence of Cold War values, postwar prosperity, industrial production, mass consumer culture and enhanced consumption, suburbanization, the consolidation of the federal welfare state, secularization, and a return to "normal" heterosexual and patriarchal gender relations. And while these topics and themes have revealed a great deal about modern Canada, a deeper understanding is needed of how people like Ida Martin experienced, and helped to shape and eschew, the social and cultural changes of this era.

The Diarist: Ida Louise Martin (née Friars)

Like many of the female diarists uncovered by Margaret Conrad and others as part of the Maritime Women's Archives Project, Ida Martin's descendants settled in the Saint John River Valley in New Brunswick.[10] The Friars lineage, to which Ida belongs, originated from Poughkeepsie, New York; according to a Friars family genealogy, Simeon Peter Friars left New York during the

American Revolution (allegedly because he had deserted the patriot army and blew up one of their powder houses) to settle in Ward's Creek, near Sussex, where he is often referred to as "the pioneer settler of Ward's Creek."[11] Ida Louise Friars was the seventh of ten children born to Simon Peter Friars and Louisa Maud Lockhart, the sixth generation of this branch of the Friars clan. She was born on 18 July 1907 at McGregor Brook, a few miles north of Sussex.[12] Ida Friars married Allan Robert Martin (or AR as he is known in the diaries and throughout this book) on 12 November 1932, and in February 1936 Barbara, their only child, was born.[13] When Barbara was four years old they moved from Westfield, New Brunswick, to Saint John, where they resided for much of their lives.[14]

Four words embody Ida's world in postwar Saint John: home, family, work, and faith. Ida lived most of her married life in a two-storey house at 213 Queen Street on the west side of the city. She and AR took considerable pride in home ownership, evident in the fact that they spent a great deal of time fixing up the house. The top flat, where they lived, was also the site of hospitality and sociability. Ida hosted many social gatherings over the years, but her favourite activity was to sit at the kitchen table with friends and family (and even strangers) and enjoy a cup of Kingcole tea.

Family members were frequent visitors at 213 Queen Street. Ida's daughter Barbara, son-in-law Sterling, and grandchildren Bonnie and Allan lived for several years in the downstairs flat and they viewed the upstairs as an extension of their home. Since Ida came from a large family, extended family members often visited. In Ida's declining years her nieces, the "Friars girls," reciprocated these acts of hospitality by visiting Ida wherever she was living after she left 213 Queen Street. As Heather Seely, one of her nieces, wrote in a guest book for Ida's 96th birthday on 18 July 2003: "Ida, you're such a sweetheart and we all love you very much. Thanks for all the laughs and wonderful songs over the years."[15]

From Ida's family we also receive a sense of her personality. As suggested by Heather Seely's reference to "all the laughs … over the years," Ida was described by her extended family as being cheerful and helpful to others. Her brother Garfield wrote the following verses about Ida in 1929:

It is your most unselfish life
Which brings us here tonight
We love you for your sunny smile

Figure i.2
Ida Martin

For heart so true and bright
We love you for your youth so gay
For wit so real and funny
And all the best we love in you
Cannot be bought with money[16]

Even after the passing of her "youth so gay," Ida never lost her exuberant disposition. Following a visit with Ida in 1999 when she was 92 years of age, friends remarked in her guest book: "Nice visit. Always so cheerful."[17]

Another important component of Ida's world was hard work. Although her dream of becoming a nurse never materialized, she transferred her caretaking skills to her immediate family, caring for her mother and father in illness and old age, as well as her siblings and extended family members. When necessary, Ida worked outside of the home to supplement the family's income. Most of the labour chronicled in her diaries, however, consisted of "just the usual work" – the continuous domestic activities required to keep a working-class household afloat.

Ida's faith was very important to her and to her self-identity. Shortly after arriving in Saint John, she began attending Charlotte Street Baptist Church and then, after it amalgamated with two other churches, Hillcrest United Baptist Church. Ida was actively involved in both congregations, teaching Sunday school, singing in the choir, and serving as a member of the United Baptist Women's Missionary Society. She tried to live her life according to the tenets of her faith, something that did not go unnoticed by the members of her faith community. As Dr Darrell C. Pond, senior pastor at Hillcrest wrote to Ida in a letter dated 11 February 1986, "Ida … thank you for the witness that you are. Your disposition is so Christ-like and you are a real blessing and encouragement to so many people and you need to know that."[18]

Diaries are rich historical sources and windows into the lives of the diarist. Keeping a diary, as Neil Sutherland has aptly noted, is akin to writing an autobiography, a way to "justify themselves [the diarist] to themselves."[19] Our analysis is in part indebted to the insights of historian Gail G. Campbell in her recent analysis of nineteenth-century New Brunswick women's diaries. According to Campbell, literary scholars were among the first to provide nuanced analyses of women's diaries, and historians have drawn a great deal from their insights into diaries' structure and style. However, historians have a different teleology than literary scholars and often ask fundamentally different questions of their sources. While the former analyzes diaries' contributions to various literary genres, historians are more interested in "what the diary reveals about the experiences of people in past times."[20] We agree with Campbell, and throughout this book we utilize Ida Martin's daily diary entries to illuminate the nature of working-class life and society in postwar Saint John. However, we also wish to stress Campbell's first point that historians have much to gain from borrowing from other disciplines, especially literary approaches to reading diaries. We argue that, despite the work of Campbell and others, most historians use diaries superficially to "verify" or "authenticate" historical events.[21] This approach tends to give short shrift to diaries, for we cannot effectively mine these sources unless we understand their form and function. With this in mind, we will examine the style and structure of Ida Martin's account book diaries, viewing them as texts and artifacts.[22]

Why Ida Martin Kept a Diary

Ida Martin began her diary-writing odyssey on 10 August 1945, thirteen years into her marriage. Why did she begin writing in her diary at this point? She may have received a diary book for her birthday on 19 July 1945. And/or her writing odyssey may have begun as a travel diary, as she left for Boston on 10 August to visit her sister, which are the first entries in the book. In any case, once Ida began her diaries, she kept them faithfully for an exceptionally long run of forty-seven years. Of the more than 500 Canadian women's diaries annotated by Kathryn Carter in 1997, only 34 span forty years or more, and only six were written by women from the Maritimes. In a similar compilation of 55 diaries and reminiscences written by New Brunswick women, Joanne Ritchie found only three diaries that covered forty years or more.[23] Martin's diary run is comparable to that of nineteenth-century social critic Sarah Jameson Craig, who grew up in New Brunswick, and kept diaries for forty-one years. Her run was not continuous, however, as she recorded entries from 1865 to 1889 but not again until 1902–19.[24] And one must not forget the prolific Lucy Maud Montgomery, of *Anne of Green Gables* fame, who kept journals for over fifty years.[25] Gail G. Campbell, in *"I wish to keep a record,"* analyzes the diaries of twenty-eight women who lived in New Brunswick. Although the span of the diary excerpts vary, collectively they cover the period from 1825 to 1906.[26]

Ida Martin did not personally articulate why her diaries became a key part of her daily life for such a long period of time. When asked this question by an interviewer from the local press, she responded "[I] simply had to write in [them] every day."[27] Like L.M. Montgomery, diary writing had become a compulsion for Ida.[28] There have been many conventions of diary writing over the centuries. In the 1500s, the literate classes used journals to reflect on public events and travels.[29] Seventeenth-century Puritans and other sectarians kept introspective accounts of their conversion experiences and spiritual growth.[30] Before the mid-nineteenth century, more men than women kept diaries, and some were published.[31] The woman writer of the eighteenth and early nineteenth centuries was governed by the societal expectation that she was to "be a family historian rather than to write subjectively of the self."[32] But as the symbolic distinction between public and private grew in the late nineteenth century, the diary became "newly private in name" as a literary manifestation of the authenticity and romanticized purity of the private sphere. As the gatekeepers of middle-class domesticity, women took ownership of the diary-writing tradition. Personal diaries had essentially become a literary manifestation of middle-class domesticity and respectability.[33] Over the course of the twentieth century, a more introspective format – the journal – emerged due, in part, to the effect of Romanticism, the Industrial Revolution, the growth of individualism, and developments in the field of psychology.[34]

Ida's diaries were closer to the conventions of eighteenth- and nineteenth-century work diaries, which combined the traditions of the account book, the daybook, the almanac, and the commercial diary; they were essentially terse accounts of the daily rhythms of work, family, and community.[35] Ida's diaries were written primarily for her immediate family, who often consulted the diaries as a window into the family's past. This was similar to Prince Edward Island diarist Mary Catherine Redmond, who kept entries of "everyday events ... and was the definitive source of information on a range of topics."[36] Although Ida's corpus was not officially a spiritual chronicle, it is probable that her record of daily work was an expression of her Christian faith. Like fellow Baptist Kay Chetley of Welland, Ontario, Ida undoubtedly wanted to ensure that the "grind of ... daily work" contributed "to some greater purpose or end."[37] Ida used her diaries to record daily work patterns, social occasions, family affairs, and later local, provincial, and national events. Some literary scholars have dismissed such diaries as aesthetically unappealing,[38] but as historians, we must embrace these often pedestrian and repetitive diaries, which reveal much about the lives of the women who wrote them. In that sense, this book contributes to the "history of the everyday," which champions the study of ordinary people and everyday rhythms.[39] It also illuminates the process of what Danielle Fuller has described as "writing the everyday."[40]

Personal Diaries

Authors have been drawn to personal diaries because of their flexibility and elasticity; they can "stretch" to meet a multiplicity of needs.[41] Diaries can be kept regularly or irregularly, for long or short periods, and can be written on any surface from a commercial diary to the back of an envelope.[42] Indeed, L.M. Montgomery used to write her initial thoughts on various scraps of paper, which were subsequently recopied into a more formal ledger.[43] Diarists had many different motivations for keeping diaries. According to Margo Culley, diaries make time "meaningful," while Harriet Blodgett suggests that they "arrest" time, albeit temporarily.[44] Diaries could also be a way for diarists to "sort out their lives" while giving their lives "purpose and direction" and helping them to deal with hardships and transitions such as poverty, old age, and widowhood.[45] Other writers use daily diaries to chart personal and intellectual growth.[46] Molly Lamb Boback's illustrated wartime diary about the experiences of Canadian servicewomen has been described as a form of "social commentary."[47] For Montgomery, journalling had multiple cathartic functions: "Keeping a diary had been a compulsion, a way to access the sheer pleasure of writing, a workshop for experiments in description, a means to escape from intolerable realities, a place to 'consume the smoke' of her furies, a way to record her triumphs without exposing the pride she had been taught to consider a sin."[48]

A prominent theme in literary studies is how diaries operate as a medium of self-construction. As one scholar has put it, "we create ourselves in the very process of writing about ourselves and our lives."[49] Post-structuralists posit that diarists create mutable and multiple selves: "a private first-person narrative is a particularly apt ideological grid for recording a subject held in perpetual conflict with itself, requiring regular revision and self-regulation."[50] Painter Ivy Jacquier's diary helped her to understand the "fluctuations of self. One never is, one has been or is becoming." As Virginia Woolf commented while reviewing her journals: "How queer to have so many selves."[51]

Many of the diaries that have been analyzed by researchers are from the nineteenth century, which was the "golden age" of diary writing.[52] In this era, middle-class women put pen to paper. The personal diary was considered an appropriate outlet for them as long as manuscripts remained unpublished and did not contribute in any way to the business of making a living.[53] In this format, personal diaries became a textual manifestation of middle-class domesticity and respectability.[54] Although both men and women kept diaries, women's texts are valuable in the sense that they provide a "particular female eye through which events are viewed and which suggests that women's position in society, their roles and their values ... give them a unique angle of vision."[55] Anthropologists Shirley and Edwin

Ardener assert, as part of muted group theory, that the dominant groups in any society determine the main forms of communication. Women, by virtue of their exclusion from power, have been forced to adopt alternative modes of communication. Thus, women turned to diaries "to validate themselves within a culture that trivialized their lives and their writing."[56] Margaret Conrad describes female diary writing as "women talking to themselves, a regular pastime in a male-dominated world where women are marginal to the discourse."[57] Moreover, Margaret Turner views the very act of female penmanship as transgressive, a form of "self-promotion" and "empowerment."[58] Indeed, by virtue of keeping a diary, women could "write themselves into existence."[59]

Literary scholars and historians have recently gravitated to a genre of women's private writing call the *journal intime*, which emerged in France in the early nineteenth century and focused exclusively on the projection of self.[60] Ida Martin's diaries do not emerge from this tradition. Although Ida's diaries may well have contributed to self-construction, they were not explicitly focused on the self; rather, her texts were ultimately written about and for her family. In that sense, she followed the same societal expectation as many Victorians; she was to "be a family historian rather than to write subjectively of the self."[61] Ida Martin's diaries are terse, yet illuminating, accounts of the daily rhythms of work, family, and community. As Joanne E. Cooper suggests, daily diary entries are "raw data" for uncovering the social lives of women and their milieu. They are closest in genre to account book diaries, a journal format that combines the traditions of ships' logs, daybooks, commonplace books, and almanacs.[62]

Account Book Diaries

Ida Martin's account book diaries consist of ten commercially produced five-year volumes. They are pre-dated with one day per page, but by providing four lines for each entry, the publishers were able to accommodate five years of a particular day onto one page. Without a doubt, Ida Martin was a dedicated diarist. Kathryn Carter argues that the account book diary's rigid temporal structure has its roots in the standardization of time in the nineteenth century, which met the needs of a more technologically driven society: "in their structures [one sees] a more atomized and standardized understanding … of the hours and moments that constitute a life." In other words, account book diaries not only reveal details about family and historical events, but the writer's "experience of time."[63]

Ida's diaries embody a complex sense of time. She records developments of kin and community in a chronological fashion, but the entries also "double back on themselves" by documenting the recurrence of family anniversaries, birthdays, and other commemorative events.[64] Pages were set aside in many women's diaries for recording birthdays, anniversaries, and "Important Events." The foreword section of one of Ida's diaries from the 1940s recommends that the diarist use the pages in the back of the book to "list the friends with whom you exchange Christmas greeting cards."[65] It was obviously assumed by the publisher that the female diarist was the keeper of family tradition.

Account book diaries are usually discussed as a genre that met the need of writers in nineteenth-century rural society. According to Catharine Anne Wilson, such brief and abrupt daily accounts reflect the rhythms of farm life, whereas urban diaries tended to be more private, "artful," and introspective.[66] However, Ida lived in an urban environment when she began her account book diaries. Perhaps she adopted this format because she had rural roots and had grown up on farms in New Brunswick. It may also illustrate the fluidity of the rural–urban interface in the province. The Martins moved back and forth between urban and rural society quite frequently. Moreover, these diaries may be a product of class. The patterns and demands of working-class life – casualism, seasonality, and economic uncertainty – were somewhat akin to those of rural society.

Ida's entries also underscore the fact that account book diaries are not confined to the nineteenth century. Perhaps the longevity of this format illustrates the survival of a nineteenth-century preoccupation with ensuring productivity. Carter argues that the account book diary provided a "useful container in which to enumerate productive moments."[67] This need to account for time well spent may have a religious imperative. For evangelical Protestants like Ida, keeping a diary was akin to prayer or reading scripture – a form of "spiritual discipline." It enabled the writer to show themselves and their God that they were not wasting time.[68] This informs what it meant to "keep" a diary: to "preserve it in good order and to be faithful and regular in making entries."[69] Wilson suggests that lapsed entries had the power to effectively "shame" authors to take action.[70]

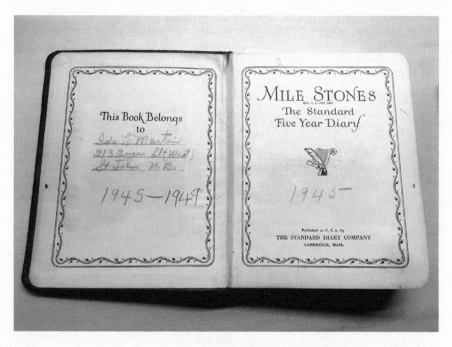

Figure i.3
Ida Martin's Diary, 1945–1949

The survival of the account book diary into the twentieth century may also be a product of the continuity of nineteenth-century patterns of work, family, and community, which were integral to the creation of account book diaries as a genre. Account book diaries embody the reality of working-class life in postwar Saint John; one had to engage in continuous hard work just to get by, as we will see in chapter 1. Whereas literary scholars once deemed such sources to be uninteresting due to their mundanity, as historians we realize that the value of account book diaries rests in their "tediously pedestrian, repetitive, and detailed" structure, which reflected the lives of the women who kept them.[71] Perhaps that is why Ida stuck with the five-year format: not only did she find comfort in the familiar and "visual pleasure" in a "uniform series,"[72] but they met her needs and mirrored her daily reality.

One can glean a sense of Ida's daily work patterns and staccato writing style in the following excerpt from her 1946 diary:

April 30: Mailed Income Tax today. I made sand[wiches] for our class meeting at Cora's.

May 1: Washed & ironed and just the usual work.

May 2: Cleaning all this am. I'm at Becks all afternoon. We went to prayer meet[ing] tonight. I went up to the Henderson's after.

May 3: Just the usual work. I hemmed Barb's new choir gown.

May 4: At Becks all day. Barb went to a party at Murphys. I did the Sat work in evening.

May 5: Worked at Becks all day.

May 6: Church and S[unday] S[chool]. Communion tonight, Mills & Verna for supper.

This minimalist writing style has been called "intensive writing," where each word carries a "large burden of information."[73] Martin describes her domestic routine as "just the usual work." Similar expressions include "cleaned all through," "worked around all day," was "busy as a bee," or worked "right out straight." These phrases are admittedly not complex; they are ordinary "because life itself was often ordinary."[74] While it is tempting to dismiss such entries as generic, or as concessions to minimalism, they often carry specific connotations with more historical context. Since at least the nineteenth century, housework has been performed according to a daily, weekly, and seasonal schedule. Some routines were daily affairs: rinsing out underwear, ironing, cooking, washing dishes, and tidying up. There was also seasonal work, such as spring cleaning, when the family would clean throughout the house, tar the roof, and take off the storm windows.

Because Ida's diaries were commercially produced, they sometimes included published pages containing verses and other "cultural directives."[75] The foreword of Ida's 1945–49 diary implies that it was meant to be used by women to record their traditional *rites de passage*:

What an easy thing to write
Just a few lines every night
Tell about the fun you had
And how your sweetheart made you glad.
Write about the party gay
In the sail-boat down the bay

The motor-trip, that perfect dance
The week-end at the country manse.
Courtship – then the wedding time
Honeymoon in southern clime
 Home again in circles gay
Till 'Little Stranger' came your way.
So day by day the story grows
As onward your life-journey goes
Lights and shadows – memories dear
These are MILE STONES of your career.[76]

Ida's life trajectory followed some of these milestones: courtship, marriage, the arrival of a "little Stranger." However, these verses were obviously designed for a middle-class audience. Ida did not use her diaries to ruminate on the "party gay," sailboats, or country manses. While she did have some modest leisure pursuits, Ida's diaries were primarily accounts of hard work. And as we will see in chapter 4, her "sweetheart" did not always make her "glad." In some ways Ida resembled female diarists in the Victorian era who often disregarded the publisher's directives and "tailored" their diaries to their own needs, thereby "imposing themselves" on the source.[77]

Self-Censorship in Diary Writing

A diary's format influenced authorial content. It is probable that diarists like Ida censored their entries to fit the space provided. The "tightly determined spatial format" of the account book diary controlled the diarist's "self-expression," for it linked "account-keeping with personal reflection."[78] On 31 December 1975, Ida wrote a longer entry than usual since there was additional space at the back, suggesting that she would have elaborated more often if she had been given more room. Ida, like many other diarists, found ways to stretch their entries. They often used the front and back pages for financial accounts and additional information. Ida also engaged in cross-hatching, a common practice in nineteenth-century diaries, wherein one turns the paper 90 degrees and writes over previous passages.[79] Ida also used intratextualities, or exchanges between different elements of the text used to create continuity between entries.[80] For example, Ida kept track of the

Springhill, Nova Scotia, mine disaster of 1956 in the upper margins of her diary from 3 to 5 November, which allowed her to trace the explosion and rescue efforts without the need to search for the information.

How did diarists like Ida decide "what to report and what to leave out?"[81] The spatial elements of the diary obviously played a role, but so too did the author's world view. According to Martin Hewitt, self-censorship was a normal part of diary writing for women and men.[82] Female diarists, for instance, have been loath to report on "sensitive issues" related to sexuality and family scandal.[83] Montgomery's journals do not "reveal how she really saw herself in times of deep introspection and [do] not trace any traits which cast her in a truly bad light. To delve into these areas would demand a measure of self-exposure that she was either unwilling or unable to undergo … She constructed herself as she wanted to be remembered."[84] When Ida's brother and his wife separated, she writes that another sibling "met me outside church with bad news of F and R."[85] Anyone familiar with the family would have known their identities, but Ida nevertheless felt the need to use discretion. She also wrote of conversations with them and efforts to help the family, but few specific details of the break-up are given. Here self-censorship served to underscore, if not protect, the privacy of the family.

Ida frequently used coded language to refer to indiscretions. As we will see in chapter 2, Ida used the term "bad" to refer to her husband's drinking.[86] Another example of a cryptic literary device was the use of revealing nicknames. She referred to one of her husband's friends as "2 face" because he was duplicitous and often took AR away from his family.[87] The most damning nickname was reserved for her sister-in-law: "Madame Queen." Whenever AR visited his sister, Ida voiced her ambivalence by writing that he was "over yonder" or "over the way."[88] Changes in handwriting reflected this enmity. Whenever Ida referred to "Madame Queen" in the diaries, her handwriting became almost unintelligible. It is almost as if she begrudged her sister-in-law the effort it took to write her name, let alone her nickname.

Ida sometimes relegated emotional diary responses to parentheses. After Christmas in 1962, Ida wrote: "We took Grandma home (a sigh of relief)."[89] After recording a dispute between AR and his sister, Ida added: "(Blamed me I know)."[90] She also referred to other intense emotions in parentheses, such as the "(heated debate)" that accompanied Charlotte Street Baptist Church's decision in 1959 to unite with other local churches.[91] Perhaps this literary technique allowed the author to have the best of both worlds; she could acknowledge that such reactions were inappropriate for inclusion in her daily discourse, while at the same time providing Ida with the opportunity to vent her frustration or disdain, albeit in a more oblique fashion.

There were topics that Ida Martin consciously refused to tackle, such as Allan Legere, a murderer who terrorized the Miramichi region of New Brunswick in the 1980s. She commented in a local newspaper article, "I just thought that was so terrible what he did to those people," but she could not bring herself to record the details.[92] Studying the avoidances, omissions, and silences of diary texts is an integral part of our analysis; as Joanne Ritchie has posited, "we can learn as much from what people don't say as from what they do."[93]

Literary Complexities in Diaries

Account book diaries are often characterized as "simple" sources, focusing on the daily and leaving synthesis and retrospection for more formal auto-biographies.[94] However, account book diaries are more complex than we might think. While Montgomery often ended her journals with a "climactic sweep," even writing "Good Bye" at the end of each volume,[95] Ida brought a sense of closure to her five-year diaries by summarizing events at the back of many of the volumes. These lists "do not privilege 'amazing' over 'ordinary' events in terms of scope, space or selection."[96] They are similar to nineteenth-century farm diaries, which contain a "flow of undifferentiated activities."[97] Perhaps this is a reflection of rural and working-class life, in which big and small events can have a profound effect on life. In any case, these lists acted as intratextual indexes with dates attached, so the reader could look back to find the original record. Like Samuel Bamford's nineteenth-century diary, Ida Martin's volumes were "retrospectively crafted documents."[98]

Another retrospective intratextual device is the narrative structure at the back of the 1981–85 diary, where Ida elaborated on the maladies suffered by her brother Garfield and her husband. Besides compiling the relevant information scattered throughout the volume, she wrote their medical histories in a more literary style than her daily entries: "[Garfield] Operated on Tuesday 21st/81. July 28th GB called. He's ready to come home. Called 15 min[ute]s later & said NO. He couldn't." Moreover, her description of a car accident in which she was involved is also written as a narrative: "July 31st left Long Reach at 8pm for home. AR hit the Guy [*sic*] Wire of ferry floats. We both got hurt.

AR chest and my face. Ambulance took us to Hosp[ital] for Xrays and we come [*sic*] home. Roy was right behind us. So he had car towed to his place."[99] Perhaps because these incidents were so traumatic, Ida thought that they were worthy of a more evocative style of expression. In the words of Rubio and Waterston, diaries and journals are "partly enigma"; some parts are carefully written, while others are a "tumble of unstructured responses to the immediacies of life."[100]

Retrospection in Ida's diaries is also a product of the process of recall and reconstruction. Since Ida mainly wrote her diary entries at night, she had to assemble the day from memory, selecting the appropriate bits to record. It has been argued that memory organizes events and activities into "scripts" that are "situational" (the daily routines and rhythms of life) and "personal" (personal episodes contained within situational scripts). This may be why many of Ida's entries take the form of personal and family experiences of daily events or "episodes."[101] Like many diarists, Ida frequently perused previous entries. The five-year format enabled this, as the reader could easily glance up to see what they had been doing the same day years before. Once Ida re-read three of her diary books at one sitting.[102] The reasons for doing this were undoubtedly varied. Perhaps diarists simply "relished the experience" of reviewing past fragments of their lives. Or maybe it was a form of escapism, a way to "get back the spirit of youthful days." Revisiting previous entries may have also provided comfort or allowed writers to make sense of their lives, to discern "[p]atterns that pointed to [their] destiny."[103]

In the process of re-reading the entries, diarists created "layered documents," editing their works as they re-read them. Indeed, "keeping a diary was a complex re-living/re-reading/re-writing process."[104] Like Montgomery, who razored pages and replaced them, erased entries, wrote over top of them, and in the typescript pinned or sewed bits together, Martin also modified the entries. She pasted over her entries for 23–4 February 1970 with new commentary. There were many times when she would clarify a mix-up between entries with the use of arrows or editorial comments. On 13 October 1967, she crossed out "Gar got Lump off Elbow" and wrote "No he didn't." In the entry for 13 May 1989, she notes "This should of been yesterday Fri OK?"[105]

The reader can also learn much from examining Ida's grammar.[106] Like the early twentieth-century diaries of Amy Darby Tanton Andrew of Prince Edward Island, words are often misspelled, punctuation is irregular, and sentences are fragmented.[107] Some scholars have identified these elements as identifiers of a "women's style" of diary writing. Irregular grammar signifies a lack of education or a life too busy to worry about such things. This "style" may also be characteristic of account book diaries, which did not provide much capacity for elaboration.[108] Regardless, much can be learned from the grammatical choices that diarists made. For example, Ida often used capital case letters for emphasis. She would capitalize to draw attention to transitions in the family economy: "ALLAN STARTED WITH STEPHENS [construction]," "Allan worked 1/2 day & FINISHED AT PORT," "WE PUT ON STORM WINDOWS." She would also emphasize important events, such as "CANADA 100 YRS OLD."[109] Capital letters could also suggest frustration: "I went to town with M. I sat in the car all afternoon. I was SO MAD."[110] Sometimes she used different coloured pens and pencils for emphasis: on 2 December 1981, she wrote in red pencil: "a Red letter Day. Constitution Passed in Commons."[111] Similarly, punctuation could be used to good effect. Inferring that AR was a reckless driver, Ida wrote in her diary: "Allan took fill up to Wardens [in his dump truck]. Barb & I went too (we were plenty scared)????."[112] One can also sense her general frustration on 20 March 1973: "AR layed [*sic*] under house plumbing from 7:30 till 20 to 12. Oh dear what a day! ! ! ! ! I combed Cora's hair, I went to S Sears & Thornes. The car works terrible!!!! I could hardly get home. Stopped 15 times." Ida also used underlining for emphasis: "<u>I'm so tired I layed down and went to sleep</u>," and "<u>Gar back in Hosp.</u>"[113]

It is important to study the handwriting of the diarist as well. As we will see in the last chapter, the most significant shifts in Ida's handwriting occur as she ages, and her writing becomes shaky. This is similar to Montgomery, who experienced great emotional distress over her husband's mental illness and her own depression, and as a result her handwriting was "spiky even shaky and difficult to read"; the "ink also varie[d] in flow, the writing varie[d] dramatically in slant and shape, and words [were] often illegible."[114] Aging and its attendant challenges can also affect the ebb and flow of diary production. Ida wrote regularly, unless she was on vacation (which did not occur very often) or was incapacitated. The longest gap in Ida's diaries occurs between mid-June and mid-August 1986, when she became too ill to write. Her last two diary volumes again resemble Montgomery's final entries. As in Lucy Maud's journal, Ida's short fragmentary entries suggest that she did not have the energy to "write expansively." The concluding entries lacked "any sense of shaping or final summation": there were a "few desultory entries" and then they essentially dried up. On 18 March 1992, at the age of 85,

Ida, like her predecessor, L. M. Montgomery, "simply-or not so simply-broke off her long habit of 'writing up' her life."[115]

Life Writing

One last factor which influences our reading of the diaries is our personal relationship to the diarist: Ida Martin is Bonnie Huskins's maternal grandmother. This project is thus a manifestation of what anthropologist Ruth Behar calls "vulnerable writing," in which one feels more exposed than usual by drawing attention to the personal.[116] Many fields, ranging from law to literature to anthropology, have been governed by "paradigms" that privilege distance, abstraction, and objectivity.[117] Historians, however, have been among the most reticent to incorporate the "I" into their research and writing.

We have decided to manage the personal by adopting feminist praxis, which challenges the "norm of objectivity that assumes that the subject and object of research can be separated from one another and that personal and/or grounded experiences are unscientific."[118] Feminist scholar Helen M. Buss, in her assessment of Rosalind Kerr's reading of her grandmother's letters in the collection *Working in Women's Archives*, argues that such work is often "discouraged by traditional scholarship, which idealizes an 'objectivity' that hides unacknowledged assumptions and biases." Feminist analysis, on the other hand, "allows for the special passion we feel for the archives of those close to us, encourages the full revelation of bias, and highlights the sophistication of the insightful readings that emotional attachment brings by an attention to theorization."[119] In other words, a personal connection to one's historical research is a positive location, for it permits us to replace an indifferent "spectator knowledge" with a more engaged "passionate scholarship."[120] Feminist scholars also point out that "each of us has a certain autobiographical impulse" and that we all have an "ethical responsibility to acknowledge and respect" our multiple locations and our interactions with the source material.[121]

A feminist approach called life writing has been adopted in this book as an organizational framework. It is defined by Marlene Kadar, as a "genre of documents or fragments of documents written out of a life, or unabashedly out of a personal experience of the writer." Life writing thus encompasses the personal writings not only of an author, but also of those individuals with a relationship to the author who engage in "autobiographical acts involved in the collection of oral histories and archival accounts."[122] As such, this framework describes and enables collaboration in two forms: intergenerational and the partnership between the authors of this project.

Ida Martin, as the diarist, is the linchpin of this life writing exercise. In placing the diaries front and centre, we support Martin Hewitt's argument that diaries are a "mode" of life writing. We must recognize, he argues, the "complex cultural, symbolic, and textual operations of the diary, and to place it at the heart of discussions of life writing."[123] But there is also an intergenerational component to this project. Ida's daughter Barbara (Bonnie's mother) intervened directly in the process of Ida's diary writing. When it came time for the selection of memories to record in the diaries, Ida was open to assistance. Barbara recalls that "almost every night Mom would sit at the back of her kitchen table writing away, and sometimes she would let two or three days get ahead of her and she would be asking [others] to help fill in where she was and what she had done to catch up."[124] This reinforces the insightful point made by Susan Engel that "memory never stands alone." The making of memory and the construction of meaning are highly contextual, intersubjective, and contested in terms of objectivity.[125]

We often assume that diaries are intensely private documents, expressions of our innermost thoughts and secrets. We have in our minds a stock image of the diary with padlock and key. However, diaries have traditionally been "semi-public" documents, circulated between friends and family and composed collectively. In the nineteenth century, "[m]others left their journals out for the family to read; sisters co-wrote diaries; fathers jotted notes in their daughters' diaries; female friends exchanged diaries; and men published their diaries."[126] Ida's diaries became a key reference in her family's efforts to reconstruct their collective pasts. The Martin and Huskins households often settled controversies by calling on Ida to consult her diaries to resolve these disagreements. This may be one of the reasons why Ida was not more introspective; she knew that other eyes would be perusing her diaries. Indeed, Ida may have felt that the diaries were not hers alone, but the entire family's.[127]

As we will see in chapter 6, when Ida became too frail to keep regular entries, Barbara functioned as an alternate recorder. Initially Barbara attempted to write as Ida, adopting her mother's voice. But eventually she and Ida collaborated, with Barbara writing some of the entries and Ida others. This mother–daughter compositional duo became even more intensely collaborative when both wrote the same entries, with Barbara usually beginning the entry and Ida finishing it. This collaboration is not unusual in diary families. When nineteenth-century Iowan diarist Emily Hawley Gillespie became too ill to write, her children took dictation and wrote in the diary for her. When she died, both children put their observations in the margin.[128] When Ida died in 2004, Barbara started her own diary as a way of maintaining this family tradition.

Granddaughter Bonnie represents the third generation in this life writing project. A key tenet of life writing and feminist praxis is "negotiate[ing] between the positions of insider and outsider."[129] Bonnie is an insider, and privy to intimate knowledge about family relationships. However, being a relative may blind her to what social distance may reveal about the diaries. That is why the involvement of Michael Boudreau has been so integral to this project. He provides broader historiographical and theoretical insights and a sense of balance in terms of assessing the importance of Ida and her diaries to understanding the past. He has helped Bonnie to see that Ida is more than her "Gram"; she is a multi-dimensional historical actor with many stories to tell. Reading Ida's diaries is a challenging enterprise. As terse account book diaries, they provide little in the way of introspection. They also do not always provide us with authentic insights, but rather a textual projection of a life. Nonetheless, if we examine them carefully as texts and artifacts, and place them in the context of other primary and secondary sources, they can provide a valuable lens into the nature of family, labour, and community in postwar Saint John.

The Backdrop to Ida Martin's Diaries: Saint John, New Brunswick

Saint John is located at the mouth of the St John River in New Brunswick. Originally populated by the Wolastoqiyik, the city and river owe their non-Indigenous name to Samuel de Champlain, who arrived in Saint John harbour on 24 June 1604, and named the river after the feast of St John the Baptist.[130] No permanent European settlement was attempted until 1630 when fur trader Charles de la Tour constructed Fort La Tour. By the 1730s, Acadians from other parts of the Bay of Fundy began settling along the river, but they were subsequently deported from the region by the British during *le grand dérangement* (1755–1763). In 1758 the French fort was rebuilt by the British and renamed Fort Frederick, only to be destroyed in 1775 by the Americans.

In 1778, the British erected Fort Howe on a hill above Portland Point. Permanent British settlement began in the 1760s with the arrival from Boston of James Simonds and James White, who formed a merchant enterprise and traded with the Wolastoqiyik, the garrison, and the British in Halifax. The Loyalists of the American Revolution had a major demographic impact on the city as they settled on the east side of the harbour in Parr Town, the west side in Carleton (where the Martins would later live), and the north side in Portland. In 1785, Carleton and Parr Town were incorporated under the name of Saint John, the first incorporated city in Canada. One year earlier New Brunswick had been carved out of Nova Scotia as a separate colony.[131]

By the early nineteenth century, Saint John's economy was expanding due to the timber trade and shipbuilding. By mid-century, however, Saint John's era of "wood, wind and sail" was being challenged by steam and iron technologies, the dismantling of British protectionism, an international depression in the 1870s, and a devastating fire in 1877. Confederation and the arrival of the Intercolonial Railway also created economic competition with central Canada and the beginnings of regional disparity. Although Saint John had received large numbers of immigrants, particularly Irish, in the late eighteenth and early nineteenth centuries, by the late Victorian period immigrants were bypassing the city for central Canada and the west, and large numbers of Saint Johners joined the regional exodus to the "Boston States." Civic boosters refused to give up on Saint John, however, and promoted the city as the "Liverpool of North America." They invested in the modernization of the waterfront and were successful in convincing the Canadian Pacific Railway to build a terminus at the port in 1889.[132]

Saint John's port gradually integrated into the Canadian economy, achieving winter port status in 1895. In 1927, the port of Saint John was nationalized, due to "the economic plight of the region," which made "nationalization desperately needed to relieve Saint John of the responsibility it could no longer afford to bear."[133] In 1936, the National Harbours Board, a Crown corporation, was established, which leased dock facilities in Saint John and other ports to shipping companies. The federal government also provided much-needed monies to repair the west side of the harbour after a crippling fire in 1931, which "proved in a sense to be a blessing in disguise," for it provided employment in the Great Depression and ensured that the west side's wharves, piers, transit shed, and grain elevators were still relatively new in the 1960s. By the time that AR began to work at the port, the government of

Canada had subsidized the seventeen-acre Navy-Island Terminal in 1934. The following decades would see the reconstruction of the Pugsley Terminal berths between 1948 and 1952 and major renovations to Long Wharf.[134]

Ida, AR, and daughter Barbara moved to Saint John as part of the "drift from country to city ... [which] intensified during World War II." It is probable that the family was attracted by the demand for longshoremen, as "wartime traffic ploughed through Saint John and Halifax."[135] The Martins may also have been lured to the city by the presence of family and friends. As Tamara K. Hareven has pointed out, family and friendship networks have often been of assistance in the migration process and in finding work and accommodation.[136] Ida, AR, and Barbara initially lived in Saint John with family friend Fred Haslam (formerly from Westfield), in a house on St James Street West until they found their own accommodation. Despite the strains that migration placed on housing availability in the city, AR and Ida bought one of the many houses in a "bad state of repair" (213 Queen Street West) and spent most of their married lives renovating it.[137]

The chapters that follow have two objectives: they will reflect on the methodological considerations involved in using diaries and they will show how diaries like Ida Martin's can intersect with and contribute to our understanding of post-1945 Canadian history. We will begin each chapter with excerpts from Ida Martin's diaries and then examine the diaries in the context of the changing contours of life in Saint John in the second half of the

Figure i.4 *Opposite*
Port of Saint John

Figure i.5 *Left*
Ida, AR, and Barbara
in front of their house.

twentieth century. Chapter 1 chronicles the challenges of "getting by" in Saint John, the role of the welfare state, as well as the strategies used by Ida to help her family survive. Chapter 2 extrapolates from Ida's diary entries her views on working-class masculinities, notably among longshoremen who worked at the port of Saint John. Cars and trucks are often associated with working-class masculinity, but in chapter 3 we argue that motor vehicles had more complex and contradictory meanings for working-class families. Chapter 4 reflects on the significance of sociability in the context of family, church, and community. In chapter 5, we reveal how Ida became more engaged with the world around her through communications systems and political discourses. And lastly, in chapter 6 we analyze Ida's diaries as a textual representation of the changes and continuities associated with aging and widowhood in modern Canada.

1

"Getting By" in Postwar Saint John

Did Sat[urday]'s work. (4 May 1946)
Just the usual work. (13 February 1946)
Usual Monday's work. (3 May 1948)
Just right out straight. (22 December 1964)
Busy as a bee. (23 December 1964)
AR just puttering around. (12 June 1977)

Nineteenth-century farm diaries focused on the daily work rituals of farm families. Industrialization and urbanization certainly changed the nature of work for many Canadians, but the family economy remained central to the survival of these families. But one of the problems in studying working-class family economies is that "[i]t is not easy to look inside the homes where women ... of the working classes worked to feed, clothe and nurture their husbands, relatives and children. The key lies in finding ... the sources that will allow us to see and understand what they were doing, how they did it, and the relationship between their daily tasks and the transformations in the wider economy."[1] Diaries provide such a window into these homes. They are rich sources that reveal the often-hidden world of the family economy to the historian's gaze. Working-class women like Ida Martin, following in the footsteps of nineteenth-century farm diarists, kept an almost daily record of the varied strategies that many working-class families employed in order to "get by," particularly before the welfare state in postwar Canada was fully developed.

The postwar period witnessed the growth and consolidation of the federal welfare state, which had a profound effect on family economies, yet working-class families like the Martins continued to function in informal communal and familial economies that had changed little since the eighteenth and nineteenth centuries.[2] Another major transformation of the postwar era was the emergence of mass consumer culture. The Martin family certainly responded to the lure of consumer culture by adopting a number of new domestic appliances between the 1950s and 1970s. However, these manifestations of the modern world were not universally or enthusiastically accepted by Canadian families for a variety of reasons.[3] Thus, while modernization spread throughout the Maritime region in the postwar period, many of the older economic and social patterns remained in place.[4]

Socio-Economic Challenges in Saint John in the Postwar Era

Working-class families faced many challenges in the postwar period, but "getting by" was even more of a struggle if one lived in the Maritimes. In the short term, the Second World War brought many benefits to the region. Much of the wartime shipping traffic came through Saint John and Halifax due to the dangers posed by German submarines in the St Lawrence. In order to accommodate this traffic, the federal government invested in the Saint John port, subsidizing the construction and renovation of graving docks, piers, dry docks, and marine railways. The arrival of workers and military personnel in Saint John increased the city's population from 70,927 in 1941 to 78,337 in 1951. This stimulated local industries and businesses. General wages in Atlantic Canada increased by as much as 21.1 per cent, while the cost of living rose no more than 18 per cent: "on balance, at the end of the war, workers had more money, better skills, and better organization."[5]

However, in the immediate aftermath of the war, Saint John experienced economic uncertainty and hardship. Perennial problems persisted such as a chronic housing shortage, and employment trends were unstable. The labour force at the shipyards peaked in 1945 at 75,000, but then shrank to 12,000. Moreover, the ports in the Maritimes, like Saint John, were primarily tasked with repairing vessels. Most new naval or merchant marine vessels were built in British Columbia, the Great Lakes, and the St Lawrence. Because of industrial concentration in central and western Canada during the war, the *Report of the New Brunswick Committee on Reconstruction* suggested that regional underdevelopment had actually worsened during the war. There were various indicators of this trend. For example, the net value of secondary industry in the Atlantic provinces after the war was only $94 per capita, compared with the national average of $405 and Ontario's $696. The number of men engaged in primary industries fell by over 50,000.[6]

Per capita income in New Brunswick in the postwar period was lower than any other province except Prince Edward Island.[7] Similarly, the median earnings of men for all occupations in New Brunswick in 1951 was $1,907, compared to $2,367 for Canada. Only Newfoundland and Prince Edward Island had lower median earnings than New Brunswick ($1,588 and $1,609 respectively).[8] In Saint John most workers (62 per cent) earned between $1,000 and $2,999 annually, while another 10 per cent made below $500. With the majority of households having only one person in the paid labour force, and an average family size of 3.7 in 1951, many residents of Saint John lived modest and, for some, precarious lives.[9] Indeed, economic insecurity forced many married couples, like Ida and AR, to limit the number of children in their families.

The opening of the St Lawrence Seaway in the late 1950s diverted many vessels from the region to Ontario and Quebec. As a result, political and business elites in Saint John began to formulate diversification plans for the city. This led to the emergence of pulp and paper mills and oil refineries in the 1960s; the establishment of mega-projects in the 1970s, such as the Coleson Cove thermal generating station, and the Point Lepreau nuclear facility; and the boom and bust cycles associated with infrastructure development. In addition, 75,000 service sector jobs were created in Atlantic Canada in the 1950s; this increased the number of women's jobs by 35.9 per cent.[10] In the late 1980s and 1990s, New Brunswick Premier Frank McKenna (1987–1997) encouraged the province and the city to pursue "Post-Fordist development strategies" such as call centres and information technology.[11]

Besides these efforts to create new jobs, Saint John engaged in a major urban renewal project in the postwar era. Housing remained in short supply after the war, and what was available was in poor condition. An ambitious "Master Plan" was designed in 1946 that outlined areas for redevelopment. In the "spirit of postwar reconstruction," architect J. Campbell Merritt contended that much of the city's housing stock was "below standard" and the city's "layout and infrastructure" were "less than desirable." In the *Potvin Report* of the 1950s, 4,000 dwellings were targeted for immediate removal and

8,000 for major repairs. Only 1,000 were judged to be in good condition. These changes to the city's landscape "significantly altered the face of several of the City's neighbourhoods." One of the "better quality planning areas" was the west side, where Ida and AR lived. It was largely residential; only 5 per cent of the urban spaces were zoned as industrial or commercial. Nonetheless, only 27 per cent of the dwellings were listed as being in "good" or "fair" shape. This probably included the Martin residence, as Ida and AR worked constantly to ensure its upkeep. This urban renewal plan also identified new suburban neighbourhoods, and several surrounding villages were eventually amalgamated with the City of Saint John in 1967, "creating the largest city, by area, in Atlantic Canada."[12]

Ida and AR remained in Saint John despite these challenges. But many people did not. While the population growth rates for Saint John were over 6 per cent between 1951–56 and 1956–61, for the 1961–66 period there was a negative growth rate of –1.33 per cent,which rose a bit in 1966–71 to –0.99 per cent but then worsened in 1971–76 to –4 per cent.[13] In some ways, this was a reflection of the larger population loss in the region. In the 1940s, 93,000 people left Atlantic Canada, and then another 82,000 in the 1950s.[14] However, some of the families who had fled Saint John were moving to the suburbs, notably Martinon and Grand-Bay/Westfield.

Paid Labour

Work is probably the most prevalent theme in Ida Martin's diaries. It seemed as if Ida was always working, or she thought that she had to. Indeed, hard work was an expression of working-class respectability. As Joan Sangster has noted in her analysis of working-class women and their families, "Honesty, hard work, and adherence to Christian values or the golden rule were all ingredients of their sense of individual, family, and class pride." Respectability was ultimately earned; although it might be symbolized by economic success, it was largely measured by "the concrete evidence of a life of hard work."[15] As a result, most respectable working-class families "frowned" on "financial carelessness and inordinate debts." Ida kept the family solvent; the front and back pages of several of her diaries were covered with financial transactions and records.[16] This frugal attitude was in part a product of the Great Depression. As Cynthia Comacchio has indicated, dramatic events such as war or economic depression "take on primacy in individual lives as in the collective

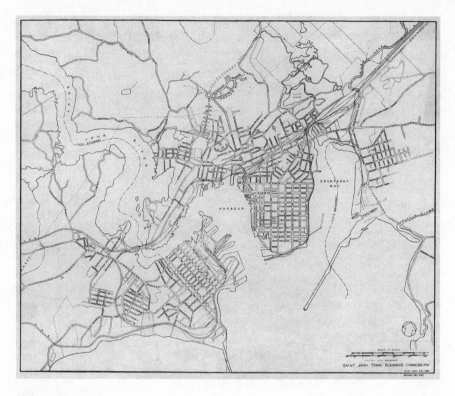

Figure 1.1
Map of Saint John, 1952

generational experience, influencing both memory and lifelong impressions of social and political issues."[17] As a young woman in the 1920s and 1930s, Ida experienced the cruelties of economic deprivation. This generational experience helped to shape her views about work and the importance of family in surviving economic uncertainty. And as will be seen in this and later chapters, Ida and AR never quite had confidence in new, or "modern," consumer goods, whether they were washing machines or automobiles. Instead, they relied on older, more dependable models, which they would often have repaired rather than discard them for newer, more costly replacements. The Martin's frugality was also a response to the challenges of "getting by" in postwar Saint John and a belief in "self-sufficiency and self-help."[18]

Ida dreamed of being a nurse, and like many single Maritime women in the early twentieth century, she was accepted as a student at the Boston General Hospital.[19] Before she left, Ida was presented with a poem by friends and family. The last verse reads as follows:

May he who watches through the night
Who guides us day by day
Love, protect, and bring you back
The girl we sent away.[20]

It would be financial constraints that ultimately brought Ida back, as she was unable to secure the loan that she needed to buy her uniform and supplies. So Ida returned to New Brunswick and began working as a telephone operator in Westfield, a rural suburb of Saint John, and married Allan Robert Martin (AR).[21]

Four years after their daughter Barbara was born, the family moved from Westfield to Saint John, where the Martins lived by the rhythms of casual wage labour, as had many working-class families since the nineteenth century. AR began working at the port as a longshoreman in the early 1940s until he retired in 1971.[22] AR's dock labour was governed by seasonality and the availability of employment. He began work in November or December, and ended in April, at which time he engaged in the informal economy and earned money by hauling loads as a truck driver. He also worked for a bootlegger in 1946[23] and by engaging in what Ida called "treeing": cutting down Christmas trees on private and Crown land and selling them at King's Square in uptown Saint John.[24] In the spring of 1956 he began casual work for Stephens Construction and Paving, which stabilized his employment pattern in the sense that he could at least anticipate work in the spring and winter. Sometimes AR's work responsibilities would overlap: in Ida's diaries it is recorded that on 23 May 1947, AR hauled mud in the morning and worked at the port in the afternoon. On 8–9 April 1958, he worked at the port during the day and for Stephens Construction at night.

Like many working-class women in this period, Ida's participation in the paid labour force was sporadic. But she also mirrored the entrance of more married women into the workforce after the war. Women comprised close to 30 per cent (5,975) of Saint John's paid labour force in 1951.[25] Ida stayed on at the telephone office immediately after she was married, and even worked there when the family moved to Saint John. In July-August 1946, she worked nights at the telephone office, often having to take the bus or hitchhike to

Westfield.[26] Working on the night shift also meant that she occasionally missed church because she was late coming home.[27] Beginning in June 1954, Ida began working at Beck's Drycleaning and continued to work there regularly between 1955 and 1957, and then again in 1962, sporadically in 1964, and between 1966 and 1968. The primary variable determining whether married women took on paid labour was usually financial, but it was "not the sole factor."[28] Ida no doubt welcomed the extra income, but she also enjoyed the sociability with the other female employees at Beck's. She also made new friends and often treated the "girls" to cookies and cakes. Ida also took in sewing from Beck's in the mid-1960s, stitching seams on her treddle machine for piecework wages.[29] But as was the case with most piecework, there was no guarantee that it would continue.[30]

Ida also earned some money at home in other ways. In 1959 Ida took a hairstyling course at the Vocational School. Although she never became a licensed hair stylist, Ida gave many people "the full treatment" when they would "pop into the house." Rarely, however, did they offer Ida money for her services. So eventually she put a jar on the table for money that she was saving for "missions" and if they wanted to contribute they could, which a few did.[31] Ida's financial contributions to the household economy, while modest, were significant in the context of AR's at times precarious employment and a welfare state that was in its infancy in the early postwar period.

The Welfare State

After the Second World War, the New Brunswick Committee on Reconstruction declared that the province had "woefully inadequate health services." A 1949 survey of public welfare services, conducted by the Canadian Welfare Council at the request of the Health Survey Committee of New Brunswick, reported that New Brunswick had the highest death rate in Canada in 1946 (10.1/1000 compared with 9.4/1000 in Canada), which was partly explained by the high infant mortality rate and the larger proportion of elderly residents.[32] The survey also noted that "with existing wage scales and lack of social insurance, few men [in the province] can make adequate provision for their families in the event of death, or total disability of the breadwinner."[33] New Brunswick had one of the most impressive wartime enlistment rates in the country but after the war one of the highest unemployment rates for returning veterans. Of the 40–50,000 unemployed veterans in Canada in 1946,

13 per cent came from New Brunswick.[34] This reality made welfare state benefits all that more vital for residents of the province. According to Margaret Conrad and Jim Hiller, the introduction of unemployment insurance "brought important benefits to a region where seasonal and structural unemployment" was "consistently higher" than elsewhere in Canada.[35] Federal unemployment insurance was compulsory in all industries except agriculture, horticulture, and forestry, the argument being that jobless periods were predictable for seasonal workers, who should therefore be able to save enough money to survive during the rough patches.[36] In New Brunswick, "where industries [were] small and where agriculture, logging and fishing employ[ed] 49.3% of the male labour force, coverage [was] not nearly as great as in some parts of Canada." In June 1949, unemployment insurance coverage for Canada as a whole was 74 per cent, while in New Brunswick it was only 65 per cent.[37] The exclusion of seasonal workers was not changed until the Unemployment Act of 1971, which made it easier for seasonal workers to qualify for benefits. AR and Ida were among the fortunate minority who did receive unemployment insurance coverage in the immediate postwar period in New Brunswick.

AR's work at the port was technically seasonal, but not agrarian; hence the Martins were able to regularly file for unemployment insurance, usually when employment at the port or at Stephens Construction ended.[38] We often assume that this welfare state benefit monumentally transformed the work patterns of its recipients. On the contrary, it merely helped them to get through particularly difficult periods.[39] It appears from the diaries that AR turned his attention to the informal economy when on unemployment insurance: for example, renovating and fixing up his own home as well as that of friends and family. This corresponds to what Rosemary Ommer and Nancy Turner have argued with regard to welfare state payments in Newfoundland's outports: they were not used as hand-outs, but as "the necessary and small sums of start-up capital that keep the informal system vital. [Newfoundlanders] insist, accurately, that they are working, even if they are not employed in the formal sector."[40]

The Martins also benefited from the Medicare plan, which New Brunswick joined in 1971,[41] as well as universal monthly Old Age Security pensions to Canadians 70 and over, beginning in 1951.[42] Furthermore, in her diaries, Ida records receiving workers' compensation cheques,[43] since AR was frequently injured on the job. For injuries and illnesses not covered by workers' compensation, Ida and AR were able to access benefits provided by organized labour, in this case the International Longshoremen's Association (ILA). As Alan Derickson has noted: "Throughout the 1950s, unions negotiated improvements in insurance protection for their members. Labo[u]r frequently won coverage of a wider range of services, benefits for workers' dependents and for retired employees ... The benefits became an important component of the postwar compact between labo[u]r and capital: management retained its prerogatives to make decisions regarding production and employment, and unionized workers gained a higher standard of living and insulation against authority."[44]

The benefits provided by the ILA were coordinated with the Shipping Federation of Canada and payable by the Equitable Life Assurance Society. Benefits included the following: hospital room and board (up to $8 daily for employees and $6 for dependents for a maximum of 31 days); additional hospital charges (up to $80 for employees and $60 for dependents); and surgical benefits (up to $200 for employees and $160 for dependents, whether performed in or out of a hospital). The total maternity and obstetrical benefits for a dependent wife was up to $50.[45] And beginning in 1971 the Martins received a port pension which continued to be paid to Ida for one year after AR's death, and thereafter she was covered for 60 per cent of the pension.[46] In 1989, the portfolio achieved a 7 per cent return, which covered only the Actuarial Assumption for the pension fund, so the Board of Trustees was unable to grant a cost-of-living increase to past pensioners. Instead the trustees decided to offer improved coverage of dental, eyeglasses, and hearing aids to a maximum of $400 per family per medical plan year, which was useful as a tax-free benefit.[47] In better years, the pension plan paid regular increases to its survivors. For example, in June 1990, Ida received an annual $30 increase in her pension benefit, bringing it to $219. She also received a cheque for five months of retroactive payments.[48]

Lastly, Ida and AR took advantage of the benefits offered by the Canadian Mortgage and Housing Corporation (CMHC), by taking out two forgivable loans as part of the Residential Rehabilitation Assistance Program. On 25 November 1980, the Martins negotiated a $1,420 loan over an amortization period of 5 years and 9 months and a second loan of $2,555 over a period of 3 years and 5 months.[49] By 22 December 1983, the $2,555 was declared to be "earned in full" as was the $1,420 in November 1986. A clerk from the CMHC ended one of their correspondences with the phrase "We trust that this section

of the National Housing Act has been of assistance to you." Ida and AR no doubt
would have responded in the affirmative.[50] In 1981 the Martins also took advantage of the Canadian Home Improvement Plan (initially established in 1936
to provide loan guarantees) to acquire a loan to pay for insulating their walls,
and to pay for aluminum storm and screen windows and the installation of an
asphalt gravel roof.[51]

Informal Economy

Despite the stability offered by formal welfare state benefits, the informal
economy was still integral to helping many working-class families "get by"
on a daily basis. And it is through Ida's diaries that this particular informal
economy is revealed. AR contributed to his family economy by engaging in
various types of non-wage labour. He was a scrounger; he brought tar home
from Stephens Construction for use on the roof of his house and he went to
the dump to find five-gallon cans for the tar.[52] He also found boards at the
landfill and in 1970 he obtained lumber from homes that were about to be
demolished.[53] In this sense, AR resembled the working-class families of the
nineteenth century, who relied on "some blend of production, exchange, purchase, and sometimes scrounging."[54] Moreover, he and Ida "lived a double
life" by continuing to partake in the informal rural economy while still living
in an urban environment. AR would frequently go clamming, lobstering, and
hunting in Chipman and the surrounding area with his friends, while he and
Ida would often pick berries in Pennfield and other locations.[55]

   Like many working-class wives throughout the nineteenth and early twentieth centuries, Ida helped her family survive by acting as the household manager and financier.[56] Household managers were responsible, not only for their
own labour, but for "reproducing the labour power of all the adults of the
household," which meant "transforming ... wages ... into food, meals, clothing, and comfortable shelter and raising the children."[57] As Bettina Bradbury
has posited, the home has "remained crucial to working-class survival, to the
functioning of the labour market, and to the wider economy."[58]

   The onerous task of "money managing and stretching" was in itself a "full-
time occupation."[59] Ida kept track of her husband's paycheques and paid his
union dues as well as his truck licences.[60] Ida would sometimes ask her
daughter Barbara to deliver these payments in person. Similarly, one of the
documents left behind by Ida is a weekly premium receipt book that recorded

Figure 1.2
AR and friend scavenging lumber, 1951

her life insurance payments. The entries show that she visited the Metropolitan Life Insurance Company office at 61 Union Street every few weeks (from
November 1964 to July 1969) to make payments ranging from 95 cents to $5.[61]
For many working-class families, "[e]xtending credit was seen as akin to ex-
tending trust, and the regular personal visits to make payments on the account made debtor and creditor familiars."[62] Sometimes Ida went herself to
the union hall to collect wages, holiday bonuses, and even Christmas turkeys,
perhaps because she wished to have full control of the family's income, for
AR, like many working-class men of his era, spent much of his time and
money engaged in conviviality with his friends and fellow workers. This was
a common strategy used by working-class wives to ensure that their husband's wages, or any bonuses, were not squandered before the family's economic needs were met. To this end, Ida would often pay the family's bills
before giving AR any money to spend on himself.[63]

Ida tried to save money for the family by opening a bank account. In her Bank of Nova Scotia passbook dating from April 1969 to September 1975, she began her savings account with a $1,700 deposit and then through a series of deposits gradually increased her investment. Some of these deposits were identified as bonds and investment certificates. By the end of her passbook she had a balance of $9,063.62.[64] There is also a receipt book which suggests that Ida extended a personal car loan to her son-in-law Sterling Huskins in 1981. In the receipts we see that Sterling repaid the loan over one year, from 16 January 1981 to 21 January 1982.

The desire for self-sufficiency was undoubtedly one of the reasons why Ida and AR entered into the quagmire of home ownership, unlike a majority of Saint Johners who rented their dwellings.[65] In 1951 there were 10,270 "Tenant-occupied dwellings" in Saint John, the majority of which (81 per cent) were unfurnished. Most tenants paid under $50 a month for rent, which usually did not include heat. In comparison, the 1951 census reported that Saint John had 2,845 "Owner-occupied dwellings"; 80 per cent (2,285) were owned outright by the residents.[66] Owning a home was a way of obtaining a "place that was theirs to control and theirs to work in – a valuable base for home production and earning," but only if the loans were paid off and the taxes paid.[67] When the Martins first decided to buy their house, they did not even know how to secure a mortgage, so they sought financial advice from the only businessman they knew: Bouche (Simon P.) Donovan, who owned the butcher shop next door.[68] They proceeded to purchase the leasehold property at 213 Queen Street West in 1949 for $3,500 and took out two mortgages – a $1,500 mortgage with real estate agent Clinton D.B. D'Arcy and a second mortgage for $2,000 with the vendor Reta Pyk, a widow originally from Sussex. Since repayment of one's debts was a sign of "personal worth,"[69] and integral to the doctrine of self-sufficiency, Ida and AR proceeded to pay off their second mortgage by 1956 and their first mortgage by 1959. They did so in small regular payments, ranging from $22 to $80. The city of Saint John finally agreed to sell the lot to the Martins in December 1980 for $2,100.[70] This was a leasehold property, which meant that the Martins leased the plot of land from the City of Saint John on which their house stood until the city agreed to sell them the land outright. This was common practice for many working-class families in Saint John.

Ida also engaged in other non-wage strategies common among working-class families, such as taking in boarders.[71] In the early 1950s, Ida took in a few single men: "Abbie and Everett," "Gordon," and "Frank Clarke."[72] In 1956, Ida boarded a handful of Canadian Pacific Railway (CPR) policemen. In January, "CPR Bill" came to board, and then two others in November. On 13 November she records: "Just looking after the men" and on 14 November: "Men still here coming and going at all hours." The next day she notes "The men all left today. They got their 6 trial trips in." In December another policeman, Len Byrne, came to stay. On 16 March 1957, CPR Bill was back and "showed them all around the sheds tonight"; he left again in April. By 1959, Ida referred them to other accommodations,[73] perhaps because she found that the income generated from her boarders was insufficient compensation for the work involved. She did receive additional income for room and board from her daughter Barbara once she began working at London Life Insurance Company from the mid-1950s to 1961.[74]

Ida also acquired another source of revenue by renting out the bottom flat at 213 Queen Street to a variety of long-term and short-term tenants. In the 1940s, they rented the flat to G. and M. Richardson, and then to A. and H. Baird. In 1951, W. and M. Snare lived in the flat, followed by G. and M. Macfarlane, who were long-term tenants from 1952 to 1959.[75] While the McFarlanes, who rented the flat for most of the 1950s, were "lovely tenants,"[76] the family who rented the flat in the early 1960s proved to be problematic. In January 1960 a man forced himself into the downstairs flat "asking for money." He eventually was sentenced to five years at Dorchester Penitentiary, according to Ida's diaries. On 22 February, one of the tenants came upstairs twice "asking for a loan of $5," which she refused both times. There was an "awful fight" downstairs in June 1962 and again on 15 August. Finally, in March 1963, the Martins raised the rent and by August, the family had moved out.[77] They were clearly too much trouble for what they were worth, and their presence may have threatened Ida's efforts to maintain a sense of respectability in her home. Another tenant lived in the flat temporarily in 1964,[78] but in 1966, daughter Barbara and her family moved into the downstairs flat and paid a modest rent.[79]

Kin and Community

The Martins belonged to an informal kin and community network which engaged in mutual exchanges of labour and services. Ida and AR frequently helped family, friends, and neighbours who were ill, in trouble, or merely in need of assistance. Tracy Friars and Heather Stilwell, Ida's nieces, noted in a funeral eulogy that "Auntie Ida's" mother died when she was 32, and Ida immediately took on the role of "mothering her siblings, especially her younger brothers. It was unlikely one ever heard her call her brothers by their full names; it was either JE or GB or LT, to name but a few. We all recall the fondness she had for her brothers and sisters, and the great fun they all had together." Similarly, Ida's niece Bonnie Britt recalled that Ida "played the role of Grandmother to the entire Friars Clan."[80]

Ida Martin helped family and friends over the years by sewing for them, cooking, cleaning house, and celebrating milestones in their lives, such as birthdays. Indeed, the pages of her diary are littered with reminders of her nieces' and nephews' birthdays, and she baked birthday cakes for many of them. At Ida's funeral, her nieces remembered "[t]he many wonderful birthday cakes she so lovingly made, with the nickels and quarters wrapped in wax paper, and the special slice that held the quarter for the birthday girl or boy."[81] Ida seemed rather hurt when she had to bake her own birthday cake in 1956, and nobody remembered her anniversary in 1978 except for her neighbour Mrs Robertson, who sent her a card.[82]

Ida's assistance to kith and kin extended to times of personal hardship. When one of her brothers left his wife and children, she made donuts for the children, went over until 4 a.m. after one of their quarrels, and even accompanied her sister-in-law to divorce court in Fredericton.[83] Ida also acted as a nurse. She dressed her brother's boils,[84] and rubbed her niece's stiff shoulders with liniment.[85] Ida also helped her female relatives when their children came down with the measles, including her sisters-in-law Florence and Mildred.[86] It is revealing that on 1 May 1990, when Ida's cousin Patsy called to say that her husband Arthur was in the hospital after suffering a heart attack, Ida wrote: "I felt terrible. I didn't have a thing to eat in the house so didn't ask her in for the night."

Many working-class women have contributed to the informal economy by babysitting for each other, and Ida was no exception.[87] In 1946–47, Ida frequently kept Wayne Richardson, the infant son of her downstairs tenants, so that they could go to work and do errands.[88] Ida also babysat her nieces and nephews: on 9 October she kept the "kiddies" – Bonnie and Janet – while her sister-in-law Ruth went shopping. She also frequently babysat Barbara Jean, her brother Russell's girl,[89] and other children in the family. In the early 1960s, Ida took care of her granddaughter Bonnie on a continuous basis while her father Sterling attended teachers' college at the University of New Brunswick (UNB) and Barbara worked: "kept Bonnie. all are working downstairs."[90] Ida also babysat when her daughter had other engagements: "Barb had to play for Prayer Meet[ing] so I baby sit. Sterl to UNB" and "Barb to church, Sterl to UNB, and I Baby Sit for 2 hrs."[91] As a result, Ida experienced most of her granddaughter's milestones: her first tooth; standing up in the crib for the first time; her first birthday party; her first time playing in the yard ("she just loves it") and the beach ("Bonnie L just loved it"); contracting chickenpox; her first glasses; her first musical solo at kindergarten; and her first day at school.[92]

Relatives and friends reciprocated; brothers George and Garfield brought her coal in 1955–56, while Faye brought her deer meat.[93] AR and his brother-in-law John frequently exchanged haircuts with their own barber sets when they visited.[94] Patsy's husband Arthur would often do their income taxes, no doubt in exchange for all of the house work that Ida did for Patsy, who was often ill.[95] Daughter Barbara helped them sort out financial and contractual matters. For example, on 12 August 1961, Ida and AR signed an agreement with Memorial Gardens Association (Canada) Ltd. to purchase two interment spaces at Ocean View Memorial Gardens in Saint John, as well as two burial vaults, a companionate memorial stone, and interment fees, totalling $803.40. They proceeded to pay off this contract in ten-dollar instalments over the next five years. This was undoubtedly a more expensive plan than they could afford. Barbara helped Ida craft a letter dated 4 July 1966 informing the company that "We have had a difficult time making the payments … as you can see by my payment record, as most payments were past due. Now, my husband has suffered a heart attack and we cannot afford the vaults, nor can we continue payments." The letter suggested forgiving the balance owing on one vault and $100 on the other. Barbara and Ida reminded the Memorial Gardens Association that they had been "instrumental" in referring family and friends but could be "just as instrumental in others not buying, when we do not feel you deal fairly with your clients." The strategy worked. Head office eliminated the cost of one of the vaults as well as the service charges, which meant that "you will not owe anything further on your account … We are under no obligation to effect a reduction but we can fully appreciate your circumstances and we are willing to do what we can to lessen the burden you must have at this time."[96] Another example of reciprocal support was practised by Ida's brothers, who often drove AR's truck for him when he was ill, as did family friend Fred Haslam.[97] AR's fellow workers took up collections for him when he was in the hospital in 1956 and again in 1966.[98]

Consumer Goods

Another major transformation of the postwar era, besides the consolidation of the federal welfare state, was the proliferation of mass consumer culture, including the peacetime retooling of munitions factories to produce domestic labour-saving devices. The Martins adopted a number of new domestic appliances between the 1950s and 1970s, including a new fridge, an electric frying pan, a floor polisher, a General Electric steam iron, an electric sewing machine, a Westinghouse toaster, a deep freezer, and eventually an oil furnace. These appliances would in some ways transform their work patterns. For example, Ida recorded preparing enough food to store in the freezer in 1979.[99] However, as Joy Parr has argued, these accoutrements of the modern world were not universally or enthusiastically accepted by Canadian families like the Martins. Ida's diaries make continuous references to the mechanical problems they experienced with the furnace and freezer in particular. In 1973–74, the Martins had a series of problems with their furnace, including leaks, smoking (which led to a sooty mess), and the "zone valve" becoming "stuck" on the furnace so that it was 85 degrees all night.[100] In 1980, the Martin's freezer broke down, filling with water, and they had to bring in a repair person from Sears. A year later, "Our (Freezer Deep) is broken down. Compressor gone." Sears eventually took the old freezer away and brought over a new one.[101]

The Martin family did not always adopt the most up-to-date models. According to Parr, this was partly because of a lack of choice in Canada, due to import controls and excise taxes, which were not lifted until the mid-1950s.[102] The newest models were also more expensive, and did not appeal to Canadians who had endured the Depression and the Second World War, and were thus "habituated to scarcity and schooled to value conservation and thrift."[103] By the mid-1980s, Ida still had an oil- and wood-burning stove. But she did acknowledge that electric stoves were good for certain purposes. In 1957, she cooked her Christmas turkey in Mrs Dryden's electric oven and admitted that "It was beautiful."[104] She also frequently cooked her Christmas turkeys in the downstairs flat that was occupied by her daughter and her family.[105] However, these new technologies were not always more serviceable. In March

1977, the power went out for 1½ hours, but she was able to finish her cooking by burning wood in her oil stove.[106] During the Ground Hog Day gale in Saint John in February 1976, the Huskins family came upstairs to huddle around the oil/wood stove: "A wild Hurricane. The worst on record. Floods everywhere, lights out, Furnace out, cold! Cold! The town is a Disaster. Huskins moved up, No School."[107]

Ida was cautious and stubborn when it came to her washing machine. Initially she did all the laundry by hand, but then purchased a wringer washer. Canadians seemed to prefer the "somewhat obsolete wringer washers" in the 1940s and 1950s, which outsold automatics three to one. In 1951, only 10.8 per cent (8,040) of the "powered washing machines" that were owned by New Brunswick residents were in Saint John households. Joy Parr suggests that the wringer washer was viewed as more durable, cheaper, and easier to repair. This pattern was not reversed until 1966.[108] Indeed, Ida did not obtain a new Hoover washer with "side by side tubs" until 1965 when her son-in-law bought it for her when he graduated from teacher's college. It was delivered as a surprise, but "she argued with the delivery man, because she said it wasn't hers. But he left it anyway. That did her for years; she never did have an automatic one."[109] However, one wonders what she thought of the new appliances, for even the Hoover spin washer broke in 1968 and again in 1974, when they had a "terrible time."[110] Perhaps another reason why Ida may have preferred the oil stove and the wringer washer is that these technologies permitted users more involvement in the work process and more control over the product.[111]

Like many women in the early postwar period, Ida was responsible for most of the domestic labour in the household. Women made up 82 per cent (14,430) of those residents of Saint John, fourteen years of age and over, who did not belong to the paid workforce. And the majority of these women (67 per cent or 11,810) were not in the labour force because they were "Keeping House."[112] Nevertheless, Ida took great pride in "Keeping House." This included every phase of the laundry process, especially ironing and line drying. Cheryl MacDonald has noted that "doing the laundry has been an integral part of female culture for generations." It symbolized the relationship between cleanliness, respectability, and "basic Christian virtues."[113] Like many women of her generation, Ida ironed everything: underpants, towels, and face cloths, and she took a modicum of pleasure from having a perfectly arranged outdoor clothesline.[114] Line drying was not only superior to machine drying,[115] but it allowed one to see the fruits of one's labour. According to a working-class woman in Depression-era Montreal, interviewed by Denyse Baillargeon, "I used to enjoy seeing my laundry hanging on the line … It's harder to see housework these days."[116]

Domestic labour was taken very seriously by Ida. In the entries for 1 May and 3 May 1946, Martin describes her domestic work routine as "just the usual work." On 4 May she records that she did the "Sat[urday]'s work in evening." A phrase such as "just the usual work" takes on added significance when one determines the context of the entry. Domestic labour was performed according to a daily, weekly, and seasonal schedule, as it had been since the nineteenth century.[117] Monday was "wash day come hell or high water!," with another full wash on Thursday. Some routines were daily affairs: rinsing out underwear, cooking, washing dishes, and tidying up, while "Ironing was constant."[118] Washing was the "most hated" of nineteenth-century domestic tasks due to its labour-intensive nature.[119] However, as washers and dryers became more prevalent, they increased the workload: "every day – potentially – was washday."[120] There was also seasonal work such as spring cleaning. On 7 April 1972, Ida began spring cleaning: "Up at 6. Done front Bedroom and BathR all before Breakfast. AR painted our Broom ceiling and 2 walls. I cleaned the rest of everything in sight. Worked right up till 7 have got most of the cleaning done."[121] AR would wash dishes occasionally, but his domestic responsibilities were what Craig Heron calls "men's work" around the house: "building, repairing, painting, or refurbishing."[122] This was not easy work, for the Martins had an old home and it required constant upkeep. Gender roles blurred in the sense that Ida often helped with home renovations. However, from the language used in the diaries Ida felt that AR was not being efficient, he was merely "tinkering." Indeed, she uses that word on 9 December 1970. On 13 June 1977, AR "was just puttering around." On 26 September 1968, he was "tearing and going on at the porch."

As Ida's diaries suggest, "getting by" in post-1945 Saint John was anything but easy. While the Martins did not live in poverty, the strategies that Ida and AR utilized, along with the all-important support from the welfare state, allowed them to maintain and enjoy a modest working-class lifestyle. But as the next chapter reveals, AR's dangerous workplace and the risks that he often took while at work, risks that were a by-product of working-class masculinity, often placed the family's economic stability, and AR's survival, in jeopardy.

2

~

Longshoring, Direct Action, and "Being Bad":
A Working-Class Woman's Perspectives on
Working-Class Masculinities

[AR] left [home] at noon and returned at 6am. I walked the floor all
   night. (18 February 1952)
AR and _____ out being bad. (20 December 1951)
[AR and his companions were] MAD ABOUT THE WAY OF BEING PAID.
   (12 February 1970)
A man fell down the hatch & hurt. (17 March 1961)
Allan got his head hurt with a flying gurney. (29 February 1947)

Ida Martin's diaries provide a lens into the ways that working-class women
viewed working-class masculinity. Ida frequently recorded details about her
husband's workplace activities and recreational behaviours. Since he was the
primary breadwinner, it was in her best interests as household manager to
know where he was and what he was doing. In the process of recording these
entries, Ida's frustrations with AR and his world sometimes crept to the
surface. In this chapter, we interpret these at times unguarded expressions
as evidence of a working-class woman's views on working-class masculinity,
views that tended to denounce many aspects of gender constructs.
    Christopher Dummit argues that workers and employers in post-1945
Canada supported the "ideology of manly modernism," which reflected a
turn toward "instrumental reason," "stoical control," and expert knowledge
as the key ideals of this period.[1] Ida's diaries, however, reveal the persistence
of older forms of nineteenth- and early twentieth-century working-class

masculinities, such as the primacy of the male as the main breadwinner; the precariousness of seasonal work; the deleterious effect of manual labour on the worker's body; the prevalence of a homosocial recreational culture; and the tendency for working-class men to revel in boyish horseplay and various forms of risk-taking behaviour. Although scholars have identified a plurality of working-class masculinities in this period (including the notion of the male breadwinner, and a masculine culture of drinking, occasionally in excessive amounts), AR and his cohort embodied the "rugged masculinity" and "radical manliness" of longshoremen who engaged in feats of "masculine strength" and partook in direct action, reminiscent of the late nineteenth and early twentieth centuries.[2] Ida's diaries provide a rare glimpse into these masculinities in postwar Saint John.

The first section of this chapter examines the nature of dock labour in Saint John. The second illustrates how Ida herself, as a working-class wife and mother, viewed and experienced working-class masculinity. Despite AR's hard labour as a longshoreman, as well as a trucker, member of a construction crew, and general odd-jobber, Ida chastised him for his irresponsibility in not working hard enough; for spending too much time with his friends; and for engaging in dangerous behaviour. We also consider the labour unrest recorded in Ida's diaries, and the impact of longshoring and other forms of manual labour on the bodies of working-class men like AR. In so doing, this chapter underscores how home and work remained intertwined in the postwar period.[3] It also illustrates the relationship between longshoring, family, and masculinity. There is a voluminous literature on the history of dock workers and longshoring, but much of it focuses on union history and labour unrest,[4] and the technological transformations of the world's ports.[5] While labour historians are beginning to examine the implications of race on the waterfront,[6] few scholars have explicitly applied the category of gender to longshoring in a systematic fashion.

Longshoring in Saint John

Like many male residents in west Saint John, AR earned a significant part of his income from working as a longshoreman at the port of Saint John. The first entry on AR's Employee Information Card for the International Longshoremen's Association (ILA) Local 273 is 1 June 1943.[7] Working at the port was often a family affair; in the Friars family collection there is also an ILA card for Ida's brother George.[8] But due to the pressures of casual labour and seasonality, AR was forced into a pattern of occupational pluralism. By June 1956, AR began working for Stephens Construction and Paving, and odd-jobbing. He also hauled fill for such customers as Chitticks, a construction business on the west side operated by George Corbett Chittick (1904–1973).[9] Nonetheless, dock work remained the most reliable and fundamental type of work in the Martin family economy.

The ILA had managed, by the early twentieth century, to partially decasu-alize longshoring by formalizing the hours of work, but families who relied on income from the port found that rhythms were still governed by "season-ality and the availability of work."[10] The employment of dock workers had traditionally been casual, due to a variety of factors such as the nature of the cargoes (some "requiring more men or greater skill than others"); the level of mechanization available; and the efficiency of "inland transport services." Port employment was also affected by "general economic conditions, by sea-sonal fluctuations in trade and by changes in the international situation."[11]

Longshoremen in Saint John, like AR, participated in the "shape up," dur-ing which workers were chosen by stevedoring companies who, in turn, con-tracted out their services to the shipping companies. AR was fortunate in being a member of a "regular gang."[12] As Gerald Mars's study of longshore-men in St John's, Newfoundland, has revealed, membership in a gang offered "considerable advantage[s]" for men like AR in the form of "insurance facil-ities." For example, gangs would collect money for a sick member or donate blood for an injured member.[13] Ida at times recorded the activities of "O'Neil's gang," "own gang out today for first," "own gang at tea boat," and "O'Neil's gang [working] then [visiting] downstairs."[14] Gang members were notified of work through notices posted on bulletin boards, in newspa-pers, and through radio announcements and telephone messages. As one ob-server notes, "The gangs never knew for sure when they would be out, so they … listen[ed] to the radio to get their information. Every night after supper it would say 'so and so' gang report for 7 p.m. tonight, or next morning."[15] Membership in a regular gang was not a "formal guarantee of [one's] 'right' to [his] position in the gang," however, and he could be "replaced by a casual at any time," and oftentimes one's gang was not called out at all. On 14 Febru-ary 1969, Ida writes: "Home at noon. They put O'Leary's gang on instead (There [sic] mad)."[16]

If one's gang was not called, then the dock worker could participate in the "open shape," where men were picked individually as "supplements." There was also the "chip system" where the foreman would toss chips into the air and if a worker caught one, he had work for that day. Both systems, however, provided little guarantee of employment.[17] Sometimes AR was hired casually. On 16 April 1968, he was called to Pugsley Wharf to work with McCormick's gang. In January 1969, AR "worked till Dinner to get boat finished then Perry called him to drive jacklift." Later in the season, "Edgar McGuire called at 9 and wanted A[R] for a gang."[18] Sometimes he worked two jobs in one day: on 19 August 1952, AR worked until 3 p.m. for O'Neil and in the evening for Green. Despite technological modernization of the port's facilities, Saint John continued with the shape-up as "its root form of hiring and dispatch" into the mid-1980s.[19] Since Saint John was a winter port, AR usually began to work in November or December until April. Cold, snow, or incessant rain often made working at the port untenable.[20] As late as 1970, a port development study showed that seasonality still affected employment at the port of Saint John: "Cargo seasonality causes considerable employment fluctuation – approximately 46 gangs (including two grain and one sugar) were employed. As a result of the seasonality, some port workers from Saint John seek summer employment elsewhere."[21]

"Obligation and irresponsibility": Ida Martin's Critique of Working-Class Masculinity

Although Ida's diaries functioned primarily as an account of what she and her family did each day, she occasionally used the diaries to critique AR and his friends. It has been established that Ida was the family's financial manager, which meant that she kept track of her husband's pay cheques, paid his ILA and truckers' union dues, and renewed his truck licences.[22] On 20 May 1966, Ida went to the ILA office in person to obtain AR's "last cheque." On 22 December 1967, she went to Stephens Construction "for our turkey" and also picked up Christmas bonuses in person. Historians have suggested that working-class wives did this to ensure that the money was not misspent. One thing is certain: Ida did not think AR was capable of doing *her* job: "AR took cheques to bank and got bawled up."[23] In other words, he became confused about cashing or depositing them. Ida at times also questioned AR's capabilities as a breadwinner. On 20 December 1967, she implied that AR was lazy

and irresponsible: "back at 8 shed after *loafing* [emphasis added] for 12 days."
Such an allegation could wound a male breadwinner's pride deeply, particularly if it was made in public.[24]

But what caused Ida the most consternation was AR's membership in a
homosocial network of associates who worked, played, and drank together.
This tradition of companionate drinking had its roots in the "rural working-
class masculinity" of early New Brunswick, where a boy's "first drink" was a
"male rite of passage."[25] In a book of lore collected by local historian David
Goss, Saint John resident Barbara Gilliland tells of the exploits of a young
AR and her father Fred Haslam when they lived in Westfield. Their pranks,
namely stealing apples, rhubarb, and pumpkins, and making daring getaways
in the process, embodied the elemental camaraderie and mischief of subse-
quent exploits.[26] AR's workplace culture – working together on paving crews
and longshoring gangs – also fostered strong connections between the men.
Brian O'Neill has noted that "Longshoremen derived much of the[ir] work
satisfaction from being with their 'buddies.'"[27] Dock workers of AR's generation tended to live in waterfront communities like the lower west side of
Saint John, in close proximity to the port. This allowed them to come home
together at lunch time and for breaks during night shifts. AR would frequently walk home with a "bunch of men and they would horse around on
the way."[28] This "hors[ing] around" was part of the repertoire of working-
class masculinity, which included "swaggering, shouting, whistling, singing,
swearing, belching, and farting in deliberately performative ways."[29]

Sometimes these close bonds were compromised by the sectorialism of
the waterfront, as workers were divided between wharves, piers, and sheds.
Stevedoring firms in Saint John also "cultivated favourites," which led to ri-
valries between the gangs. Indeed, in 1954, Ida records a "row" between "AR's
and Charleton's gang."[30] More often than not, however, socializing and drinking reinforced homosocial bonds. According to sociologist William Sonnen-
stuhl, "occupational drinking cultures present liquor as normative rather
than deviant." Dock workers (and a number of other manual labourers)
"earned reputations for on-and-off-the-job drinking."[31] Several scholars have
argued that working men like AR and his companions viewed their status as
breadwinners as an entitlement to recreational time away from home.[32]
Working-class men in Saint John did not construct their drinking culture
around the iconic local tavern, as elsewhere, for the public consumption of
alcohol in New Brunswick as late as the early 1960s was still illegal. According

to Stanley Mills, this created "guilty drinker phenomenon," where the imbiber had to consume in private locations "or in fields, alley-ways, dance-halls, and gravel pits."[33] For AR, drinking was relegated to the workplace and a number of unofficial private locations. In 1955, AR was drinking on a German boat in port. He also was "over to Pugsley's [Wharf] but didn't work but was?." In September 1958, he "worked but [was] LOADED." On 4 March 1961, AR was "working but ? Late for supper."[34] Drinking was used by many longshoremen as a basis for assessing masculinity and solidarity. As Gerald Mars notes, "Men are judged as men by how well they carry their drink and by how generously they spend money on drink." And those longshoremen who did not drink were often viewed by their co-workers as loners.[35]

Ida's opposition to AR's drinking exploits meant that when he drank at home, he usually did so alone. On 17 March 1960, "AR bad. Still sitting out front [during a snowstorm] when I came home." At other times he drank in the garage ("terrible in eve[ning]. Stayed in garage") or in the truck ("Down in truck till 12pm").[36] By the 1970s, three of five people in Atlantic Canada admitted to drinking alcohol, which was still primarily consumed at home. However, this consumption rate was still below the national average, although Atlantic Canadians paid the highest prices in Canada for alcoholic beverages and spent a greater percentage of their disposable income on them.[37] According to Mark Rosenfeld, working-class wives like Ida became concerned when their husbands' drinking and carousing were "done to extremes."[38] However, in Ida's case, she was more sensitive due to her Baptist faith and her membership in the Women's Christian Temperance Union.[39] The following excerpts from Ida's diaries underscore her uneasy relationship with AR's drinking:

> 5 June 1946: "not working today but went over and was drunk all day."
> 24 January 1948: "Didn't work. He and _____ to hockey and came back (souced)."
> 24 January 1951: "AR lied – wasn't working but?"
> 12 July 1951: "AR [and] _____ on a bat? I walked floor till 1/4 to 4am."
> 15 December 1951: "didn't work but were bad."
> 20 December 1951: "AR and _____ out being bad."
> 21 December 1951: "didn't work partying til 3am."
> 18 February 1952: no port work due to a storm, but "AR and _____

left at noon and returned at 6am. I walked the floor all night."

28 March 1952: "with ____ boozing til 2am."

4 April 1953: "AR away with _____ and ????"

24 June 1953: "went to ui and boozing the rest of the day."

16 April 1956: "AR? Who with? Till 2am."

27 March 1957: "AR terrible bad. Got a roast of meat somewhere? I don't know where."

22 December 1958: AR "worked ½ day got? And got [Christmas] tree. I don't know who with."

5 April 1960: "AR off all day so I guess he watch TV and?"

These entries are another example of intensive writing, as examined in chapter 1. The blunt, minimalist entries require decoding. In most of these entries, AR is drinking with someone else, often identified by a blank space in the diaries. Perhaps Ida thought that it was inappropriate to include the proper names of her husband's friends in her diaries. Alternatively, she may have been so angry with AR's associates that she could not bring herself to mention them by name. In another entry she refers to one of AR's friends as "2 face," perhaps because she saw him as duplicitous.[40] Ida also accuses AR of deception: he "lied – wasn't working but?." It is clear from this entry that Ida uses the question mark to signify that she does not know the details of her husband's whereabouts. Like many working-class wives, she probably had "some knowledge of [her] husband's recreation away from home, though not necessarily the details."[41] Another pattern that emerges is that drinking often occurred during periods of under- or unemployment, or when applying for unemployment insurance. Craig Heron posits that turn-of-the-century workers may have looked forward to "bouts of joblessness," for they provided more opportunities for "male companionship."[42]

Ida also used code words in her diaries to refer to AR's binges. Three times in the entries above, Ida uses the word "bad"; either AR is bad or he is "being bad." In Ida's vocabulary, this usually meant that AR had been drinking.[43] In the 12 July 1951 entry, she describes AR and his companions as being "on a bat"; other colloquial phrases include being "tipsy," "caned to the eyes," and "souced." On one particular day when AR was extremely intoxicated, he was "full, full, full, disgusting," and on a better day "a little? but not too much."[44]

It is obvious that the "profoundly contradictory tendencies in working-class masculinity – between self-indulgent irresponsibility and deeply ingrained commitments to collective solidarity owed to family and work-mates" still had relevance in the postwar period.[45] According to family tradition, AR did not drink as much after his daughter's marriage in 1960, realizing that he was aging and had missed out on much of his family's milestones. The diaries bear this out. Instead of imbibing, Ida records him as turning to household chores. In 1964, he did not secure work at Stephens, so he "worked at car fenders," put "rain coating" on the "woodshed etc.," and painted the front of the house. In January 1965 he did not secure work at the port, so he repaired the gas boiler. In August, he fixed a hole in the roof and "renewed" the brakes on the "Chevy."[46]

Radical Masculinity on the Waterfront: Contested Definitions of Manhood

Ida used her diaries to record key pieces of information about ILA Local 273. This Local was founded in 1911, when competing waterfront unions in Saint John merged and voted to affiliate with the American-based International Longshoremen's Association.[47] Ida records meetings and elections in her diaries. On 10 March 1964, AR worked at the ILA election, came home at 4 a.m., and then worked all day and half of the night. On 17 March he was back to the polls for a recount. Four years later AR "went over to vote for ILA Pres" and in 1970, he "work[ed] til noon at 3 shed then an Election of Officers for ILA. All men voted back in office. Ronnie Smith President."[48]

Ida also chronicled incidents of unrest among the longshoremen. She did so because the strikes, walkouts, and general disputes with the employer directly affected the family economy, of which Ida was the steward, along with her husband's life and how she viewed working-class masculinity. An example of this can be found on 12 February 1965: "A Riot started at the waterfront. No one working all day," and then on 13 February: "A RIOT at the waterfront for rights of parking. No 1 work all day." On 12 February, approximately 1,000 longshoremen and 500 CPR truckers walked off the job to protest the loss of their usual parking lots, which were filled with new cars assembled for export. Saint John had turned to foreign and Canadian-made automobiles as one of its primary cargoes and had thus expanded storage facilities. It is not surprising, therefore, that cars would receive preferential treatment as cargo.[49] The dock workers were undoubtedly frustrated by the attitude of port managers like J.R. Mitchell of Halifax, who noted that "the cargo gets preference." Saint

John longshoremen also complained that the parking lots were the last to be ploughed, and if they parked elsewhere they were ticketed. Union executives made it clear throughout this dispute that they did not condone the walk-off and they tried to convince the men to return to work.[50] The dispute was eventually settled on 15 February when the National Harbours Board (NHB) and Local 273 agreed to study proposals for extra parking areas, as well as plans to expedite snow removal and to reduce fines for illegal parking.[51]

Five years later, on 12 February 1970, Ida noted that "AR worked till dinner then came the WALKOUT." This time the issue was a new payroll system. Instead of obtaining their pay from local stevedoring firms, as had been the custom, the cheques were now compiled and issued by a centralized computer network in Montreal. The men argued that there were frequent delays in receiving their pay, and if the cheques were not picked up in time, they were sent back to Montreal to be reissued the following week. This grievance was aggravated by the workers' "branch plant relationship to Montreal." According to Edgar Dosman, who interviewed Local 273 members in the 1970s, "memories of 'domination' by Montreal when Saint John and Halifax were primarily winter ports remain[ed] vivid."[52] The longshoremen of Saint John had been severely affected by the rationalization of the shipping industry. In 1903, the Shipping Federation of Canada was founded. It was comprised of "deep sea and coastal shipowners, agents, charterers, and operators" which provided services to and from eastern Canadian, St Lawrence River, Great Lakes, and Arctic ports. The Shipping Federation negotiated collective agreements with workers in Saint John, Montreal, Quebec, Trois-Rivières, Halifax, Toronto, and Hamilton. Beginning in 1968, a consortium entitled the Maritime Employers Association (MEA) represented shipping agents in these ports.

This alliance of eighteen employers seemed bent on "drastically alter[ing] the traditional way of doing things" on the waterfront, including transforming the "amorphous ILA" into a "structured and flexible industrial-type work-force" or "bwf" (basic work force). Labour activist James Orr remembers the MEA as "hatchet men" who were intent on "hammering us into the ground."[53] This led to labour unrest on the waterfront in the mid-1970s, including the first "complete shutdown of the port" in sixty years in 1974 and participation in the "Saint John General Strike" in 1976, when workers took to the streets to protest wage controls imposed by the federal government.[54] Three Atlantic directors sat on the MEA, but the head offices were still in Montreal, so the

MEA was "branded" as an "outsider" by local workers.[55] This sense of regional alienation was accentuated during the payroll dispute by the employer sending workers' cheques to St John's, Newfoundland, instead of to Saint John, New Brunswick.[56] As Ida proclaimed in her diary, her husband and his work mates were "MAD ABOUT THE WAY OF BEING PAID." At a union meeting to discuss the issue, several members were fined by the local for expressing their anger too vociferously, and for drunk and disorderly conduct.

It is clear that longshoremen, as illustrated by these two incidents, expressed their radical manhood through such forms of direct action as swearing and shouting, refusing to work, and walking out. Indeed, the longshoremen of Saint John were known as men who "responded with actions not words." In that sense they emulated the radical manhood of labour activists like Robert Gosden, who once said that "Talk was cheap. What mattered was action." Even writers and intellectuals who believed in "talk," such as Maritime socialist Colin McKay, did not accept lethargy or insouciance. As Ian McKay remarked in an open letter to Colin McKay: "You were marginalized, but you did not take it lying down: you argued with the world, you mobilized counter-opinions, you treated with a scoffing irony the supposedly authoritative view points of the bourgeoisie and its numerous intellectual allies."[57] Since at least the late nineteenth century, industry has partnered with unions like the ILA to contain this form of activism and replace it with a more acceptable and temperate form of manhood.[58]

The waterfront and union hall were arenas for the negotiation of "contending definitions of what it mean[t] to be a man."[59] One prominent area of contestation was drunk and disorderly behaviour. The records of unions like the ILA and the Railroad Brotherhoods contain lists of members who were "reprimanded, suspended and expelled" for excessive drinking and engaging in raucous behaviour.[60] Throughout the early twentieth century, Local 273 regularly disciplined their members for such transgressions as "fighting, drunkenness, disorderly conduct, and breaking their hall's windows and furniture (and even its stove on one occasion)."[61] In the 1939 *By-Laws of Local No. 273*, the motto is recorded as "Sobriety, Truth, Justice, and Morality."[62] One wonders whether the union's campaign to produce abstemious men was successful in the long run, for officials continued to battle inebriation and disorderly conduct well into the 1960s and 1970s. As illustrated previously, AR had been drinking at the port, although he was never formally reprimanded for being drunk and disorderly.

The leadership of Local 273 also insisted that the men treat their union officers with more respect and decorum. During the payroll incident, President Ronnie Smith tried to set the tone at one of the meetings by fining himself $10 for swearing.[63] Smith also filed a complaint against Brother Kenneth Thibodeau for giving him a "hard time" at the wharf: "He tried to explain to Brother Thibodeau about the central pay system. But Brother Thibodeau did not let him explain, he just kept hollering louder, and told him he should have been at the pay centre when the trouble was going on trying to get their pay. The President stated he was at a meeting at the time and he told the Business Agent to call him if he was needed. He is charging Brother Kenneth Thibodeau with maligning him as he … felt he should not be treated as such."[64] This insistence on formalism and deference did not sit well with many of the dock workers in Saint John, who were becoming disenchanted with the ILA due to its conservative tendencies, as well as allegations of corruption and connections to organized crime.[65] Workers more generally felt that their unions were becoming "less attentive to needs at the local level, thus weakening grassroots connections and stifling spontaneous worker self-activity."[66] Thus it is not surprising that longshoremen like Thibodeau refused to capitulate during the payroll incident. He explained to the union that "he had a hard time getting his pay at the Data centre, and thought that the President should have been the[re] to look after this."[67] Labour activist James Orr explained that Saint John longshoremen had always seen themselves as "partners on the waterfront"; now they were being reduced to the status of union members and employees.[68] As a result, longshoremen, including AR, clung to direct action and the "rough justice of casualism."[69]

The Body and Working-Class Masculinity

The "body" has been a central component of working-class masculinity since at least the nineteenth century. Manual labourers require physical strength and stamina to do their jobs, and these qualities have subsequently been adopted as emblems of their manhood. As Thomas Dunk notes: "Workers prove their worth as men by their ability to withstand dirt, noise, danger, and boredom. Working conditions are 'read' as a challenge to masculinity, rather than as an expression of the exploitation of capitalist relations of production."[70] Similarly, in her study of gold miners in the Porcupine camp near Timmins, Ontario, Nancy Forestell suggests that workplace accidents and injuries reverberated beyond the worksite to the home, the working-class family economy, and the community.[71] Ida's diaries record the arduous working conditions of longshoring, as well as the toll that they took on AR's body. She also chronicles the challenges of this hard life for aging port workers, like AR, and their families.

Although waterfront work was "complex and variegated," depending on whether one was a pier man, a deck man, a hold man, a winch man, a hatch handler, a trucker, or a freight handler, all of the work was physically demanding.[72] Sometimes AR worked the crane or drove the jack lift.[73] Most of the time, however, he was a hold man, below decks, loading and unloading cargo. Ida records AR unloading such cargo as tea, coal, sulphur, fertilizer, grain, pulp, bananas, sugar, and flour. The banana stocks that Saint John longshoremen unloaded weighed approximately 250 lbs each and they carried 18–20 stocks an hour. The fertilizer and raw sugar often hardened and thus the dock workers had to use picks and shovels to unload it. The flour bags weighed 90–240 lbs each and the men had to carry them while walking on top of the cargo.[74] Often Ida could tell what her husband had unloaded that day by the state of his clothing: in March 1953 she washed his work clothes, which were covered with flour.[75] Longshoremen also had to endure the "intense cold on the docks. Sometimes the guys' faces would freeze because of the freezing wind and weather, so they had to dress according[ly]."[76] The *Evening Times Globe* acknowledged the brutal working conditions faced by dock workers in a photo caption on 14 January 1957: "Cold Spell Doesn't Stop Port Workers." The *Globe* was clearly appreciative because the port of Saint John was recovering from a ninety-one-day CPR strike. The caption concluded with further proof of the longshoremen's physical strength: "Bags [in the photo] are raw sugar and weigh 260 lbs each."[77]

The waterfront remained a hazardous work environment well into the postwar period. Although the state and the ILA instituted improved safety standards, many accidents and injuries continued on a regular basis, particularly as the labour force aged.[78] Like mining, longshoring remained a dangerous occupation.[79] Ida Martin kept a running tally of the men that she knew who were hurt or killed at the port: those who were hurt included her brother Gars, her husband's friend Delbert Carr (who was injured on his "last load"), Ottis McCallum, Ronnie Smith, Roy Ferris, and Alex Baird (who "got foot hurt at PORT").[80] On 17 March 1961, she noted that "A man fell down the hatch & hurt." Those who were killed included Edison Maxwell (who expired

Cold Spell Doesn't Stop Port Workers

Despite bitterly cold weather on the Saint John waterfront, longshoremen were busy unloading sugar. At right, Raymond Humphrey and Fred Sanders, about to sling his baling hook over his shoulder, pause for a moment's rest, while at left, Art Harrington and Mickey Joyce ease bags of sugar onto a truck as an unidentified man watches from the deck of the Greek freighter Heron II tied up at Pier 10. Bags are raw sugar and weigh 260 pounds each.

Figure 2.1
"Cold Spell Doesn't Stop Port Workers"

in the "hold of ship at 13 shed"), James Le Clair from South Bay, Irvine Moore (whom she referred to as "Mr. Moore"), and Ken Middleton. Ida helped the Middleton family by cooking for them and attending the funeral. The names of these longshoremen who were killed on the job appear on the longshoremen's monument erected at Pugsley Wharf in 2003 by Local 273.[81]

AR was not immune to such dangers. He and a fellow worker were nearly buried alive in the grain hatch at the port. He was also injured several times, but Ida did not always specify the injury: on 27 December 1946, "AR hurt at 3 in afternoon & taken to Hosp[ital]. Fred [Haslam] & I went to see him." Shortly thereafter in January 1947 he hurt his leg and was out for nearly a month.[82] Only twenty-five days after returning to work, "AR got his head hurt with a flying gurney."[83] On 27 April 1948 "AR worked on flour today. Skinned his shoulder." On 3 June 1952 AR was injured while working at Long Wharf, and two days later, according to Dr. Baird's diagnosis, "Ribs not broke, mus[cle] pulled away." Later that year, while "out at Long W[harf] with Fred's gang," he "hurt his knee." AR was again forced to stay home for several weeks in the winter of 1955–56 due to a cracked bone in his foot.[84] AR "got his leg hurt a bit" in 1960, his shoulder in 1961, and his little toe in 1969.[85] Then on 26 March 1970, while working at 9 shed, AR again hurt his back: "A sling of

Figure 2.2
International Longshoremen's Association,
Local 273 Longshoremen's monument, Saint John

lumber hit him a glancing blow." Not surprisingly, AR's body was covered with bumps and bruises, and gouges from his longshoreman's hook.

Dock workers were also subjected to health hazards such as inhaling diesel fumes or being contaminated by dangerous cargoes such as cyanide.[86] Grain and flour were detrimental to AR and his companions because "everything was loose and the breathing was bad. They ... tied handkerchiefs around their nose and mouth, and dad would wheeze for days after." After working with grain shipments, "everything he wore was full of grain dust and kernels, right into the creases of his skin. His face would be yellow and just two eyes looking out at you ... When he would be home at 11–12, he would dread to go back and face it again [at] 4A.M."[87]

AR suffered from general bodily aches and pains due to the continuous physical exertion of port labour. By the early 1960s his feet were becoming "awful sore" and he had to be fitted with arch supports.[88] Yet because physical weakness was a "visible sign of failure" according to the tenets of working-class masculinity, and a "threat to working and breadwinning" for aging labourers,[89] he tried to mask the symptoms and the cause. His working companions later told Barbara that he would say to them on the way home from work: "I'm just going to stop a minute here and enjoy the stars out tonight ... they are so bright and beautiful ... whatever excuse he could manufacture so they would go on ahead and he could stop and then crawl at his own pace. As time went on, he would take a lunch on this shift" so that he would not have to walk home.[90] This underscores the paradox of dangerous work; it both reinforced rugged masculinity as well as undermined it, especially for those who took "pride in and dr[a]w social prestige from the physical strength and agility attached to their work as well as their role as family provider."[91] As a result, dock workers generally tended to "carry on work at an age when it constitutes an excessive effort for them."[92]

In a newspaper advertisement promoting the port of Saint John in 1952, the port is anthropomorphized as a robust young male rising above the wharves and elevators. This imagery is similar to the tribute ads sponsored by employers during Labour Day festivities in the nineteenth and twentieth centuries, wherein the worker is portrayed as "white ... dignified, powerful, and proud." Organized labour also "celebrated the muscular young man" in advertisements and cartoons.[93] The picture as well as the subheading for this advertisement draw a connection between the vitality of youth, the hopes for postwar peace and prosperity, and Saint John's potential as a modern industrial centre: "Saint John offers All Modern Facilities for the Exchange of Products between Canada and All Countries of the Peace-Loving World." Like the Labour Day tributes, moreover, Mr Port City is a "solitary figure," with no evident class solidarities or union affiliation,[94] despite the contentious history of labour activism in Saint John.

Despite Mr Port City's youthful vigour, he was not representative of the waterfront workforce. By the 1960s, port boosters turned from images of youth to the productivity and reliability of their mature labour force. In a promotional pamphlet, the National Harbours Board asserted that the Saint

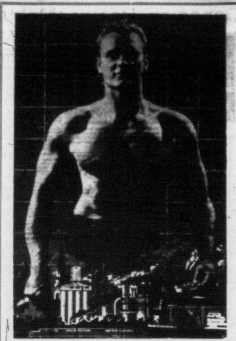

The PORT of SAINT JOHN

Canada's

Ocean Gateway

Open Year 'Round

SAINT JOHN offers All Modern Facilities
for the Exchange of Products between Canada and
All Countries of the Peace-Loving World

Old Square Riggers used to make Saint John their Home Port — and she is proud to
possess a cherished tradition which has been passed down through generations of
sailing men. With further development year by year, Saint John has now a Modern
Harbor occupying an important place on Canada's Commercial Maps — and throughout the British Commonwealth.

···· ······ ···**PHONE 3-1408**···· ······ ····

Saint John Iron Works Ltd.

Manufacturers — Marine and Industrial Repairers

• BRASS and IRON FOUNDERS • BOILERMAKERS • BLACKSMITHS •
• MACHINISTS • ELECTRIC and ACETYLENE WELDING •

—VULCAN STREET—

SAINT JOHN, N. B.

Figure 2.3
"Mr. Port City," 1952

John port had a "longstanding reputation for productivity," which was based largely on "good management-labour relations. Port councils and advisory boards continuously seek out new methods to improve their performance. Ask what we can do for you?" In the modern era of the postwar labour compromise, employers were more willing to acknowledge the contributions of workers to overall productivity: "Saint John's port work force has a reputation – known to all – for the day-to-day production."[95] This was a manifestation of the "modernist project" with its emphasis on efficiency and productivity. While it is not surprising that the NHB and the MEA pushed for "more flexibility and productivity,"[96] it is interesting to see the longshoremen themselves embrace the vocabulary of manly modernism. In the early 1960s, in order to ensure their survival in the face of mechanization, longshoremen engaged in a public relations campaign to show that they were still handling cargo efficiently. For example, in 1962, it was reported that Saint John dock workers established "what is considered a record for fast loading. In seventeen hours they put 336,933 bushels of wheat aboard the vessel *Irish Spruce* from Dublin. Two miles of conveyor belts were used." They would continue to "break records" in grain handling and "container movement" throughout this period.[97] How were aging workers like AR able to keep up in this era of increasing modernization? Given their age, they probably did not operate the Munck cranes, nor would they have been involved in RO/RO operations.[98] Instead, aging workers continued to handle much of the "break-bulk" cargo in the 1960s/early 1970s. Since "not all commodities were suitable for containerization," many longshoremen like AR still engaged in manual labour much as they always had.[99] Although total cargo increased over the years, the amount of "container traffic" remained low, with liquid bulk (petroleum), dry bulk, and forest products dominating, cargoes that required traditional loading/unloading methods.[100]

During the celebration of "Port Days" in Saint John in 1970, several stories appeared in the local press praising the technological transformations at the port. Saint John, it would seem, was undergoing a process of mechanomorphosis. The only overt suggestion that workers might be part of this process was a photograph of a robust yet older longshoreman hauling cargo on his back. Juxtaposed with this image of traditional working-class masculinity was the caption: "An efficient up-to-date labour force second-to-none in any port is one of the Port of Saint John's biggest assets ...Vincent (Baldy) Kane is shown here hefting a sack of seed potatoes."[101] This highlights the transitional nature of this period at the port. AR's aging cohort, while dominant

Figure 2.4
A longshoreman

AN AFFICIENT, up-to-date labor force second-to-none in any port is one of the Port of Saint John's biggest assets. The longshoremen's high hourly cargo handling rate has been responsible for attracting more than one cost-conscious shipper to this port. Vincent (Baldy) Kane is shown here hefting a sack of seed potatoes.

for much of the twentieth century, would increasingly find themselves on the outside looking in at the changes underway in Saint John.

Ida Martin's diaries reveal that older forms of working-class masculinity persisted into the postwar period in Saint John, including participation in a homosocial recreational culture, risk-taking behaviour, and a commitment to direct action as a form of labour unrest. This can be attributed to the persistence of the relations of production that created and sustained such masculinities. Modernization was uneven on Saint John's waterfront; aging longshoremen like AR (who retired from the port in 1971) continued to load and unload cargo alongside the emergence of containerization and other forms of technological innovation. And while the foundation of Saint John's economy has shifted over the years, it has always relied on large companies such as the Irvings, employers and unions headquartered in Quebec and Ontario and the United States, and the coffers of the provincial and federal governments. Thus it can be argued that working-class masculinity in Saint John was, and continues to be, informed by a history of regional dependencies.

Furthermore, Ida's diaries remind us that the recreational and risk-taking behaviours associated with working-class masculinity had very real and often negative consequences for families, and therefore should not be romanticized. Ida spent many nights worrying about her husband, and about the implications that his behaviour would have on her family. Moreover, the diaries document the deleterious effects that hard and dangerous labour had on the bodies of aging workers like AR. In this regard, AR finally filed for his port pension at the age of 67 because he was "just wore out,"[102] which reinforces Craig Heron's argument that "[w]orking-class men literally wore themselves out in pursuit of their masculinity."[103] At the same time, however, as the next chapter will discuss, working-class men like AR found a degree of comfort in another element of working-class masculinity, namely the quintessential symbol of twentieth century masculinity and modernity, the automobile. Indeed, as will be explored in chapter 3, "tinkering with cars," as Ida's diaries demonstrate, was also a key component of working-class culture and the family economy in postwar Saint John.

3

Dump Trucks and "Chevys": Gender, Class, and Motor Vehicles in Working-Class Life and Culture

Got dump [truck]welded and [AR's] eyes were sore from watching.
(13 September 1945)
I went to Edna Crawford's tonight, the Chevy and I. (17 March 1964)
[AR] tinkering with car – did something to brake drum. Lost brake fluid.
TERRIBLE DAY. (8 April 1974)
[AR] and ___ speeding out at Purdy's. (29 May 1946)
Couldn't drive at all with [AR] in [the car]. (4 August 1963)

In Ben Bradley's study of car culture in British Columbia, he perceptively notes that the passenger car was the twentieth century's "quintessential *object*."[1] So it is not surprising that motor vehicles figure prominently in the diaries of Ida Martin, either in the form of trucks used by her husband AR, or a succession of cars owned by herself and her husband, other family members, and various friends and acquaintances. Ida's interest in motor vehicles was initially surprising, as the literature indicates a strong relationship between motor vehicles and masculinity. According to David Charters, "our culture has invested [machines] with gendered meanings and values." Boys are more likely to be socialized into "tinkering with cars" and generally "deriving [more] pleasure from technology."[2] For Ida, the motor vehicle embodied "myriad layers of meaning."[3] One of the reasons for her interest in cars and trucks is that they tapped into what she viewed as some of the worst excesses of working-class masculinity, as described in the previous chapter. At the same time, Ida was proud of her family's vehicles, no doubt seeing them as symbols of status and mobility. In this sense,

cars and trucks were an important component of working-class life and culture. They were also a vital source of income for the household, and as such
were a key component of the family economy. Working-class women like Ida
had "complex and contradictory" feelings toward motor vehicles.[4] On the one
hand, advertisers and most male drivers devalued her as a "nervous woman
driver." On the other hand, when Ida finally learned to drive in mid-life, the
car became a symbol of liberty and freedom that allowed her to explore Saint
John and parts of New Brunswick.

This chapter will explore the gendered and class dimensions of cars and
trucks in working-class life and culture. This will be accomplished in part by
drawing comments and insights from Ida Martin's diaries on the central, yet
sometimes overlooked, role that vehicles played in working-class families' lives
in modern Canada. While scholars have revealed the centrality of motor
vehicles (notably trucks) to the rural farm economy and the symbolism of
cars to the country's burgeoning postwar consumer culture and middle class,
more light needs to be shed on the place of vehicles in the urban working-
class family economy and to the construction of working-class masculinity.
By the mid-twentieth century across North America, the middle class had fully
embraced the automobile and it increasingly became accessible and necessary
for working-class families.[5] Similarly, as Ida Martin's diary entries suggest,
several aspects of vehicle ownership – driving, repairing ("tinkering"), and
cleaning – were closely intertwined with gender identity and stereotypes in
the postwar era.

The Working Class and Motor Vehicles in Postwar Society

Automobiles became a symbol of "the good life" in the postwar period. By the
end of the Second World War, one in ten people in Canada operated a passenger vehicle. By 1945, "the dream of automobile ownership was ... second only
to home-ownership." By 1960, two-thirds of Canadian households owned automobiles; Canada had thus become a "motorized nation."[6] In New Brunswick
in 1960 there were 106,167 registered passenger vehicles. Throughout the 1960s
and 1970s, the number of automobiles in the province continued to grow,
reaching 252,915 in 1980.[7] The now-classic studies of Middletown (Muncie, In-
diana) by sociologists Robert and Helen Lynd, published in 1929 and 1937, provide us with some indications of the significance of automobiles to
working-class Americans. By the 1920s and early 1930s, the Lynds argued that

Figure 3.1
Ida and AR in front of a truck, circa 1940s

the motor vehicle was "an accepted essential of normal living." Later on in the 1930s, car culture had "more symbolic meaning to the working-class than to the business class."[8] We argue that this significance extended into the postwar period. The Martins often worked on their cars and trucks, polishing them, and posing with them; On 2 October 1962, Ida "shined the Chevy" until her husband came home. And when Ida and AR bought a Chevrolet in 1972, they took it to Sussex to show it off to her sister and husband.[9] Frequently AR would take his grandchildren for drives in his truck. On 14 October 1972, he took his grandson AD for a ride, who, according to Ida, "loved the truck." Ida also kept track of the cars bought and sold by her family members and friends. In 1961, her brother Row was in to "show me his new truck." In 1962, family friend Eileen gave them a ride in her Falcon convertible. In 1974, Mel "came in to show me her 72 Datson sta[tion] wagon."[10]

The advent of mass-produced vehicles democratized mobility for the working-class family. As Virginia Scharff notes, "the private motor car is a form of transportation that gives the driver latitude in choosing where to go, and when to make the trip."[11] The experience of travelling outside of one's community was for many Canadians, including Ida, an "antidote to the routines of everyday life."[12] Ida recorded occasional Sunday drives, and while the Martins did not generally go far afield, the diaries reveal a number of trips to visit family in Sussex, Minto, and Havelock. On 22 November 1966, Ida picked up Cain and Laura and drove to MacGregor Brook in the vicinity of Sussex "where I was born" and then to Snider Mountain and back to Cains for dinner. On 31 August 1974, they went for a summer drive to see the construction of the new "Nuclure [nuclear power] Plant" at Point Lepreau. Many times Ida and AR used their car to go berrying or picnicking. Having a car also meant that the Martins participated, in a limited capacity, in postwar leisure culture. On 29 May 1968 they bought their first camper trailer and a few days later (15 June) went on their first camping trip. In July they took their granddaughter and her friend camping at Webster Beach on the St John River,[13] and in 1974 they bought Barbara and Sterling's old trailer.[14]

The Martins, along with their family and friends, were rarely able to afford new vehicles. While some may have bought new cars on credit and instalment plans introduced in the postwar period, most bought and sold their cars among themselves, or contributed to a booming used car business. By the mid-1920s, when the market had become saturated with mass-produced cars, most dealers in North America began selling more used cars than new vehicles. This helped to create a "wider cross-section" of automobile owners.[15] The propensity of working-class Canadians to buy used cars also reinforced a general pattern in working-class consumerism that Joy Parr has identified; they frequently preferred used and older models. Oftentimes the explanation was financial, but many also privileged reliability over novelty. The Martins bought only Chevrolets (or "Chevys" as Ida called them), which they considered the most reliable and affordable. They bought their '64 Chevrolet in 1966, their '69 Chevy in 1972, their '74 Impala in 1976, and a '78 Malibu in 1982.[16] They did most of their own repairs, including putting on new brake shoes.[17] Ida kept track of vehicle expenses; the back of her 1966–70 diary includes a list of the car parts they were forced to replace, including tires, mufflers, and brake pads.

AR operated a series of dump trucks over the years, either his own or those belonging to Stephens Construction. In the city directory, AR was employed

Figure 3.2
AR repairing a car

as a trucker in 1941 and a general driver in 1943.[18] He had his own truck in the 1940s and used it to haul loads for various employers. Due to the importance of trucks as a source of income, they are often recorded in Ida's diaries. She describes AR painting his truck, selling the truck, and installing a new motor.[19] When AR began working for Stephens, he drove their trucks, but she still differentiated between them in her diaries. In 1959, AR drove the "Red Truck." On 25 August 1967, No. 20 truck broke down so AR had to drive "old No 6." By November he had his own truck back. In 1970, AR obtained Tom's truck, a "newer one." She also knew when the truck was in the garage.[20]

The trucks belonging to Stephens Construction were often in a state of disrepair. In the heat of August 1960, the truck's generator broke while paving the Harbours Board property. On 1 May 1967, AR "got gassed in an old truck his own no go." One month later, on 1 June 1967, AR "broke axel [*sic*] of truck then something else and then something else gave way. He's awful tired tonite." Two months later "another Spring" in the truck broke.[21] On 28 April 1975, a wheel came off the truck, rolled down the street onto "some man's lawn, thru fence." In May, after a two-week delay, he finally found a part that he needed. AR would sometimes work on his vehicles in the middle of the night with Ida's assistance. They did so to avoid the extra costs associated with taking their vehicles to a mechanic.

Trucking was also a means of earning a living for Ida's brothers. In 1945, her youngest brother Russell bought a three-ton Ford truck to haul sand from a local beach. When brother Jim returned home from the war, he also bought a truck and they went into business together. Eventually they incorporated as RE and JE Friars in 1960, specializing in dry-bulk freight. When Jim retired in 1976, Russell was joined by sons Bill and Peter (who left the business in 1984) and Glen. As of 1995, they had twenty-five employees and served the Maritime provinces and New England. Their fleet included one dump truck, ten highway tractors, one boom truck, and six van body trucks, as well as sixteen trailers for hauling rock, lime, cement, sand, fish feed, wire, cables, poles, and general freight.[22]

Gendering Motor Vehicles

The association between motor vehicles and masculinity dates back to the "industry's forefathers," notably Henry Ford, who viewed himself as a "humble-farm-boy-turned mechanic," more "schooled in the machine shop ... than the classroom or boardroom."[23] Men with rural roots, such as AR, saw the operation and repair of farm machinery as a "defining element of masculinity," and thus viewed the introduction of automobiles to the homestead as a masculine domain.[24] Lydia Simmons, who was raised in the red hills of Mississippi, reflected that "one thing set me apart from my brothers. The car. As far as my father was concerned, women rode in cars and otherwise didn't go near them. Boys? Growing old enough to learn to drive, getting behind the wheel for the first time was a rite of initiation into adult American society."[25]

What of women who took the wheel? The literature on female automobility in the late 1910s and 1920s views the automobile as an "engine of liberation" for women. Once cars became cheaper and more accessible, and the introduction of the electric starter removed the need for physical strength to turn the crank, "women began to move." According to John Gordon, "It was the automobile as much as the Second World War that liberated women."[26] L.M. Montgomery often used the automobile in her fiction as a "powerful symbol of freedom" for women. Valancy Stirling, the main character in Montgomery's 1926 romance *The Blue Castle*, was a woman "teetering on the edge of spinsterhood," who "conquered her fears of the world facilitated by the mobility and freedom Barney Snaith's car provided her." However, Montgomery herself never learned to drive, so we must not "overestimate the car's transformative impact on gender identity."[27]

When "women stepped up to take the wheel," they "invaded a male domain," according to Virginia Scharff, and thus had to "combat both subtle and overt resistance."[28] This is manifested in the social construction of the dangerous "woman driver." Almost immediately, critics portrayed her as a bad driver: indecisive, timid, incompetent, and emotionally unstable. Regardless of how sensible a female driver may be, she still belonged to the category of the bad woman driver.[29] The female driver was also perceived as dangerous because she was contributing to the "collapse of standards of conduct between the sexes" and the "degeneration of the nation's morality." By taking the car out for a drive, she was neglecting her responsibilities at home; she was driving with "reckless and wild abandon;" and she was using the car for dating and "unchaperoned automobile parties" where sexual activity could occur.[30]

By the end of the 1920s and then again in the post–Second World War period, the automobile industry, advertisers, and critics worked to reconcile mobility with female domesticity. Women were portrayed using the automobile to "fulfil their family roles" notably to shop and chauffeur other family members. The motor vehicle became a part of "homemaking." It has been suggested that cars "did little to reduce women's domestic responsibilities," but rather added more responsibilities and expectations.[31] In the postwar era, the car was seen as a technology that "renewed [the] importance of family life." Nuclear families could go on outings in the car and thus spend more time together. The "companionable, hierarchical family, once set on wheels, would arrange itself without conflict or even conscious effort into what would become an archetypal configuration: a man behind the wheel, a woman in the passenger's seat, and children enjoying the ride in the back."[32] The motor vehicle also embodied some of the highlights of postwar middle-class masculinity: domesticization, suburbanization, and consumption.[33] Moreover, gendered distinctions tended to coalesce around two poles: "automotive function" (which was identified with "masculine" concerns such as technological prowess, power, speed, and service) and "form" (identified with "feminine" preoccupations such as luxury, comfort, style, and safety).[34]

Critiquing Motor Vehicle Masculinity

Ida Martin could not afford to be concerned about luxury or style when it came to cars or trucks. Her diaries also reveal that the distinction between form and function was more nuanced than one might think. Although automotive technology was supposed to be a masculine concern, Ida kept track of the mechanical status of their vehicles, probably because she needed to for the sake of the family economy. Upon returning from a family trip on 24 August 1965, she recorded that the car had gone 1,600 miles, had used $26.27 in gas and 10 quarts of oil. In 1971, she included her diagnosis of the car trouble: "A nut off the fly wheel fell down in the pan and caught upon the cogs going around."[35] It is interesting to note that Ida also sometimes questioned her husband's mechanical expertise when tinkering with their vehicles, and found his preoccupation with cars and trucks to be rather exasperating at times. On 12 September 1945, she complained in her diary that AR "frigged at truck," which does not suggest much confidence in his abilities. On 8 April 1974, she noted, "AR tinkering with car – did something to brake drum. Lost brake fluid. TERRIBLE DAY." One can sense her ridicule on 13 September 1945 as she writes: "got dump [truck] welded and [AR's] eyes were sore from watching."

A more serious concern for Ida and other working-class women was the risky behaviour that their husbands engaged in when driving their motor vehicles. This clearly overlaps with Ida's concerns about AR's risk taking while working at the port (as seen in chapter 2). Reckless driving was common for men like AR, who grew up in rural society. According to Lydia Simmons, one of the rites of passage for young men in Mississippi was to "roar down narrow crooked country roads like a 'bat outa hell' … And before one left home, one had to have at least one tremendous wreck driving while drunk or flaunting one's life as a daredevil, and survive it. Otherwise, one was not a man."[36] Ida and Barbara accompanied AR in the truck for a run in 1948; "AR took fill up to Worden's. Barb and I went too (we were plenty scared???)." What do the question marks mean? Perhaps they suggest that Ida regretted bringing her daughter along on this trip? AR was known to take risks behind the wheel. In the absence of cruise control he would place a stick on the accelerator, wedge it under the dash, and then put his feet up on the dash.[37]

Figure 3.3
AR standing in front of a Ford truck, 1948

When AR took the truck on the road, he often imbibed. AR and his brother-in-law, who had accompanied him on a trip to Campbellton, New Brunswick, telephoned Ida while inebriated. Ida also noted the following in her diaries: "Took ?? to Minto and drunk all day till 1/4 to 3 in am and landed back"; "AR on a drunk all day out to Barnseville"; "AR and ____ spreeing out at Purdy's"; and "terrible bad he and others to drive in."[38] On 23 September 1953, AR and a friend left for Fredericton, but were "[a]rrested and [j]ailed that nite," probably for driving while under the influence, and she bailed them out of jail the next morning. This episode clearly upset Ida: "I was sick all day." Sometimes imbibing led AR to miss work: "AR and _____ boozing all day. AR missed work. They hit a car coming over from town." In 1960, "AR smashed Truck Up by Cath[olic] Ch[urch] He's ???."[39] Again, Ida is using blank spaces and question marks when she does not know the details of her husband's exploits or feels too embarrassed to record them. AR was not alone in causing car accidents due to drinking and driving. As Christopher Dummitt has noted, the "shiny golden age of the automobile had a rusty underside."[40]

Ida was also concerned about the effect that trucking had on AR's body. Even after he retired from the port, due to age and ill health, AR continued to work at Stephens Construction. He eventually suffered a heart attack in 1973, which kept him at home until May 1974.[41] AR continued to endure a series of accidents and other health issues as a result of his work. In the fall of 1974, he "fell off his truck & hit his side on running Board broke 3 ribs & top of femur. He had a terrible night." But he was back at work within twenty-six days.[42] On 4 November 1974, AR took his truck to get the clutch repaired and had a difficult time walking to the car: he was "all in." Stephens thereafter assigned him tasks with fewer physical demands. This could be interpreted as a tactic to "get the old m[a]n out of the way,"[43] or perhaps they were legitimately trying to accommodate his diminishing capabilities. His tasks included working as an "acting mechanic" for the trucks and rollers, and putting handles on shovels. Finally in December 1975, his truck licence was downgraded, so he had to return it.[44] In 1976, AR retired from Stephens, although he continued to do renovating and other manual work at home, despite his bad heart.

Ida as Driver

Like many women of her generation, Ida never learned how to drive until later in life. She obtained her driver's licence on 4 September 1962 at the age of 53. In that same year 178,722 New Brunswick residents possessed a licence to operate a motor vehicle.[45] Ida's reticence to drive was due to the above-mentioned construction of the "nervous woman driver" and perhaps the fear of driving that AR's exploits had instilled in her. When Ida was practising for her driver's test, she clearly lacked confidence. However, it is interesting to note that she was most flustered when her husband was in the car; compare her first test with the American Automobile Association (AAA) when she "did real good" (27 June 1962) to her driving lessons with AR two days later when she "did terrible." As Scharff has noted: "Ridicule and discouragement are potent political weapons, and no doubt many women were deterred from driving in part because they or persons close to them believed that no woman could manage an automobile."[46]

Nonetheless, Ida persisted and obtained her driver's licence. Yet it is telling that even after she had her licence, Ida continued to be nervous when AR was in the car; on 4 August 1963, she "couldn't drive at all with AR in [the car]." But overall, improved mobility did seem to have a transformative effect on her. In the diaries, the automobile seems to "come alive" as a driving companion.[47] On 4 September 1962, she noted: "The Chevy and I went to Colbrook" and on 17 March 1964 "I went to Edna Crawford's tonight, the Chevy and I."

The only exposure which Ida and AR had to other makes of cars besides Chevrolets was when family and friends brought them over and took the Martins for a spin. These cars included a Dodge Dart, a Mercury Meteor, a "Toroyo" (Ida probably meant Toyota, her first introduction to a Japanese-manufactured automobile), a Plymouth Aries, a Pontiac, a Volara, an Omega, and a Buick. But the strangest automobile in Ida's estimation was when her daughter and husband bought a 1959 "Volks" or "Voxwagon." On 22 April 1962, Ida's niece drove her to church in the 'V waggon': "lots of laughs." On 16 May 1964 she drove the little black beetle for the first time: "some funny." The only time that Ida bought a new car, which was not a Chevy, was in 1986, when she bought a new Dodge Omni.[48] At this point in her life she was an elderly widow looking for a smaller and more fuel efficient car, but the Omni fell apart within a few years, no doubt reinforcing her suspicions about newer vehicles.

AR and Ida were in a car accident on 31 July 1982, which is described in the back of Ida's 1981–85 diary; "left Long Reach at 8pm for home. AR hit the Guy wire of ferry floats. We both got hurt. AR's chest & my face. Ambulance took us to Hosp[ital] and we come home. Roy was right behind us so had car towed to his place." The next day Ida recorded: "We are hot looking Ducks. I'm Black as a crow. Had people coming & going all day." When they went to see the Chevy, she was surprised by the damage: "Oh me!!!" She and AR did not start to recover from their ordeal until a week after the accident.[49] AR never drove again; Ida became the primary driver. She transported AR to church on 22 August 1982 and took her first drive to Sussex after the accident: "AR went too" (14 March 1983). Ida's tenure as the sole driver signifies the irony of the nervous woman driver construct; recent studies have indicated that women have more stamina for long-distance trips and are actually better and safer drivers than men.[50]

Cars and trucks occupied a central place in the Martin household and in working-class culture and life generally. While owning a vehicle was generally associated with middle-class status, such was not the case for Ida and AR. The fact that Ida and AR did not purchase their cars until the early 1960s speaks to the minimal prosperity that many working-class families in Saint John (and elsewhere in the Maritimes) experienced. Nevertheless, the Martin's experience with automobiles demonstrates that vehicle ownership in the postwar era had become a "universally accessible" option for all but the poorest members of Canadian society.[51] Ida and AR used their vehicles for such leisure activities as camping, picnics, Sunday drives, and visiting family and friends, but they did not take extended vacations beyond New Brunswick. In this sense, they tended to view their cars and trucks in more utilitarian terms, rather than as solely a means of leisure. Indeed, vehicles were key to the working-class family economy and automobiles were a reflection of and helped to construct working-class gender roles and identities, especially masculinity. But in spite of the constraints that established gender roles imposed upon women, the car also afforded women such as Ida an opportunity to escape the confines of the home and the neighbourhood (although she tended to remain in the province), thereby allowing some women to create a life – a world – beyond what their families and society had prescribed for them. It is to this social life (or worlds) that Ida forged that we turn to in the next chapter.

4

~~

Sociability: Ida's Worlds

Busy all day with Explorers. Made lunch and cocoa – 22 girls.
   (8 October 1946)
AR drunk. We went to choir practice. (2 May 1946)
We went to church and got to laughing Bonnie [her niece] and I.
   (16 April 1962)
Barb and Eilleen had Blind Dates but they weren't successful. Tee, hee!
   (28 June 1956)
I made a B cake for John. We had a nice supper. Sterl & kiddies up.
   We had a good game of checkers & to bed at 12. (8 March 1977)
Little Boy's eyes healed this morning in Calvary a miracle. (1 April 1973)
Praise God for his Wonderful Peace he brings. (5 April 1976)

The postwar era introduced an array of social and cultural experiences
to many Canadian families. These avenues of sociability included family
vacations (facilitated by the automobile and later commercial air travel),
rampant consumerism (epitomized by the shopping mall), professional
sporting events, along with television and movies (most of which was produced by Hollywood). Depending on the amount of disposable income that
families had, the opportunities for social interaction and entertainment
were countless. But many working-class families who, like the Martins, had
limited financial resources could not regularly partake in many of these
leisure pursuits. This meant that older forms of sociability, notably faith

and church-based events and organizations for Ida Martin, not only persisted in the postwar era, they often overlapped with some of the modern
forms of leisure.

As Magda Fahrni has argued in her analysis of Montreal families during
the reconstruction period, "The popular conception of a postwar family –
prosperous, suburban, secular, and nuclear – clearly coexisted with other
family realities."[1] The Martin household did resemble the dominant pattern
of the postwar period in that they were a nuclear family. However, in Ida's
diaries, the Martins lived in "intersecting geographies of daily social life,"[2]
wherein opportunities for heterosociability existed alongside active homosocial recreational networks. In this sense, Ida's diaries resemble the patterns
of visiting and family life recorded in nineteenth-century diaries.[3] Ida's diaries differ, however, in that they provide a lens into the sociability of her
daughter Barbara. Barbara (Bonnie's mother) was born in 1936, too early to
be considered a product of the Canadian baby boom, which began in 1946
and ended in 1962. Thus Barbara's first child Bonnie also missed the boom
generation by one year.[4]

Moreover, Barbara's world does not resemble the idealized postwar portrait in that she grew up in a working-class family and much of her sociability
revolved around the church. In her analysis of the oral histories of two Canadian women from the postwar period, Isabel Campbell has stated that
"[w]hole life oral history testimonies expose complexities and contradictions
with regard to idealized families, generational differences, and polarized
gender roles that might remain otherwise hidden when relying primarily on
archival sources."[5] This may be the case, but "archival sources" such as diaries
can reveal similar levels of complexity and nuance in the social worlds of the
postwar working-class family. And while more is now known about these
social worlds, our knowledge about them in a Maritime context remains relatively limited. This chapter, therefore, hopes to broaden our understanding,
through Ida's social activities, of the social worlds of Saint John's working-
class families.

Heterosociability

In the mid-1940s, Ida, AR, and Barbara enjoyed the leisure opportunities of
postwar Saint John. Although income (per capita and regional) lagged behind
in the Maritimes, residents still enjoyed an improved standard of living than

previously and spent more of their money on leisure.[6] Ida, AR, and Barbara often pursued leisure activities in fluid ad hoc groups. In January 1946, Ida went "over town" with Mrs Riches and "her Ma" to the Barn Dance Broadcast. Two months later, she went to "the show" with Linda and then to the Maritime Farmers broadcast at 8 p.m. "Then the boys came over and we had music." The following month, Ida again attended the Maritime Farmers radio program after she finished cleaning. In July 1946, Ida "[w]ent to Lynch's show [the circus] with AR and Fred," and in August she took the ferry from the west side to King's Square to listen to the Shriners Band.[7] The west side ferry ran from Rodney Slip to the foot of Princess Street. Established in 1789, the ferry saw reduced ridership in the postwar period, due to ice flows and increased car ownership, and ceased operation in 1953.[8]

The Martins liked to attend movies. Movie theatres were popular before the onset of television. There were over 1,800 theatres in Canada by the 1950s.[9] On 19 June 1946, Ida went to the "show" with her brother-in-law Murray. In September of the same year, "AR kids & I to Gaiety," and then again on 4 October, "AR Barbs and I" went to a "show at Gaiety," a movie theatre on Main Street West. A few days later on 19 October 1946, "Barbs AR Geo Janes and I to show had midnight snack at Janes." Early the next year she also records attending a hockey jamboree, then a show at the Capitol (a theatre near King's Square in uptown Saint John).[10] As Ida and AR aged, they went out to the movies less frequently, although they occasionally attended movies to mark special events such as their anniversary, or for Ida's birthday, as they did on 6 July 1955.[11]

Like the New Brunswick women diarists of the nineteenth century studied by Gail G. Campbell, Ida and AR's sociability was grounded in an "endless round of visiting and being visited."[12] The Martin kitchen was a hub of hospitality, welcoming many family members, friends, and neighbours. Their sociability was centred in the household but "not bounded by it." Ida and AR also frequently visited family members, friends, and neighbours.[13] The purpose of their visits could be work-related (as illustrated in chapters 1 and 6), when Ida and AR helped a number of family members with home renovations. In that sense, there was a fluidity between work and play – between the family economy and sociability – just as there had been in the nineteenth century.

Visiting also created a geography of sociability. As mentioned in chapter 1, Ida had family in New England. While Ida's sister Marguerite Fanjoy (née

Friars) and her family lived in Boston, Ida visited by train, sometimes alone, at other times with Barb or other family members. As we postulated in the Introduction, she may have begun her diaries as a travel journal, for the first entry she made in her diaries was on 10 August 1945 when she and her brother George (GR) left for Boston on the train. While there, Ida frequently shopped in Central Square, visited friends and family, rode the subway, attended Tremont Temple Church, and even attended the dog races.[14] In 1947 and 1949, she spent late December/early January in Boston, enjoying the ice follies, hockey games, and other leisure activities. Ida also visited Boston with her two brothers and a niece in April 1961.[15] When Marguerite and family moved to Sussex, New Brunswick, Ida and AR spent a great deal of time with them, travelling back and forth on a regular basis. During a visit with Marg and John on 10 April 1973, Ida recorded that they "laughed most of the day." They also frequently travelled to Minto to visit Ida's brother GR, wife Ruth, and her two nieces Bonnie and Janet, and vice versa. On 31 May 1953: "Friars arrived from Minto. We had a crowd coming and going all day."

Sometimes sociability could be intergenerational in nature. In the summer of 1946, AR and his brother-in-law Jim took two truckloads of children to Loch Lomond Lake for a swim. A few days before that, father and daughter went fishing together.[16] Despite these opportunities for hetero- and intergenerational sociability, Ida, Barbara, and AR also participated in their own homosocial communities. As noted in chapter 2, AR's homosocial network encompassed his fellow longshoremen and truckers with whom he worked and played. Sometimes Ida resented the time that this took away from their family. On 10 August 1951 Ida wrote, "Barb lonesome for her father." Sometimes the nuclear family members went off in multiple directions; on 20 June 1953, Ida recorded that "Barbs to Lorneville. I went to car races. AR to Bill's stag party." But the main nexus for Ida's and Barbara's sociability from the mid-1940s onward was the church.

Church

Postwar Canada is often associated with the rise of secularism. According to John Webster Grant, the church in Canada experienced a boom during and immediately after the Second World War, but by the dawn of the 1960s, "Christendom was dead."[17] Recent historiography suggests, however, that Protestantism continued to exert a significant influence in postwar society, both in terms of its effect on public life and institutions, as well as on the private realm of the family.[18] Grant acknowledges that the "end of Christendom did not imply the end of Christianity, or even the diminution of the influence of the church on its members or even society."[19] This chapter explores the continued centrality of Christianity for working-class adherents like Ida Martin. Ida's strong Baptist faith will be analyzed as a form of "lived religion," wherein one's beliefs and religious life are interpreted as part of "lived experience."[20] For believers such as Martin and her Baptist community, "religion was not something that was limited only to an hour on Sunday, or to a particular edifice, or to certain ritual events"; it was an important part of "everyday life."[21] This analysis of lived Protestantism will also contribute to our understanding of the role of religion in the lives of working-class women, for as Catherine Gidney asserts, we still know little about "the intersection of working-class women's history and religious history."[22]

Although Ida became a Baptist, her family history reflects the significant legacy of Presbyterianism in the nineteenth and early twentieth centuries. Her parents were married in the Presbyterian Kirk in Sussex in 1895 and buried in Kirk Hill Cemetery, along with most of the Friars clan.[23] Ida was baptized in Chalmers Presbyterian Church in Sussex in 1908 and was married in the United Church parsonage in Millstream.[24] Sussex could be called a "hotbed" of Presbyterianism for many of the leaders of the Presbyterian Church in New Brunswick, such as Reverend Andrew Donald, originated from or practised in Sussex and the surrounding area.[25] Why then did Ida eventually turn to the Baptist faith? It was in one sense fortuitous. When the family moved to Saint John in 1940, Ida and Barbara stumbled into Charlotte Street Baptist Church because they were late for service at the United Church. By the end of their first service, Ida had joined the choir and several other committees, and she never looked back.[26] She subsequently used her diaries to record the institutional history of her church, including the date when Charlotte Street Church voted to amalgamate with Fundy Heights and Ludlow Street Church (3 June 1959) to form Hillcrest United Baptist Church, noting that it was "a heated debate"; the "big meeting" to organize the new church (29 June 1959); the first time that the three churches met together (18 October 1959); the turning of the sod of Hillcrest (6 June 1960); the last service at Charlotte Street (17 September 1961); the laying of the cornerstone of Hillcrest (28 May 1961); Hillcrest's official opening (24 September 1961); and the burning of the building's mortgage papers (3 February 1977).

One suspects, however, that something more than mere chance governed Ida's decision to attend and subsequently to remain in the Baptist church. Ida would have been comfortable in the company of Baptists due to their moderate theology and the long history of collaboration and co-operation with the Presbyterians in nineteenth-century Sussex. Mainstream theology among Maritime Baptists tended to focus on "personal religious experience," not on a "specific religious ideology," thus avoiding many of the theological controversies that were "raging" in Ontario and the west.[27] Most Presbyterians in Canada had shifted away from "strict Calvinism" and so were much more open to criticism of the Bible than the American and Scottish churches.[28] Thus, it is not surprising that Protestantism was marked by considerable "denominational fluidity" during this era.[29] Ida's parents reflect this legacy of pluralism; on their marriage certificate, her mother is recorded as a Presbyterian and her father as a "Free Baptist."[30] For many years in nineteenth-century Sussex, Presbyterians and Baptists (and sometimes Anglicans and Methodists) met for services in the Roachville Meeting House until they had organized their own congregations.[31] It is fitting that when Ida Martin's mother, Louisa Maud Friars, died in 1939, her service was conducted by a Baptist pastor, Rev. Joseph Griffiths of Hampton Baptist Church, and Rev. L. Judson Levy from the Sussex United Church.[32]

Ida's decision to become a member of Charlotte Street Baptist Church also illustrates the significance of gender in determining denominational affiliation. As Hannah M. Lane has argued, evangelical church membership was primarily a decision made by adult women like Ida. Ever since the Reformation, "women have formed the majority of voluntarist church members in churches that often offered women opportunities for expression, association, or leadership not available elsewhere."[33] Another explanation for Ida's attachment may be due to the strength and vibrancy of the Baptist tradition in the Maritimes. By 1901, Baptists were the single largest Protestant denomination in New Brunswick and Nova Scotia. G.A. Rawlyk has referred to the Maritimes as the "Baptist heartland of Canada." "In no other part of Canada," Rawlyk asserts, "have Baptists formed such a large proportion of the population or had such a profound influence on the existing popular culture."[34] It may also be argued that the Baptist faith articulated for Ida Martin a world view that at least partly guided her actions. An enticing characteristic of the Baptist Church for its members is that it became an avenue for action. Prior to 1914, the Baptists had the "richest tradition of social concern of the three principal Protestant denominations." In an effort to "preserve the church's importance in society," the Baptists were much more adept at uniting the sacred with the secular. This action-based platform continued to be officially articulated at the Baptist Convention as late as 1940.[35]

As a faithful Baptist, Ida would have attempted to follow the activist teachings of the church in whatever way she could. An excellent example of this action-based agenda is the United Baptist Woman's Missionary Union (UBWMU), to which Martin belonged. Maritime Baptist women had performed missionary work overseas and at home since the early 1870s. After the First World War, they were involved in "projects galore," ranging from helping female missionaries in India to supporting sanatoriums in the Maritime provinces. Ida was active in the UBWMU from 1946 until the conclusion of her diaries. She not only attended meetings, but also gave devotionals,[36] and led the group in prayer on 5 April 1976, after which she declared "Praise God for his Wonderful peace he brings," which is the closest she came to making an overt spiritual declaration in her diaries. In 1978, she attended a convention in Grand Manan, New Brunswick,[37] and in December 1978 she was made a Dominion Life member, receiving a gold pin from the Dominion Committee of the Baptist Women of Canada. The life membership was instituted in 1939 to recognize individuals who embodied a lifetime of service. The pin that Ida received was inscribed with the letters BMDLM: "Baptist in name, Missionary in purpose, Dominion in constituency, Life in duration and Membership the responsibility. Thus it symbolizes all which we represent, all for which we work and all which we believe."[38]

The Baptist church in Saint John provided a vibrant social network for Ida, her daughter Barbara, and later Barbara's family. As Lynne Marks has noted for Protestants in late nineteenth-century small-town Ontario, notably Baptists, "Faith, social responsibility, personal ambition, and a desire for community" drew some into active involvement in their local churches.[39] Ida attended not only the women's missionary society, but also prayer meetings, Sunday School, and two services on most Sundays. In 1977, both she and her grandson AD received perfect attendance awards in Sunday School. In 1957, Ida was appointed the convenor of the church's Sunday School picnic.[40] She also gave the Sunday School lesson on 24 February 1980: "Thanks to the Lord."[41] In her diaries we see pastors and guest preachers come and go. We also see references to exceptional sermons, as when Reverend Darrell Pond "excelled himself" or when he "preached up a storm."[42]

As an evangelical, her diaries were also tallies of how many were saved and baptized.[43] On the other extreme, she noted when not many came to church because of the Super Bowl.[44]

Moreover, she recorded the intersection of family and church life, notably when her son-in-law Sterling gave his testimony and was baptized and became a deacon,[45] when her grandson was dedicated,[46] and when she first took her granddaughter Bonnie to church as an infant or to Baby Band as a two-year-old.[47] In the 1940s and 1950s, Ida sang in the church choir and sat on the music committee. When she was no longer in the choir in later years, she still kept track of the senior and junior choirs and recorded when the senior choir was "clapped back for an encore."[48] Ida also helped out with Daily Vacation Bible School,[49] and engaged with the Baby Band, an organization that provided opportunities to train "children from their earliest years to be active co-workers with God in the bringing in of His Kingdom throughout the world,"[50] and Mission Band, an initiative begun by the UBWMU in 1874 to educate children on missions.[51]

These activities often meant a tremendous amount of work. In the 1950s and 1960s, Ida was involved with the church's benevolent committee. At Christmas, she often went "benevolent shopping" and then packed hampers for shut-ins, for the poor, and for overseas missionaries.[52] Ida recorded collecting for the Bible Society in 1970 and washed and ironed baptismal gowns in 1981.[53] This volunteer labour would continue into old age: in 1985, at the age of 78, she made sandwiches for the Baby Band in the morning and cookies for the missionary party in the evening.[54] Ida also cooked for the church groups in which her daughter was involved: "Busy all day with Explorers. Made lunch and cocoa – 22 girls" and two days later she was " busy all day with CGIT [Canadian Girls in Training] – went down and prepared lunch and cocoa – 15 girls, 3 leaders, 6 quarts of milk."[55] However, the relationship between work and religious sociability was a fluid one, as it was in the familial context. Being a leader of Baby Band meant picking up prizes, writing invitations, and organizing parties, but it also meant mixing with the other leaders socially.[56] As a choir member, Ida not only attended practice, but also had the choir to her house for a "social."[57] In 1981 as a missionary society member Ida "done up 15lbs of stamps for the leprosy mission" and sent a missionary parcel to India. And she also brought five women home for tea after the missionary meeting in March 1968.[58] It is quite clear that Ida enjoyed church-related functions. "We went to church and got to laughing Bonnie [her niece] and I." At the Ladies Christmas Party in 1978, she recorded that one of them dressed up as Santa and they all "had a Ball."[59]

Ida's moral outlook and sociability extended beyond the church proper. On 8 March 1946, she joined the Women's Christian Temperance Union,[60] due no doubt to many Baptists' negatives views on alcohol and her own experiences with AR's drinking. According to her diary, she became president of her chapter in 1947.[61] She attended rallies and conventions, but most of the meetings were held in the living rooms of the members. She records attending temperance meetings in the homes of Mrs Todd, Mrs Henderson, Mrs Hargroves, and Mrs Fullerton.[62] Daughter Barbara received first prize in a temperance essay contest in 1946.[63] Although the temperance movement in the postwar Maritimes lacked the "institutional base" of its nineteenth- and early twentieth-century roots, it could still "rely on a network of Baptist and United Church ministers and congregations into the 1950s and 1960s to carry out its activities."[64]

Although Ida and her daughter became very involved in the activities of the church, AR did not. This is consistent with many of the working-class families that Lynne Marks explored in late nineteenth-century rural Ontario. While the demands of the family economy may have united these families, as Marks concludes, the "values of a shared Christian domesticity appear to have been far less significant in most working-class homes."[65] Some diary entries accentuate Ida's and Barbara's religious world as a counterpoint to AR's: On 2 May 1946 "AR drunk. Went to choir practice,"[66] and on 20 February in the same year, AR was "drunk all day" so Ida "[w]ent to [a] prayer m[eeting]." Despite the Protestant church's call for the involvement of more adult males in the religious life of the church and the family, the dominant perception remained: mothers were primarily responsible for "spiritual care-giving." Postwar husbands and fathers tended to skip church and neglected religious life at home. According to Tina Block, "[f]amily religion remained very much the preserve of women in the postwar world."[67]

It is interesting to note that AR did eventually turn to the church later in life. After his daughter's wedding, he attended services with Ida a few times. In 1962, she noted that "[w]e both went to church"; the next week: "AR & I to church this am & evening"; and in early December "We 3 to church [Ida, AR, and niece Bonnie]." He also went to Hillcrest Church in 1977 to see his grandson baptized.[68] By the early 1970s, however, AR was not attending the Baptist church with his wife and daughter, but instead migrated to Calvary

Temple, one of the many Pentecostal congregations growing at this time.[69] On 29 May 1982, he was baptized at the Full Gospel Assembly.[70] AR's insistence on attending another church illustrates the continued existence of separate social worlds, although Ida did occasionally accompany him in the evenings. On 9 April 1972, she attended the junior choir cantata at her own church, went with her son-in-law to a gospel concert in the afternoon, and then attended Calvary Temple with her husband in the evening. She clearly had mixed feelings about Pentecostalism. On the one hand, she was impressed that a healing occurred at the church: "Little Boy's eyes healed this morning in Calvary a miracle."[71] She also acknowledged that many gave witness for Christ at the services; "20 coming forward at one time."[72] However, she was not used to the more free flowing nature of Pentecostal worship, noting that there was no service per se, just "confusion confusion," and that they tended to last a long time: "AR went over to the charismatic service home at ¼ to 12 ugh!!" She also commented on the performance of the pastor at Calvary: "real excited. Took off coat, threw it on floor etc."[73]

Generational Sociability

In addition to revealing the social world of the church, Ida's diaries provide a glimpse into the emerging social worlds of her daughter Barbara. Although Barbara was not a baby boomer, she did come of age in Saint John in the 1950s. One characteristic of the experience of young people after the war was a longer time spent in school. While Ida and AR did not earn high school diplomas, their daughter Barbara completed high school, and in 1955 she graduated from the Saint John Vocational School with a certificate in commercial education (with an emphasis on typing and short-hand). Ida kept track of Barbara's teachers and her progress in the classroom. She also became involved in the Home and School Association.[74] In 1947 and 1948, Ida baked cookies for the Home and School Association and for a Valentine's Day party at La Tour School on the west side of Saint John. According to Barbara: "I was so proud of her when I was in primary school, anything the teachers needed or wanted, she was there ... making costumes or whatever. One time she made all of grade two into flowers. I was Miss Rosebud."[75] She also made costumes for the winter carnival and school closing.[76] As always, Ida ensured that social intercourse was mixed with work in equal measure. On 1 February

1947, she had the Executive of the Home and School Association in for tea, and on 10 May 1948 she invited the teachers to dinner.

Ida also became a chronicler of Barbara's emerging social life, revealing the increasingly youth-centred nature of postwar society. In 1946, Ida recorded when Barbara started her music lessons, when she went to the movies with her friends, and when she skinned her face while roller skating.[77] After the war, historians have noted that youth in Canada spent more time than ever before "in the company of their peers."[78] Ida kept track of Barbara's various friends and the many birthday parties that she attended. For Barbara's eleventh birthday, Ida hosted a party for twelve girls.[79] Ida continued to follow her daughter when she started at Saint John High School on 4 September 1951, when she graduated in June 1954, and then went to Vocational School, graduating on 30 June 1955.[80] Barbara had a series of jobs until she started more permanently at London Life in June 1955. She continued to live with her parents, paying them a monthly rent.

Given Ida's involvement in the church, many of Barbara's formative years were spent there. Teen culture in the 1940s and '50s is typically considered to have revolved around the secular world of movies, dance halls, music, and clothing. But the "teenager" experience was not a uniform phenomenon; in Barbara's case it was also shaped by religion. In Ida's diaries, an important marker of Barbara's youth was her involvement in the church. Ida recorded when Barbara was baptized (10 February 1946), her first Sunday in the choir (15 February 1946), becoming a member of the CGIT (14 May 1947), and in later years, her involvement in the Baptist Young Peoples Union (BYPU), becoming president on 19 September 1955. Many young people from the BYPU met at Ida's flat after their meetings for sing songs and parties. On 28 January 1955, the youth played and sang until 12:30 in the morning. Ida usually liked her home being a hub of activity, but it clearly annoyed her on 2 October 1955: "12 kids in for a sing song ... Cross about kids in." She also worried when the youth were at "Main St [church] singing then out till 3am nearly crazy worrying."[81]

As Barbara became a teenager and young woman, she continued to associate with a peer group of female friends who experienced a great deal more latitude than young unmarried women in previous decades. For example, Barbara and three of her friends left Saint John for an unchaperoned trip to New York City 17–26 July 1959. A more common symbol of teenage culture in the 1950s is dating. Barbara dated many different people over the course of the mid- to late 1950s. Mary Louise Adams argues that dating became more competitive beginning in the 1930s, when young men and women "wanted to have as many dates as possible." For a woman to be "popular," she had to be seen as "valuable and in great demand."[82] Ida lists many of Barbara's courters in the pages of her diary, usually with no commentary. But sometimes Ida expressed her displeasure: on 25 February 1958, Barbara was "Out with paint dealer. I'm some mad," and in April of the same year, "some Thomson fellow came to get Barb but I wouldn't let her go with him." A year earlier, "Barbs out with Gagetown soldier me worrying my head off."[83] On 4 July 1958, Barbara dated McKiel in the afternoon and Spence in the evening. Another characteristic of dating in this period was that it was often enjoyed as part of a group activity. Barbara and her friend Eileen dated young men together. On 12 June 1958, Eileen, Barbara, and two "fellows" went fishing at St Martins. Two years earlier, Ida could not contain herself: "Barb and Eilleen had Blind Dates but they weren't successful. Tee, hee!"[84] Barbara also emulated the teen culture phenomenon of "going steady" in 1959 with a young man from England named Spencer, who took her on picnics and to the drive-in, and brought her roses; in essence they engaged in a formal courtship. In early December, Spencer went back to England for a visit, returning on 15 January 1960 with a tea service for Barbara (no doubt for her trousseau) and presents for Ida and AR. However, shortly after he returned, they "broke off going steady."[85] What had happened? Over Christmas, a quiet young man named Sterling made his way into Ida's diaries for the first time on 21 December 1959, as he came to the house to help put up their Christmas tree. He would become a constant presence in the Martin household. Sterling recalls that he was "at 213 Queen Street every night of the week until all hours, and hearing the coughing coming from Ida's bedroom, which would begin at around 1AM. That was no doubt my signal to be on my way."[86] Barbara and Sterling were engaged on 21 July 1960 and married on 24 June 1961.

Ida then proceeded to record the matrimonial traditions of the late baby boom era in Saint John, with an endless string of showers and weddings, including Barbara's and Sterling's. Many of the wedding showers were designed to meet the specific needs of the young couple. Barbara had both a linen shower and a cupboard shower, to fill her pantry.[87] Barbara displayed her gifts in her parents' flat.[88] After many preparations, "everything went off lovely" at the wedding on 24 June 1961. When their friends Butch and Sandra were married on 7 October 1961, Barbara and Sterling engaged in the wedding tradition of chasing the newlyweds: in Ida's words, the "[k]ids followed them to Pen[n]field came home and got supper and after them again." When Barbara's cohort began to conceive, another round of baby showers followed, often called "Stork showers" in Ida's diaries.

Another interesting postwar social practice that emerged in Ida's diaries in the mid-1960s are home parties, during which a particular product was sold to the attendees. Barbara attended a jewellery party on 10 April 1969, a clothes party on 4 November 1969, and several Tupperware parties in February and March 1966. Barbara hosted her first Tupperware party on 15 February and made $73. This would be followed by others hosted by Barbara's friends. The advertisements for Tupperware promoted an image of the postwar user as a "white middle-class Everywoman," yet most women who became hostesses were working class, due to the opportunities Tupperware provided in generating an income and because they purported to stretch household budgets by keeping food fresh, a particular concern for lower-income families. Regardless, one cannot overlook the opportunities that Tupperware parties provided for sociability, especially for homemakers who may have felt isolated and who may not have had many respectable places to gather outside of church.[89]

In June 1966, Barbara, Sterling, and their three-year-old daughter Bonnie moved to the bottom flat of 213 Queen Street,[90] where they would remain until 1986. For that period of time, the border between the two households became fluid, creating a climate of intergenerational support and sociability.[91] Sterling remembers "being out in the yard doing things on a Saturday morning, and about 10 or 10:15 the upstairs porch window would open and Ida would announce that tea was ready. Or at other times all I had to do was go upstairs and inquire if there was tea going, and it always was!"[92] A typical example of intergenerational sociability was the birthday party for Ida's brother-in-law John Fanjoy in 1977, which was held in her flat. She recorded that the Huskins cooked a turkey in the oven downstairs and "I made a B cake for John. We had a nice supper. Sterl & kiddies up. We had a good game of checkers & to bed at 12."[93]

This intergenerational sociability also applied to the relationship between grandparents and grandchildren. Scholars have identified different "styles" of grandparenting; Ida could be considered an amalgamation of the "influential" grandmother (she was involved in the lives of her grandchildren, lived close to them, and saw them often) and the "surrogate" grandparent (she helped to parent and take care of her grandchildren).[94] Ida and AR often took their grandchildren for picnics or to see the animals at the Rockwood Park Zoo. Whenever Bonnie and AD went away with their parents, Ida recorded missing them in her diaries. When the Huskins went camping for the first time at Oak Point 18–24 June 1971, Ida recorded "Kids [by which she meant all four of them] away real lonesome." And when the Huskins left for a vacation in Ontario later that summer, she felt "Lonesome, Lonesome, Lonesome."[95]

Ida's diaries reveal that her social worlds tended to revolve around her faith and her family. Both were extremely important to Ida; indeed, they were central to her identity as a working-class woman in postwar Saint John. Moreover, by exploring Ida's worlds through her faith and family we can see how some working-class families in Saint John negotiated the economic and cultural changes that unfolded in this era. And like Ida, these families relied upon one another, and for some the church, for a measure of stability, conviviality, and solace. Ida's religious life, in particular, is an important reminder that the wave of secularism that accompanied modernity did not completely wash away individual faith and the place of the Christian church in Canadian society. Moreover, as Ida's diaries clearly indicate, faith and family were closely intertwined, to the point where each strengthened the other. But as the next chapter will highlight, faith and family were not the only aspects of Ida's worlds. Through the new communication medium of television, Ida would engage in the world of politics and other social and cultural developments in post-1945 Canada.

5

Assessing the Social and Political Engagement
of an "Ordinary" Woman

Gars [brother] and AR didn't work all day [due to storm], so we watched
    the trip around the world. John Glen of NSA orbited the world 3 times
    in less than 3 hours. (20 February 1962)
wrote 8 premiers tonite. (25 January 1979)
A Red Letter Day. Constitution passed in Commons. (2 December 1981)
Hostages in Iran were freed. They were held 444 days. (1981–85 diary)

One of the most obvious patterns in Ida's diaries is their thickening over time,
both literally as she crammed more and more information into the diaries,
and figuratively, as she began to move beyond the bounds of family to record
more information about the world around her. By the mid-1950s, Ida was
beginning to record global issues such as the space race and the Olympics,
national highlights such as the introduction of the new flag, and formal
political activities including federal, provincial, and municipal elections, and
significant constitutional developments.

How do we explain this thickening in the diaries? In an attempt to answer
this question, this chapter borrows from Gerald Friesen's *Citizens and Nation:
An Essay on History, Communications and Canada* by interrogating the effect
of communications systems on the articulation of Ida's world views and
political concerns. Friesen argues that we need more analyses of the ways in
which "ordinary people" (like Ida) have contributed to the shaping of the
image of the nation. He contends that "in societies [like Saint John that are]
peripheral to great imperial centres, the crucial measures of adaptation and

community-building – the acts deserving of the term 'historic' – are those undertaken by ordinary citizens."[1] How do we uncover the achievements and contributions of the non-elite? Friesen suggests that we can understand a great deal about ordinary people by placing them in the context of the communications systems they use(d) to express themselves. In other words, acts of communication, whether oral, written, print, or electronic formats, establish a "framework" for understanding ordinary people's construction of self, of community, of politics, and of citizenship. This chapter examines the influence of textual/print and electronic communication systems in facilitating the political/social engagement of Ida Martin, the importance of the diary in this process of meaning making, and the ways in which electronic media shaped Ida's evolving interest in politics and the world around her. It also analyzes the filtering process – how ordinary citizens like Ida sifted through the information and what they eventually articulated. In so doing, this chapter will help us to better comprehend how some Canadians interpreted "significant" historical events and gave them meaning. This is particularly important in Ida Martin's world, since she had limited access, for financial reasons, to such mainstream publications as *Chatelaine* and *Maclean's* magazines. This suggests that the influence of these magazines, which Valerie J. Korinek has superbly revealed for suburban Canada, was somewhat muted in parts of urban, working-class Canada.[2]

Textual and Electronic Communications

By putting pen to paper, Ida was invoking the legacy of what Friesen calls the "textual-settler society," a communication system characterized by the "alphabet-letterpress-print revolution."[3] By writing in a commercially produced five-year diary, Ida was also following the dictates of "print capitalism." Her commercially bound diaries limited the amount of space that she had at her disposal, and they also had embedded within them certain values or cultural directives. These verses were printed in Ida's 1945 diary:

What an easy thing to write
Just a few lines every night
Tell about the fun you had
And how sweetheart made you glad.
Write about the party gay,

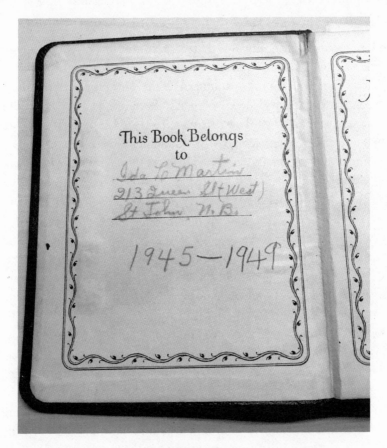

Figure 5.1
Ida Martin's Diary, 1945–1949

In the sail-boat down the bay;
The motor trip, that perfect dance,
The weekend at the country manse.
Courtship – then wedding time,
Honeymoon in southern clime;
Home again in circles gay,
Till 'Little Stranger' came your way.
So day by day the story grows
As onward your life journey goes
Lights and shadows – memories dear.
These are the MILESTONES of your career.

Ida did not reflect the commercial diary's presumption that she would be middle-class. She could not afford sailboats, "weekends at the country manse," or to "honeymoon in [a] southern clime." However, in accordance with the commercial diary's view of women's life course, Ida's entries in the mid-1940s were written largely from the perspective of her family. She made no explicit references to the Second World War, but rather recorded its effect on family members. She mentioned when her brothers were discharged from the service and when her injured brother Jim returned from overseas. She recorded making sandwiches for the soldiers' socials and taking out war bonds.[4] A similar pattern can be discerned in the front pages of her 1950–55 volume, wherein Ida inscribed a series of dates accompanied by the phrase "Lost Junior." "Junior" was her nephew, the son of her sister Marguerite, who lived in the United States. Junior served in the Korean War and these are the dates when he was lost overseas. But there is no explicit reference to the Korean War in the diaries.

By the mid-1950s and peaking in the mid-1980s, Ida moved beyond the "milestones" identified in these 1945 diary verses, including more non-local and political content. In that sense, as a consumer, Ida did not unquestioningly accept the messages of modern consumerism, such as the verses printed above. Was Ida simply becoming a more confident diarist? Or was she taking more of an interest in the world around her when Barbara left home and she was contemplating an empty nest? Or is there another explanation?

The introduction of electronic media in postwar Canada helped to expand Ida's world. A large cabinet radio occupied the back porch at 213 Queen Street. Ida and AR were still listening to the radio in the 1970s, probably because they spent most of the summer months in the back porch. While there are a few references to the radio in Ida's diaries, the entries are more useful for charting the introduction of television in their home. In November 1955, Ida and AR bought their first TV set. Although TVs arrived later in Canada than in the United States, they were part of the entertainment and consumer culture landscapes by the early 1950s. As David Harvey notes, television was an integral part of the promotion of a culture of consumerism.[5] In 1953 alone, over seven million televisions were sold in Canada. These sets received three to five channels, depending on location and antenna. By 1960, there were fifty-nine stations in Canada capable of reaching over 90 per cent of the population. English-language private and public stations were available in all provinces by the mid-1950s. Throughout the Atlantic region, people often reminisce about the postwar period as the time when they saw their first television program.[6] Douglas Owram argues that the arrival of a new TV set in a neighbourhood was "an event."[7] In 1954 and 1955, before they bought their own TV, Ida, AR, and Barbara frequently visited neighbours and family members to watch their sets. When they obtained their own TV, they also had visitors, often Barbara's teenaged friends.[8] The advent of television generated a demand for the appropriate furniture for the living room: TV tables, stands, lamps, and comfortable couches. These purchases were recorded in Ida's diaries.[9] The Martins were able to afford their first TV set due to the credit and instalment plans that were becoming increasingly accessible for working-class families after the Second World War. In accordance with their notions of thrift and self-sufficiency, they paid off their TV purchase in six months.[10] By the mid-1950s, the price of an average television had declined from around $400 (20 per cent of an average annual income) in 1952 to $170–$190.[11]

The Martins did not immediately buy a colour TV when they became available. Instead, they obtained another black and white set from their daughter in 1965, and a smaller one in 1970.[12] By preferring a cheaper black and white set, they once again reflected the cautiousness of their class and generation. Despite their affordability, black and white sets still generated expenses: at the back of her 1956–60 diary, Ida kept track of the numerous TV tubes that burned out and when she replaced them. In 1969, Barbara and Sterling went to visit one of Barbara's friends, Eileen, to see her new colour set. But they would not purchase their own until 1972, at which point Ida admitted "reception was wonderful." In September 1978, she records having cable installed.[13]

Although Ida did not watch as much television as her husband, they did watch a few programs together. Ida and AR did not share many activities in common, so this was important "together time." Ida recalls in her diary in January 1956 that "we all stayed to watch the late show" and in September 1965, they "[d]id nothing but watch TV all night." On 20 July 1973, it was a "real funny evening on TV" and 3 December 1976 was a "good night on TV."[14] What did they watch? As mass entertainment became more popular in the postwar period, Canadians were "more exposed to US culture than any previous generation."[15] Ida and AR frequently watched American TV classics such as *Bonanza*, *Ed Sullivan*, and *Carol Burnett*.[16] However, they also watched Canadian programs, notably *Front Page Challenge* and the *Tommy Hunter Show*. On 16 April 1973, she recorded in her diary that the *Tommy Hunter Show* was "real good." On his twentieth-anniversary episode in 1985, he played a "lot of the old ones [songs]."[17] According to Paul Rutherford, Tommy Hunter was popular because he "embodied the simple ways of times past, and the anguish of ordinary people."[18] She also records watching *Don Messer's Jubilee*. This show began in Halifax in 1957 and came to network television as a summer replacement program. It eventually earned a space on the winter schedule, due to popular demand. In November 1961, it was the most popular show on Canadian television, even ahead of hockey and *Ed Sullivan*. Don Messer was particularly popular in the Maritimes, capturing 96 per cent of the potential Maritime audience at its peak. Programs like Don Messer and Tommy Hunter appealed to Maritimers because the entertainment was comfortable and familiar, and the stars were seemingly real people, neither "fashionable nor debonare." As a result of Don Messer's exposure on TV, Ida went to see him when he made a special appearance at the local Sobeys in 1960, and she attended a resurrected version of the show in 1986.[19] Ida records watching a few sporting events, including the 1958 victory of the "Moncton fellow," boxer Yvonne Durrell and she watched the Olympics and the Grey Cup, but primarily *Hockey Night in Canada*, which usually ended up near the top of the rankings in the winter months.[20]

However, the "promise of television was best realized by actuality broadcasts of special events."[21] In actuality broadcasts, ordinary people like Ida could watch the events as they unfolded. In that sense, TV was the "most accessible vehicle of communication yet devised."[22] Ida was particularly persistent in tracking the space race; in 1960, she watched "Spudneck go across the sky twice." On 20 February 1962, she records that "Gars [her brother] and AR didn't work all day [storm], so we watched the trip around the world. John Glen of NASA orbited the world 3 times in less than 3 hours." She records on 23 July 1969, "3 men splashed down from 1st walk on moon." In April 1970, she watched the "moon fellows" go into space and "give their account of themselves in space ship." She continued to keep track of the Apollo 14 mission. In July 1971, "I watched fellows on moon most of the day" and again in April 1972 "3 astronauts left for the moon – John Young, Tom Mattingly, Charles Duke." She also mentioned the "splashdown of astronauts in Skylab" in 1973.[23]

Television broadcasts allowed ordinary people like Ida not only to receive a glimpse of the final frontier, but to "see other parts of the world that their ancestors would never have had an opportunity to see."[24] Ida watched the

Pope's address to the United Nations in 1965, the peace treaty being signed between Israel and Egypt in 1979, Anwar Sadat's assassination in 1981, and the Olympics in Korea in 1987. She also noted when the "hostages in Iran were freed. They were held 444 days."[25] She was very aware of American developments, given the amount of American coverage she would have been exposed to. She recorded the assassinations of President John F. Kennedy, Senator Robert Kennedy, and Martin Luther King, the swearing in and resignation of President Richard Nixon, the debate between Jimmy Carter and Ronald Reagan, and the shooting of President Reagan.[26]

Politics and Constitutional Developments

What is perhaps most surprising about the diaries is the visibility of formal partisan politics and mega-constitutional developments. There is a small yet expanding literature on women and politics in Atlantic Canadian history, but it tends to either analyze the involvement of women in formal politics (local, provincial, or federal),[27] or their role in formal and informal political activism – for example, signing petitions, joining voluntary organizations, and engaging in letter-writing campaigns.[28] Ida Martin was certainly not a politician nor was she a political activist. She represents the majority of ordinary women (and men) in Canada, both historically and in the present day, who have never been directly or actively involved in formal or informal politics (beyond voting) or political activism. Does this mean that we should consider them to have been politically unengaged? Political scientist Don Desserud argues that "Throughout New Brunswick history, women have shown considerable skill and determination to find alternative means to express their political concerns."[29]

One of Ida's methods of engagement was simply to watch and record. She recorded many elections: American, Canadian, provincial, and municipal. Indeed, election returns were one of the most watched forms of actuality broadcasting. After watching Pierre Elliott Trudeau's narrow victory over Robert Stanfield in 1972, Ida concluded that it was "some exciting."[30] She also stayed up until 1am to watch Joe Clark's 1979 victory over Trudeau, and then Trudeau's landslide win over Clark in 1980, which she watched until 2 a.m.; "[t]ired" is what she wrote the next day.[31] In the back of her 1976–80 diary, she records in more detail Joe Clark's fall from grace. Ida was glued to the TV all day and night in 1984 as John Turner was elected as Liberal Party leader

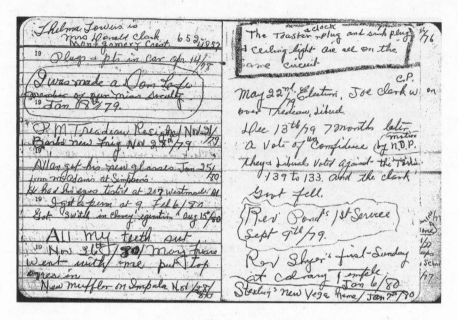

Figure 5.2
Diary entry, 1976–1980

and thus as prime minister.[32] A few days later she watched the debate between John Turner, Brian Mulroney, and Ed Broadbent, and then Mulroney's majority win in 1988.[33]

Ida kept especially close tabs on constitutional developments, primarily the constitutional repatriation round of the late 1970s and early 1980s. She watched the "Premiers 10 at Ottawa" on 31 October 1978. On 6 February 1979, Ida "[s]at most of the day watching Trudeau and Premiers on Constitution." In the front of her 1981–85 diary, she notes: "New Canadian constitution signed by Q Eliz in Ottawa: April 17, 1982." In the same volume on 2 December 1981, she notes in red pencil "A Red Letter Day. Constitution passed in Commons." Then on 4 February 1982, coming full circle, she records once again watching the premiers' conference.

This attention to constitutional events on television can be understood by considering the "drama" of these affairs, which attracted constant media coverage.[34] Constitutional negotiations were by their very nature "all-consuming affairs," taking up more and more of citizens' attention. Traditionally a form of executive federalism, wherein a constitutional elite of

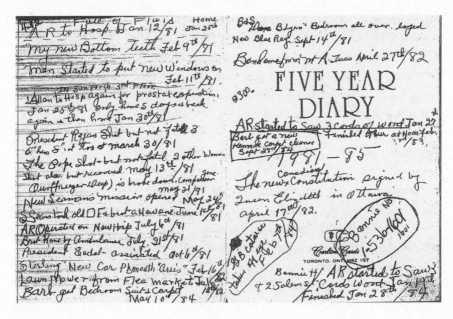

Figure 5.3
Diary entry, 1981–1985

elected officials and prominent bureaucrats determined the fate of the nation, the repatriation saga incorporated citizens' demands in the process. Anthony Hampton, in his analysis of the response of New Brunswick citizens to the Meech Lake Accord, argues that our historiographical understanding of mega-constitutional politics is bifurcated; on the one hand are those studies that focus on constitution making from the top down, from the perspective of executive federalism; and on the other hand, there is a literature examining citizens' responses. Hampton argues that we must look beyond this bifurcation, for while the citizens involved in the constitutional debates were not the constitutional elite, they were still usually educated professionals, with political connections.[35]

What of others, like Ida Martin, who did not fit this profile? We must find room for her in our analysis of such events. Friesen concurs, suggesting that immersing oneself in the outpourings of communication media like television coverage allows "ordinary people" like Ida to learn how to "participate in the institutions of the state."[36] Similarly, in his analysis of the TV media coverage of the Iran-Contra affair, David Thelen shows that viewers used their analysis of the coverage to dialogue with others and eventually begin a phone and letter-writing campaign. By so doing, he asserts, they were creating a "more participatory democracy" and demanding the "right to be heard for themselves."[37] According to her diaries, Ida felt strongly enough about the constitutional affairs that she wrote each of the premiers regarding her concerns; on 25 January 1979, she noted "wrote 8 premiers tonite."[38]

Filtering, Sorting, and Reorganizing: Ida's Lists

Participants in communications systems are not uncritical receptors of the information they are receiving. Instead, they "actively filter, sort, and reorganize information in personally meaningful ways in the process of constructing an understanding of public issues."[39] By analyzing the front and back pages of Ida's diaries we can see how she assimilated and organized the material. She used the front and back pages to create lists. She used these lists almost like an index, to reflect on the events of the previous five years. It is interesting to see how these lists changed over time. In the back pages of the 1945–49 diary, Ida included the names of Barbara's teachers and details of her family's finances. Family affairs continued to dominate the lists in Ida's 1971–75 diary. However, in the 1976–80 list, we see significant changes, with a chronology of political developments. Similarly, in the 1981–85 list, we see mention of constitutional developments. The political nature of the latter two lists is no doubt due to the emergence of major constitutional events and increased media coverage of them.

Another characteristic of the lists, besides an increase in Canadian political coverage, is the seamless nature of the transitions between the local, provincial, national, and international, the personal and political, as well as the mundane and the spectacular. Ida makes no distinctions as to their relative importance or significance. A useful metaphor is that of a textual collage, a non-linear arrangement of various contexts, all of which contribute to a representation of Ida Martin's social and political self. Marilyn Ferris Motz argues that nineteenth-century rural diaries also adopted this form of organization: "What appears to us to be incongruously combined ideas reflect a culture in which holidays, weather, and death do not belong in separate compartments, a culture in which one does not keep separate accounts for work and personal life, but combines all activities into a whole measured only by units of time, not social categories."[40] Working-class women like Ida (especially those with rural roots) would have organized their worlds in a similar way. Feminists have also suggested that women chroniclers possess a more "unified sensibility" than do male authors; they are less likely to "split one aspect of experience off from another."[41]

A difference between Ida's diaries and the nineteenth-century midwestern diaries studied by Motz is that the latter do not very often mention national and/or political events. Margaret Conrad makes the same point about eighteenth- and nineteenth-century Maritime women's diaries: "Instead of ordinary lives forming the backdrop of history, the so-called 'big' political events are reduced to rumours and abstractions while the daily rhythms of life continue to occupy centre stage."[42] However, Gail C. Campbell contends that the nineteenth-century New Brunswick diarists that she examined were definitely cosmopolitan, especially those who travelled, such as sea captains' wives.[43] Ida's diaries are similar, perhaps because of the periodization. The postwar era introduced frameworks (i.e., international affairs and constitutional developments) not available in the same way to her earlier counterparts. Ida integrated these postwar frameworks into her textual persona.

Postwar English Canadian Nationalism

One piece of Ida's textual collage is a concerted effort to come to terms with the growth of English Canadian nationalism in the postwar period. In the diaries we see a recognition of Canadian nationhood not only through the recording of elections and constitutional developments, but through the lens of cultural nationalism. In the back of her 1961–65 volume, Ida writes: "Canada's new flag unfurled all over the Dominion (Red Maple Leaf). The red ensign done away with." Moreover, on 1 January 1967, Martin wrote, "Canada 100 Yrs Old. This is Centennial Year," and on 1 July 1984 she noted: "Canada 117 years old."

While postwar national culture officially focused on promoting an autonomous nationalism, separate from Britain and the United States, Ida's Canada was still a very British one. In that sense, her diary contributes to the ongoing construction of Britishness in postwar Canada. Like many other Canadians of British heritage, Ida was opposed to the adoption of the maple leaf flag, probably because she thought it detracted from Canada's British heritage and its connection to the monarchy. Also, like many anglophones of her generation, Ida followed the British royal family closely in her diaries; she kept track of their vital statistics and often listened to or watched their marriages and coronations. On 6 November 1951, she recorded: "Princess Elizabeth and Duke of Edinburgh here. We saw her 3 times ... thousands lined the streets." In 1953, she went to a movie theatre with a friend to see the coronation of Queen Elizabeth. She also awoke at 6 a.m. to watch Princess Anne's wedding in 1973.[44] And on 29 July 1959, she stood with her daughter and neighbours on Sand Cove Road in Saint John to see Queen Elizabeth when she visited the city. Ida also notes that during the visit of Prince Charles and Lady Diana in 1983, her daughter, son-in-law, and grandchildren joined the "70,000 over town" to see them.[45]

Ida's Britishness also had a New Brunswick flavour. On 27 June 1960, Ida recorded in her diary that the "first French premier" had been elected in New Brunswick's history – Liberal Louis Robichaud. On 21 January 1966, Ida records signing a petition against the Robichaud government. These two tidbits reveal much about the nature of New Brunswick's Britishness. It is not surprising that Ida would sign a petition against Robichaud, for as an anglophone, with a Loyalist heritage, living in the self-proclaimed Loyalist capital of Saint John, Ida was a typical Conservative Party supporter, as was her family. Her husband frequently worked for the Conservative Party during elections and went to Conservative Party meetings. Barbara often typed voters' lists for the party, and she and her husband worked at the polls. This activity may have helped to raise Ida's political awareness. In light of AR's labour activism at the port of Saint John (as discussed in chapter 2), his support for the Conservative Party may appear somewhat ironic. But AR was not "radical" or necessarily ideological. Instead, similar to some other union members, he was pragmatic in his politics. Moreover, AR voted for the Conservatives more out of tradition than strident partisan loyalty. William Cross and Ian Stewart have noted that in New Brunswick "the province's two linguistic communities were each closely identified with (and supportive of) a single political party – the Francophone community with the Liberals and the Anglophone community with the Conservatives."[46]

Ida's identification of Robichaud as French, or more accurately Acadian, also reflects the increasing visibility of ethnicity in provincial politics. Robichaud attracted the ire of many anglophones during his first term as premier by appointing an Acadian majority to his cabinet, by expanding francophone employment in the civil service, and by laying the foundations for the creation of the Université de Moncton. Indeed, many anglophone New Brunswickers complained that Louis Robichaud's victory represented a "French takeover" of government and the province generally. During his election campaign in 1963, what had once been religious and ethnic "undertones" quickly became "overtones." Most controversial during his second administration, for anglophones like Martin, was his Program of Equal Opportunity, a massive restructuring of New Brunswick's political infrastructure. Because Acadians had previously been disadvantaged in New Brunswick, they received the most benefit from this program. As Cross and Stewart have argued, "What might in other jurisdictions have been construed as a straight forward modernization initiative became, in New Brunswick, an exercise in inflaming ethnic passions."[47] In his last administration, Robichaud would continue to inflame passions by introducing legislation to make New Brunswick an officially bilingual province, the only one in Canada.

Martin continued to record provincial politics in her diary. On 26 October 1970 she noted Richard Hatfield's victory over Robichaud and Hatfield's victory again in a close election in 1978, which, according to Ida, she "watched all evening."[48] Ida also took note of Hatfield's less stellar moments; in 1975 she watched a TV special on the Bricklin car "fold up," which was one of several "white elephants" championed by regional leaders to promote economic development.[49] She also watched the "Hatfield case" on TV in 1985, a reference to Hatfield being charged with criminal possession of marijuana, after thirty-five grams of the drug were found in his suitcase during a routine inspection of luggage during that year's royal visit by Queen Elizabeth II. He was acquitted of the charges.[50]

Another piece of Ida's textual collage was her continued interest in regional and local affairs. She recorded various events which have special significance to the region; there are references to the Irving company (i.e., one of its tankers running aground in 1962, one of its trucks running into a train at the pulp mill crossing in 1966, and the explosion of an Irving gas station in Saint John in 1974).[51] She wrote entries on the opening of the Saint John Harbour Bridge in 1967, travelling past Fredericton to "Macnequac" [Mactaquac] to see the new power plant and dam in 1966, and the capture of the Miramichi serial killer Allan Legere in 1988. Although she mentioned his capture in the diaries, Ida admitted in an interview with the Saint John *Telegraph-Journal* that his reign of terror was one of the events that she could not bring herself to record on a more regular basis, as if doing so would have given his actions some sort of legitimacy. All that she wrote was "Murderer Legere caught."[52]

Ida followed municipal elections and watched Common Council proceedings on the local cable station. To illustrate the continued overlap between the familial and the political, it is interesting to note that Ida frequently mentioned municipal affairs when members of her family were involved. She recorded the election of Mel Vincent (who was married to her niece) as a city councillor in 1973 and 1974 and his unsuccessful run for mayor in 1976. On 5 May 1983, Ida mentions that her nephew Peter Friars visited to ask for votes for Vincent. In 1980 she attended a gathering to watch cousin Roy Friars's unsuccessful bid to become a councillor. Ida also watched Bucky Haslam (her good friend Fred Haslam's son) speaking before Common Council in 1980 about the rat infestation at the Lorneville Dump.[53]

As is evident from these comments, Ida possessed an abiding interest in politics and political events. And while Ida was not a political activist per se, her textual engagement with local, national, and international politics challenges the gendered stereotype of women in postwar Canada being politically disengaged.[54] Multiple forms of communication (print, radio, and television) influenced Ida Martin's social and political engagement with the world around her. However, she was not overwhelmed by the cultural directives of commercially produced diaries or television coverage. Moreover, it must be recognized that her primary medium of engagement continued to be diary writing. To return to Gerald Friesen's study, many of his informants continued to communicate their sense of time and place through written memoirs, regardless of the dominant communication system they were meant to represent. It is ironic and intriguing that historians still consult textual materials like diaries for evidence of other innovative technologies. Indeed, diaries and other textual sources still retain their importance because of the potential they provide to express oneself socially and politically. By becoming a "self-appointed chronicler" and creating her own textual collage, it may be argued that Ida Martin was using her diary to define a place for herself in the larger body politic.

The complex relationship of women to the body politic, as revealed in Ida's diaries, indicates that a reinterpretation of the significance of women's diaries is in order. In the 1970s and 1980s, feminist scholars argued that women's diaries represented the centrality of the domestic. However, while the familial and the local continue to be important contexts in Ida's diaries, they were melded into a more substantive and messier postwar collage. Perhaps we should begin to view women's diaries as a medium that helps us to understand the more complex relationship of women to their wider social and political communities. As Marilyn Ferris Motz notes, diaries can "provide insight into the way women interpreted and responded to their immediate environment, as well as to the national and international milieus, and to elite and popular culture, in order to create themselves on paper and in person." Although Ida lived in a small, somewhat marginalized region, like American midwestern diarists Lucy Keeler and Harriet Johnson, she was "far from being isolated and provincial." Instead, she used her diaries to establish herself as a "citizen of the world."[55] And as the concluding chapter will assess, Ida also used her diaries to recount, and give meaning to, her final years as she grappled with the challenges of widowhood and old age.

6

Textual Representations and Interventions:
Widowhood and Old Age

AR took a spell and died at once. We went over to Hosp[ital] was there
    till 10pm. Barb & Sterl slept up here. (13 February 1985)
Sterling up tonite & had a long talk about his house & what would be
    best for me. Mind is in a turmoil. (14 October 1985)
I ate supper alone. Lonesome. (13 January 1986)
[Mrs] Buston & I sat out all afternoon & again tonight. (25 August 1987)
Tired to death for Quilting so much yesterday. (29 August 1989)

Elderly men and women are the "most invisible to the social historian."[1]
Unpublished diaries, according to Deborah van den Hoonaard, "may give
a clearer picture [than most sources] of what [elderly women] write primarily for their own purposes."[2] What do Ida Martin's diaries reveal about
widowhood and the process of aging? The themes covered in this chapter
reinforce Ann Martin Matthew's argument that widowhood in the twentieth century has been characterized by both continuity and "profound
change."[3] Ida Martin's diaries also illustrate the significance of wellness to
the experience of aging, and the importance of community and intergenerational collaboration. Moreover, this chapter places Ida's experience
within the larger context of the literature on aging and the elderly, and also
reveals how, as Ida aged, her diary writing became a collaborative project
with her daughter Barbara. This collaboration suggests that writing a diary
was not always a solitary endeavour.

In her in-depth and incisive study of widows in nineteenth-century Montreal, Bettina Bradbury does not gauge women's grief during the "first days" of widowhood. To do so, Bradbury argues, "would require different sources and different sensibilities."[4] By turning to Ida Martin's diaries, this chapter will utilize one of these "different sources" to chronicle Ida's at times difficult transition from "wife to widow." Occasionally Ida's writing about her life without her husband AR was inchoate and, as was her style of writing, perfunctory: "AR took a spell and died at once." But a close reading of her terse diary entries reveals the profound sorrow that Ida felt over the death of her husband, along with a degree of acceptance of his passing as part of divine will: "I ate supper alone. Lonesome."[5]

Widowhood

Ida became a widow in 1985 at the age of 78. She was a few years younger than the largest proportion of widows in the 1981 Canadian census, who tended to cluster in the 85–89 and 90+ age cohorts. Popular culture has often depicted widows as "hags."[6] This image of widowhood is informed by a history of negative attitudes toward unattached women as well as the aged. However, as late as the last quarter of the nineteenth century, "widowhood and old age were not synonymous."[7] Many women could expect to die in childbirth or become a widow at an earlier age.[8] Elderly widows became more common in North America in the post–Second World War period, due to longer life expectancies and supports provided by the welfare state. As a result, widowhood was a more predictable stage at the end of the life course. In the postwar period the proportion of widows aged 65 and over living alone doubled from 16 per cent to 32 per cent.[9]

Widowhood was a significant rite of passage for many women of Ida's generation. Part of this transition was economic in nature. As mentioned in chapter 1, Ida was privileged compared to many other working-class widows in terms of receiving a pension from her husband's union, the International Longshoreman's Association, as well as a death benefit of $3,000.[10] This was a marked departure from the nineteenth-century when many working-class widows could rely only on their families or charity to fill the financial void left by the death of a husband and breadwinner.[11] Moreover, Ida continued to practise the fiscal talents she had learned as the family's financial manager by keeping track of her money and investing in bonds. In her diary entry for 15 November 1983, Ida recorded depositing seven matured bonds. A few months later, a $10,000 investment certificate was renewed, two new bonds purchased, and a mature one cashed in. Ida also recorded buying two $500 bonds on 5 November 1985.[12] Like other seniors in postwar Canada, Ida also received federal Old Age Security (OAS), income supplements, Canada Pension Plan payments, health care plans, and other social services, which enabled elderly women and men like her to live independently for a longer period of time than was previously possible.

It has been suggested that the elderly as a group in North America lived "materially better" in the twentieth century than in "any other time in history."[13] As James G. Snell notes, by 1951, the "elderly had 'come of age' in Canada. Society had recognized their needs with a proliferation of programs ... and with a universal old age pension."[14] Ida's bank books in the 1980s and 1990s show regular ILA and welfare state benefits; for example, in July 1996, when she was 89 years old, she received $390.76 from the ILA pension, $261.82 from CPP, and $574.81 from OAS. Her bank account total hovered between $3,000-$5,000 during this period.[15] It must be remembered, however, that public pension plans are tied to labour force participation. Since few women of Ida's generation worked for long periods in the paid labour force, few widows received benefits, and if they did, it was much less than the amounts received by men.[16] As a result, over 31 per cent of Canadian widows 65 and over lived at or below the poverty line in 1981. This is four times as many women as men.[17] This is partly due to their lower pensions and accumulated savings. But it is also a reflection of the fact that widows have consistently outnumbered widowers over the course of the nineteenth and twentieth centuries, from a 3 to 1 ratio in industrializing Montreal, to 5 to 1 in Canada's 1981 census. Widowers have been more likely to remarry, often to single women or younger widows.[18] In this case, Ida Martin resembled many other women of her generation and did not remarry.

Another significant component of the widow's rite of passage was the actual death of the spouse. It is curious to note that there are no explicit outpourings of emotion in Ida's diaries. AR's passing is embedded in the usual narrative of details that characterize these diaries; on the day he died, 13 February 1985, Ida records that he complained that his arms were hurting, so she placed hot packs on them. He then proceeded to church "but took a spell and died at once. We went over to Hosp[ital] was there till 10pm. Barb & Sterl slept up here." The next few entries are also taken up with general busy work: she recorded seeing "a lovely crowd at Funeral Home," and a large turnout at the funeral; she travelled to Ocean View Cemetery for the interment and to see the gravestone; talked with her friend Fred Haslam about the port pension; went to the funeral home to pay the expenses; purchased the memorial; and transferred the automobile registration into her name.[19] While she did not delay in packing up AR's clothing on 20 February, Ida did take a bit longer to put away her condolence cards (which she did on 12 April).

Why does Ida not express a more overt form of grief over the passing of her husband? Perhaps the work of making arrangements was a welcome diversion from the reality of the loss. As van den Hoonard has shown, many widows like Ida also coped after the death of their husbands by "keeping busy."[20] Ida's response may also be due to the conventions of diary writing. Given that this was a work diary, perhaps Ida did not see it as respectable or appropriate to use them as a vehicle for emotional outpouring. We may, therefore, need to look to other sources for evidence of how Ida was coping with her husband's death. For example, in a letter to Ida from the pastors of Hillcrest United Baptist Church a few weeks later, they noted "Ida, we know that you are going through a time of struggle as you adjust to AR's home going. We know that it is hard during this adjustment period, but we also know that God's grace is sufficient to see you through these times, no matter how tough they are."[21] Indeed, it may be argued that Ida's Christian faith, as examined in chapter 4, gave her a measure of comfort to accept the inevitability of death.

Another reason for her lack of emotional engagement in the diaries may be that AR's death came as a relief of sorts, after such an extended period of ill health. AR had health issues for many years, which escalated in the last few years of his life. As chapter 2 has noted, the type of paid labour that he performed at the port and with the construction crew took a toll on his body over time. Even when he officially retired from the workforce, he did not stop doing physical labour. He turned his attention to the hard work required for the upkeep of an older home. He and Ida engaged in a regular round of indoor and outdoor chores, such as tarring the roof, painting, putting on storm windows and doors, cleaning the flu, wall papering, and fixing appliances. Beginning in 1976, both worked constantly for several months at the complete renovation of the downstairs flat inhabited by their daughter, son-in-law, and grandchildren, knocking out walls, plastering, flooring, and

Figure 6.1
Ida and AR in later life.

painting.[22] Moreover, in a variant of the family economy model, they helped
various family members in the 1970s with maintenance work; Ida's brother
Row needed help fixing his apartment and the Friars Trucking company used
their labour to renovate their building in Havelock.[23] Ida also recorded cleaning and wallpapering at the homes of her sister Vera and sister-in-law Florence. In the winter of 1976, they cleaned sister-in-law Muriel's house when
the pipes froze; as Ida noted, we "worked our heads off."[24] Ida and AR were
still part of a centuries-old pattern of working-class interdependence and a
belief in the necessity of hard physical labour.[25]

This physical labour became increasingly difficult as Ida and AR aged and
dealt with various health issues. By early February 1979, Ida complained of
arthritis in her hip, which plagued her for the rest of her life. On 11 September
1984, Ida recorded in her diary that she could not clean her house because of

the pain. On 24 June 1985, the arthritis was such that "I did not one thing all day. [D]idn't even go downstairs." This is quite an admission for a woman who saw physical labour as part of her Christian duty. At around the same time as Ida's first mention of her arthritis, AR had a "heart spell."[26] In early May, the physician's prognosis was "not good at all" and he was sent to the hospital for a cardiogram.[27] Throughout the fall and winter of 1979 he continued to suffer from "bad pains," "a real stress in the chest," and difficulty breathing.[28] At 2 a.m. on 12 January 1981, AR was transported to the hospital by ambulance because of fluid in his lungs, returning home on 20 January. This was the beginning of a series of hospital visits. He was home for only five days when he went back into the hospital on 25 July for a prostate operation, returning home on the 30th, at which point Ida "acted as nurse all day." On 3–4 July he again returned to the hospital for a hip replacement. This was followed by a heart attack on 7 July and another hospitalization. In mid-September and early November 1981, AR continued to have trouble breathing. On 25 June 1982 AR had a "Black out at breakfast." Ida herself also had "a spell" on 18 July.[29]

Despite their ill health, they would not stop working, which undoubtedly worsened their conditions. They were battling against the persistent conception that associated the elderly with "uselessness": "[p]eople were judged to be 'old' when they were no longer able to care for themselves adequately, and when their physical capabilities were perceived to be markedly declining."[30] Only a few weeks after AR's heart attack, he experienced "Distress in chest" from being "up on roof." A few days after AR's blackout in June 1982, he overtaxed himself by attempting to fix the furnace: "A Terrible Day. AR got sick trying to fix the furnace. It was off 30 days and finally He gave up and Blake Mackenzie came and fixed it (Oh Dear)." In the fall, he was "up in attic all day running a new line to kitchen. He's tired out and so am I."[31] In July 1982, Ida and AR suffered from the injuries they sustained in the car accident described in chapter 3. Although this resulted in AR giving up driving, he would not cease to work at home. On 7 February 1983, "AR had a bad day. Pain in chest but he still was out at the wood [chopping and stacking] awhile." On 20 August both Ida and AR had a spell: "AR not that good. I had a little spell down on step." By October, it was becoming more and more difficult for AR to engage in regular chores; he could not cut the daisies, weed, or put oil in the car.[32] It is also not surprising that Ida developed an ulcer in March 1984.[33] The stress continued unabated; on the evening of 10 April 1984, AR "Fell on floor, but came to. Fell again 9:30 but rallied again. I'm exhausted." On 29 August AR went back to church for the first time in four weeks. Five months later, AR died of a massive heart attack.

A month after AR's death, Ida eventually admitted that it was "real lonely" in the flat.[34] Up until this point, she had been surrounded by family and friends. On the night of AR's death, her daughter and son-in-law stayed overnight. On the night of the funeral "Marg [her sister] and I slept together. GB [her brother] slept in AR's bed." Many family and friends visited; four hundred signed the guest book at the funeral home. Others helped in whatever way they could; Fred Haslam delivered the cheque from the ILA and Don Mills helped her with paperwork; and sister-in-law Mel took her to the cemetery. It was not until several weeks later that the reality began to sink in. On 5 October, Ida recorded "Stayed all alone tonite for the first time."[35]

Leaving the Conjugal Home

Although Ida did not always overtly express her grief over the loss of her husband, she did record confusion and turmoil about the realization that she would have to leave her conjugal home at 213 Queen Street. One of Ida's most introspective entries was her "long talk" with her son-in-law on 14 October 1985 about "what would be best for me [in terms of living arrangements]. Mind is in a turmoil." The following day, after looking at seniors' apartments, she noted again: "my mind is in a turmoil tonight."[36] Sterling, Barbara, and the two grandchildren had lived in the flat underneath Ida since 1966, but after AR's death they decided to purchase their own residence. In a letter to her niece Janet in Oakville, Ontario, Ida clearly struggled with mixed feelings about the prospect of leaving 213 Queen Street:

In the early fall when the Huskins decided to buy a home of their own, it took the wind out of my Sails and I've never got it back. In fact the gale is getting worse as the time draws nearer. They move the last of the month. Can you stand a letter with a little grief in it? 'O.K. Listen.' I've been so Happy and Barb & Sterling have been so good to me. I never thought the time would come to move, But still I'm so happy for them, All their friends which are many have their own homes and so many are up that way. South Bay, Almanac, Martinon, & Grand Bay, Theirs is Martinon a sweet little yellow bungalow. Sterling can walk to his school and Barb will only be 15 min[ute]s coming in to work. But oh, everything will be so different. It will be so lonely here and to try to get a Tenant this time of the year is hard, It will have to be kept heated Tenant or not. I had 2 wks of a terrible upset cried all night and most of the day when no one was looking. Everyone would say you'll have to get an ap[artmen]t somewhere. Well that was the very thing that would send me spinning.[37]

The literature on widowhood suggests that it was not unusual for widows to struggle with the notion of moving on, for they "derive comfort from the many memories and associations of the conjugal home." Part of the struggle was also the prospect of moving to long-term care institutions, which were expanding in the postwar period.[38] In Ida's generation, the family had taken care of the elderly. Or if they did not have family, they turned to friends or charities. Indeed, Ida's mother died when she was 32, so, according to her nieces, "she took on the role of mothering her siblings, especially her younger brothers." Her father S. Peter Friars had also passed away at her house on 29 October 1946.[39] By the 1980s, it was still the case that only a small percentage of the elderly resided in hospitals or nursing homes. In 1986, only 5.4 per cent of men and 9.1 per cent of women in Canada lived in institutions.[40] Ida and her siblings came of age during the Great Depression, and the spirit of self-reliance that the hardships of this period instilled in some members of this generation meant that they did not relish the idea of "being a burden" and preferred to live independently for as long as they were able.[41]

Nonetheless, home ownership appears to have been a burden for some widows, due to the costs of maintenance and the fears of living alone.[42] This was certainly the case with Ida. She encapsulated the conversation that she had with her brother Jim over this issue in the letter to her niece:

Jim [I said] I can't stay alone, and I can't do anything with the furnace if anything happened to it. And I'm afraid of the water freezing etc etc etc and if anything happens one has to crawl under the house for the shut off, so you see what a whirl my mind was in. AR knew every pipe which one it was and where it went so he didn't worry. However in the last month my furnace has been acting terrible it was off as much as it was on. So finally they put a new motor on and it was OK. In a couple of wks after water kept seeping out on the floor

... they found [what] was needed. Oh my! I was all in by this time. He cleaned the furnace and pipe too. So I don't know what else could happen. I'm kind of timid at night alone in this city there's so many break & enters. So I got a new old fashion Storm Door made for the door at the foot of the steps at the Back. No Window just so I can bring it to and a big HOOK on the inside just like a Barn-door but its much safer.[43]

Ida had asked her brother George, who was a widower, to stay with her, but he declined for much the same reason; he refused to leave his house in Minto, New Brunswick. One of the young men from Hillcrest Church, Karl Conrad, eventually came to stay with Ida until he moved into his own apartment on 13 January 1986, at which point she recorded: "I ate supper alone. Lonesome." Susan Hicks, a student nurse, moved in a few days later.[44]

Ida remained at 213 Queen Street for approximately one year, until November 1986, when she moved into Hillcrest Village, a seniors' complex associated with the church, where she stayed for nine years. Barbara eventually sold the property on Queen Street in June 1989.[45] Ida was initially resistant to living at Hillcrest Village, noting "I don't like them [the apartments]" when she first viewed them. When she moved in, however, she noted that her apartment was a "sweet little place."[46] Some scholars have argued that transitioning into age-segregated apartment complexes is an acceptable compromise for many elderly persons like Ida, for they provide a sense of security, community, and a modicum of independence. Moreover, as she aged, Ida's life trajectory was similar to many widows in nineteenth-century Montreal who "faced diverse illnesses, patterns of decline, and changing needs for care."[47]

Eventually Ida's health deteriorated to the point where she could not stay alone in her apartment and she moved into a special care home, Seely's Lodge in Martinon, where she remained for another nine years.[48] This move detrimentally affected Ida's finances, for it required a much larger monthly rental payment. At Hillcrest Village, Ida began with a rent of $300/month, which increased every year. However, effective 1 April 1995, she received a rental subsidy from Hillcrest Village Inc. of $80 per month, which reduced her apartment rent from $365 to $285.[49] Ida was not able to enjoy this rental reduction for long, for in her bank book after 29 September 1995, there is a note in Barbara's handwriting: "Closing out Hillcrest Village." The new rent for Seely's

Lodge began at $1,280/month, peaking at $2,000 in 1999. Part of this demand for increasing rent was due to the state's neo-liberal agenda in the late 1980s which slashed its public support of such institutions.[50] It is interesting to note that despite her expenses, Ida still tithed the church $5 a week, continued to buy birthday and Christmas gifts, and on 12 July 1999 donated $48.10 to Kosovo Refugees.[51]

This chapter does not seek to romanticize nursing homes and similar institutions. It will, however, show that some individual owners and workers within the system cared for and cared about their clients. It is clear from family sources that the owners and workers at Seely's Lodge treated Ida with affection and tried to create a family atmosphere for her. In the eulogy for Ida, her nieces note that "Auntie Ida was made to feel part of the family at the Lodge and was blessed to be loved and embraced by people who became like family, to both her and Barb. We would be remiss if we did not mention the very special relationship that Auntie Ida had with Jan [Seely, owner and operator of the lodge] and her family, Mary and others." The closest relationship that Ida developed at the lodge was with Mary Guimond, a worker who frequently wrote in Ida's guest book:

> You were the first person I saw this Mother's Day morning when I arrived at work at 8am. I'm so very glad you live here and I'm so glad that I help look after you. Happy Mother's Day to a fine lady. (10 May 1999)
> Another year has come & gone. So glad we are still together at Seely Lodge. (30 December 2000)
> Happy 94th Birthday to a great lady – So happy to be here with you Ida. (18 July 2001)
> Happy Birthday again to my special lady. (18 July 2002)
> Happy Birthday Ida – who would have thought we would still be here after six years. You are my special 'Gram' to me. (18 July 2003)
> Merry Christmas to my best Gram – Another year has come & gone – and here we are again. Love ya! (24 December 2003)

On 12 August 2004, Ida was sent to hospital after a stroke, where she would remain until she died on 11 October. At Ida's funeral, Jan Seely, owner and operator of Seely's Lodge, was an honorary pallbearer. Barbara noted in Ida's guestbook that "Those who are grieving the most are from the Lodge."[52] Ida's time at Hillcrest Village and then at Seely's Lodge helped to ease the transition from wife to widow. But what remains somewhat uncertain is the extent to which Ida fully embraced life as a widow.

Wellness

In many ways, Ida's textual experience of growing old is much like Katie Pickles's description of mid-nineteenth-century widowhood as a "life-phase of conflicting emotions."[53] In her study of widows in contemporary Canada, Deborah van den Hoonard notes that after the disruption of grief, some widows find an "unexpected ability to learn how to do new things." In Pat Chambers's words, they find new opportunities which are "not confined to the rhythms dictated by their husbands' preferences."[54] One of Ida's complaints about her husband was that as they grew older he never took her out anywhere. As a result (as we noted in chapter 3) Ida bought a car of her own in 1986 to improve her mobility, and she enjoyed frequent lunches with her friend Marg. They often ended up at the Fairport Restaurant in Saint John, which was near the seniors complex. On 19 July 1988, Marg picked up Ida for a birthday lunch at the Fairport. When they arrived, there were six other women there from Hillcrest Village for a surprise party. Ida also continued to engage in the life of the church, regularly attending services, prayer meetings, and other special events. Gerontologists argue that membership in a faith community is a significant comfort for widows already active in the church.[55] She received many visitors in her apartment, ranging from immediate and extended family members, to friends and church members, much as she had at 213 Queen Street. Ida frequently spent evenings in Martinon with Barbara and Sterling, as well as with her other relatives in Saint John, Westfield, and Minto.

Ida also discovered a new sense of community in Hillcrest Village. She frequently took part in the activities organized by the complex. In her diaries, she recorded going "downstairs" to the common room for church services, bible studies, and sing songs. She was a member of the Seniors' Club, which organized special events, such as art classes, and concerts performed by such groups as the Loyalist Cloggers, a ukulele-playing group, and her nieces, the Friars girls, who sang and roasted Ida on 1 February 1990: "what a night."

The Club hosted a party the previous year on 16 February 1989, replete with a tableau entitled "Mock Wedding": "we had a great time."[56] In 1992, Ida saw a "funny movie" downstairs and then sat in the corner with a coterie of other women from the complex. Ida spent much of her time sitting in the hallway "with the ladies," or going outside when the weather was nice; "[Mrs] Bustin & I sat out all afternoon & again tonight."[57] In that sense, she resembles a widow interviewed by van den Hoonaard: "you walk through the halls and everybody acknowledges everybody else. It's a little community."[58]

Ida also spent a lot of time quilting with the other women. In her diaries, she kept a tally of the number of quilts that they had produced; by 24 December 1990 (the last time that Ida mentioned quilting), they were working on their 78th quilt. In this sense, Ida and her fellow quilters challenged the myth of seniors as unproductive and passive members of society.[59] Sometimes, however, Ida would overdo it: "all in today. Quilted too long." Or she quilted until her fingers were sore. At such times she would simply go down and sit with the quilters. On 29 August 1989, she admitted that she was "Tired to death for Quilting so much yesterday" so she went downstairs to watch. She found that the quilt had been finished, "so we had a sing song."[60] On 1 February 1989, Ida had a "banner day," combining various forms of community sociability; in the morning her nephew Peter Friars visited, followed by the pastor and his wife, with whom she had a "real nice chat." In the afternoon she quilted, and in the evening went downstairs with Barbara and Sterling to see the cloggers.

Yet no sooner had Ida begun to enjoy these new opportunities, when her health took a turn for the worse. Not long after Ida's move to Hillcrest Village, she became very ill with shingles in 1986, and ended up in hospital for an extended stay. As a result, she was unable to keep her daily diary entries. Even after she returned home, her entries from 1987–90 contain almost daily complaints about the pain in her side due to the recurrence of shingles. In March and April of 1987 she recorded visits to the pain clinic and to the hospital for needles. She was also hospitalized from 29 June to 4 July 1989 for cardiac troubles. Her shingles frequently interfered with daily life. On 27 September 1987, she "didn't do too much today. My side hurt terrible." On 11 February 1988, she could not quilt because of her shingles. When the same thing happened again on 18 June 1990 one of the seniors brought her a piece of cake "from the Quilting Bee." On 7 August 1989, one can see the effect that pain was

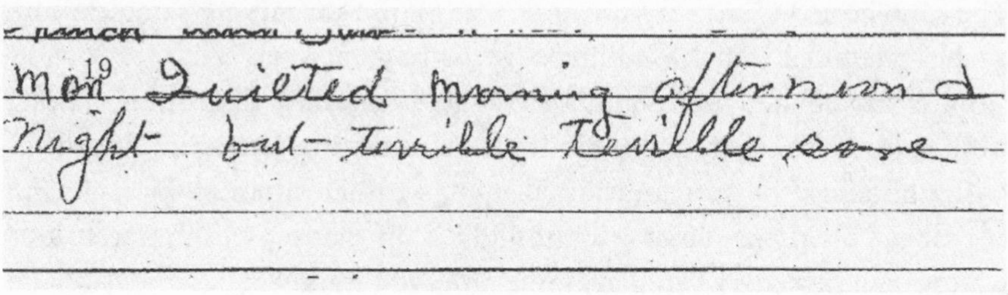
Mon 19 Quilted morning afternoon & night but terrible terrible sore

Figure 6.2
Diary entry, 7 August 1989

having on her handwriting. This reinforces the point made by many researchers that physical health is the "single most important contributor to the quality of life" for the elderly.[61]

We would like to suggest that the deterioration of Ida's health was also at least partially due to the cumulative effects of "cohort attrition,"[62] the simultaneous death of many of her family members and peers. Ida lost two of her brothers – Ora and Len – in 1966 and 1967.[63] However, most of her loved ones passed in close proximity to one other. Her eldest sister Vera died on 30 April 1980 and her brother Garfield on 5 April 1984. Both exhibited considerable agitation as they declined, which was difficult for the remaining siblings, including Ida. Vera asked Ida to take her in, but given her own health problems, Ida refused. Eventually Vera was placed in a hospital where she was "carrying on frightful. I was exhausted when I got home." Eventually she died in a nursing home.[64] Garfield suffered from a stroke and seizures, and lashed out at those around him.[65] The following year (1985) was particularly painful for Ida: after the death of AR on 13 February, her cousin Roy passed away on 4 May, and her closest sibling Marguerite on 27 June.

In Ida's diaries, the deaths of her siblings were narrated in the same everyday fashion as the passing of AR. For example, when Marguerite died, Ida noted "kind of busy all day … lots of people in."[66] However, she was more forthcoming after Roy's funeral. After church she went over to his wife's house where "we talked and cried 2 hours."[67] Her other siblings would die within the next few years. George contracted cancer in the early 1980s and died on 4 November 1988: "GB died this am." As with the others, Ida recorded that she was "Busy all day." There was a "Huge crowd" at the funeral in Minto, and George's house was filled with "wall to wall people all day." George's funeral took a toll on her; after arriving home at 9 p.m., she was "some tired." Her other two brothers – Jim and Russell – died on 12 February 1993 and 25 December 2000 respectively. This occurred after she stopped writing in her diary, so she did not record their deaths. Nonetheless, experiencing the loss of most of one's significant others in such a short span of time surely had a tremendous effect on Ida's physical and mental health; it must have seemed like her whole past and life were disappearing. We do not think that it is a coincidence that Ida was hospitalized a year after the deaths of AR, Roy, and Marguerite, and continued to suffer from shingles and other maladies for the rest of her life.

Shared Authorship and the Mother–Daughter Bond

One last theme to be addressed is what Ida's diaries reveal about the centrality of the mother–daughter bond, especially in old age. It also provides important insight into the nature of diaries. We often assume that personal diaries are intensely private documents, expressions of one's innermost thoughts and secrets. Ida herself had diaries with a lock and key. However, as Kathryn Carter has argued, diaries have traditionally been "semi-public" documents, sometimes circulated between friends and family and composed collectively; "Mothers left their journals out for the family to read; sisters co-wrote diaries; fathers jotted notes in their daughters' diaries; female friends exchanged diaries; and men published their diaries."[68] In the case of Ida's diaries, daughter Barbara often took over as diarist, especially when Ida was incapacitated by poor health.

Barbara's first intervention in her mother's diaries was in the 1951–55 volume, when she would have been about 15 years old. Barbara wrote her name in the front pages of the diary and listed a number of birthdays at the back of the diary, as Ida often did in her other volumes. On 1 January 1951, Barbara also wrote entries when her mother was away, but when Ida returned, she indignantly wrote over her daughter's entries. Undoubtedly as a result of this intervention by her daughter, Ida wrote "No Trespassing" in big capital letters at the beginning of the diary. Ida obviously viewed the role of diarist as *her* self-appointed responsibility and resented Barbara's intrusion.

When it came time for the selection of memories to record, however, Ida was more open to collaboration. According to Susan Engel, "memory never stands alone"; the making of memory and the construction of meaning is

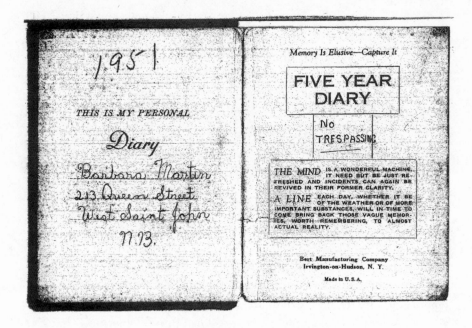

Figure 6.3
Diary entry, 1 January 1951

highly contextual and inter-subjective.[69] When Ida was hospitalized in 1986 and could not write in the diaries herself, Barbara became an alternate recorder. Barbara kept daily entries for her mother from 17 June until 26 July. Ida wrote an isolated entry on 27 July, in which she indicated that she was "real tired," but thereafter Barbara took over again until 18 August. Ida did not begin more regular entries until 16 December when she was feeling better. Barbara's shared authorship is not an unusual practice in diary writing. For example, Sarah Jameson Findon's memoir was typed by her youngest daughter, who also filled in some of the details of her mother's life. Similarly, Catherine Anne Wilson writes about a poignant episode from 1859 in Ontario when Benjamin Crawford's son completed his father's daily diary entries after Crawford had suffered a stroke. Later his father would dictate entries to his son. After his father had died, his son continued to write in his father's diary until the end of the year in order to bring to a close forty-nine years of diary keeping.[70]

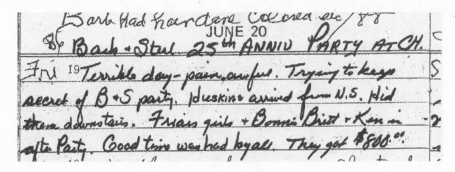

Figure 6.4
Diary entry, 20 June 1986

Literary scholars posit that diarists create multiple and mutable selves. While there are multiple Ida Martins in the pages of her diaries, a new persona emerged in the last few years of the diaries, a textual self which we call "Barbara/Ida" (which ironically and appropriately is Barbara's full name). Barbara, as principal diarist for a time, attempted to adopt her mother's voice and would record the kinds of events that she thought her mother would have recorded had she been able. On 20 June 1986, Barbara/Ida described Barbara and Sterling's 25th anniversary party at the church, an event which Ida would have attended and written about in her diary if she had been well. Instead, Barbara wrote on her behalf: "Barb & Sterl 25th ANNIV PARTY AT CH[URCH]. Terrible day – pain awful. Trying to keep secret of B & S party. Huskins arrived from N.S. Hid them downstairs Friars girls & Bonnie Britt & Ken in after Party. Good time was had by all. They got $800."[71] Ironically, some of the entries recorded information that the singular Ida could not have possibly known, given her disorientation due to pain and medication. For example, on 17 July 1986, Barbara/Ida wrote the following; "Hate this place. Feels like a conspiracy going on. Can't separate reality from dreams. Barb in all morning trying to see Doctor." Obviously, this entry recorded Barbara's experience and diagnosis of Ida's medical condition. On 15 July 1986, Barbara/Ida noted that Ida's personality had changed due to the medication and she was "not aware of anything [she was] saying."

At other times, the Barbara component of Barbara/Ida used the diaries as an opportunity to vent, much as Ida had done on her own. On 27 June 1986,

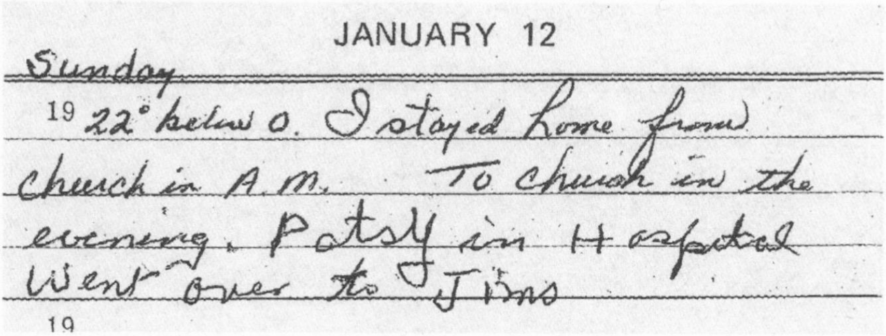
JANUARY 12
Sunday
19 22° below 0. I stayed home from church in A.M. To church in the evening. Patsy in Hospital Went over to Jims
19

Figure 6.5
Diary entry, 12 January 1992

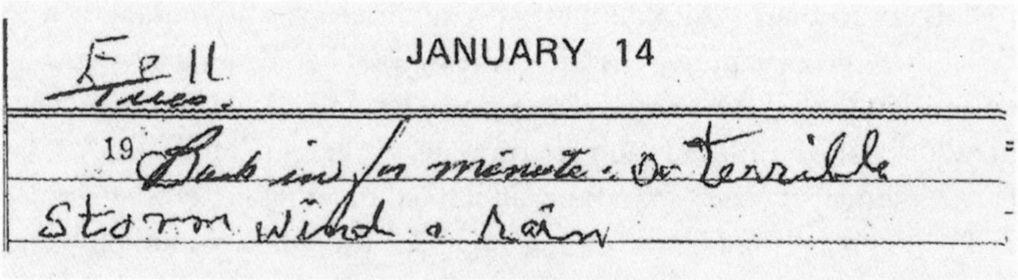
JANUARY 14
Fell
Tues.
19 Back in for minute. Terrible storm wind & rain

Figure 6.6
Diary entry, 14 January 1992

"Barb disgusted" at not being able to contact the doctor. "They [Barbara and husband Sterling] don't know whether to go on trip to England or not!" After Barbara and Sterling returned from their trip, Barbara/Ida wrote brief descriptions based on others' recollections of what transpired while Barbara was away (expanding the boundaries of collaboration). This record keeping after the fact reveals that not all entries in diaries are written on the day indicated in the diary. In the entry for 30 June (the day when Barbara and Sterling were actually flying to England), it is recorded that "I [Ida] cried all day," undoubtedly an insight shared by others upon Barbara and Sterling's return or discovered during telephone calls to check in on Ida.

Barbara again filled in for her mother in 1992, when Ida became too frail to keep daily entries. Beginning on 2 January 1992, both she and Ida acted as a tag team, with Barbara writing the entries for 2, 9–11, 13, and 20–5 January,

JANUARY 19
Sunday came over & took me home
Jim 19
Didn't go to Church
Over to Jim & Millie's for
a few Days.
19

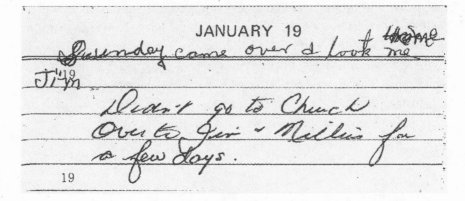

Figure 6.7
Diary entry, 19 January 1992

JANUARY 27
19 Mon Cancom lady here. Barb in
& did my hair & I had a bath.
Cousins in for registration & 6.00 fee
19

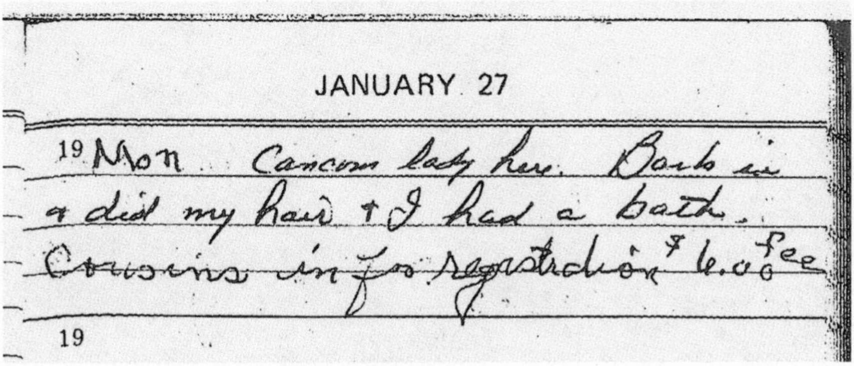

Figure 6.8
Diary entry, 27 January 1992

while Ida wrote on 4–5, 7–8, 15–18, and 26 January to 5 February, and from 11 to 19 February. This mother–daughter duo became even more intensely collaborative on 12, 14, 19, and 27 January, when both mother and daughter wrote in the same entry; Barbara usually began the entry and then Ida finished it. In some respects it is not easy to discern where one voice ends and the other picks up, which underscores the emotional strength of this mother–daughter bond. Due to this collaborative effort, Ida and Barbara managed to keep daily records for most of January and February, with only a handful of blank entries. It is obvious, however, that it was becoming much harder for Ida to keep daily entries faithfully. Her handwriting was becoming much shakier, and by February her entries were much briefer. By mid-March she was able only to record the day of the entry; indeed, there are no entries after 19 March 1992. At the age of 86, Ida Martin finally gave up her role as family recorder. Barbara now keeps a journal, specifically to continue maintaining a record of her family's history, and in order to ensure textual continuity with her mother's diaries and to keep Ida's spirit and memory alive.

Conclusion

Cleaned all through & tidied drawers etc etc. Washed a bit.
   (5 January 1949)
[AR] working at port today. He, Hartley, and Eddie went to a party
   at Clarendon, got home at 3:30. I was in to Mrs. Kempster's.
   (29 July 1949)
Usual Sat[urday]'s work. Barbs went to get her hair done. Rob[er]t[son]
   & Kathleen Bradshaw in for an h[ou]r. We 4 went to see Bud Abbot
   at Strand. (12 March 1955)
Mrs Pike Came in & I payed her our last payment on the house.
   (20 March 1956)
OUR 1ST FIRE IN NEW STOVE. Busy cleaning thru. Fanjoys
   arrived at 2:30. I had to cook for Barbs this evening & Marg
   & I cleaned all her silver. Boys played checkers. (28 March 1974)
Quilted awhile this AM. SD got me groceries. Quilted again this
   after[noon] and again tonite. My fingers all so sore, picked
   to pieces. (4 February 1989)
I didn't go to church this AM. Just frigged around & read. Church
   tonite downstairs. (26 January 1992)

Ida Louise Martin died on 11 October 2004. Her funeral was attended by
immediate and extended family, friends, neighbours, and community and
church members, all representatives of Ida's overlapping social worlds. Barbara wrote afterwards in Ida's guest book: "Life goes on but doesn't feel the

same. Ida Martin was a wonderful mother and grandmother and I was a lucky gal to call her Mom!"[1] Mother and grandmother were only two of the roles that Ida had played over the course of her life; she was also a wife, household manager, sister, aunt, friend, worker, Christian, and temperance society member. And perhaps most importantly of all, Ida was a devoted diarist. In transitioning in and out of these roles, Ida is not necessarily extraordinary in the context of her time and place. Nor did Ida believe that she was exceptional. What is extraordinary, however, is that she kept daily diaries from 1945 to 1992 and that these accounts have survived. In *Writing Herself into Being: Quebec Women's Autobiographical Writings from Marie de l'Incarnation to Nelly Arcan*, Patricia Smart contends that the significance of women's personal writings is that "they are, quite simply, the voices of women who dared to express themselves in writing and whose writings were preserved." Smart suggests that the autobiographical writings of the Quebec women that she has analyzed have been preserved because the authors were the "daughters or wives of influential men."[2] But this is not the case with Ida Martin's diaries. These diaries are important because they were penned by a working-class woman and they have survived because she insisted on passing them down to family members who preserved, analyzed, and wrote about them.

This book has taken the form of a series of critical essays that are meant to accomplish two things; first, to provide insight into postwar Canadian society, and thus contribute to several interlocking historiographies; and second, to illustrate the interpretive benefits and challenges of using diaries as historical sources. With regard to the first objective, one of the major underlying themes in this analysis has been the tension between change and continuity in the postwar period. This tension manifested itself in various ways in the lives of many working-class families in Saint John, as illustrated in Ida's diaries. For example, the Martins continued to use nineteenth-century survival strategies in order to "get by" in postwar Saint John, but paired them with the introduction of welfare state benefits. They also participated in the expanding consumer economy by purchasing appliances and automobiles, but still frequently relied on older and more durable models. The diaries also highlight the coexistence of older forms of masculinity such as "rugged" and "radical" manliness, which relied on manual labour, homosociability, and direct action, along with more modern forms such as union respectability, and the manly modern's focus on efficiency and production.

Figure 7.1
Ida Martin in later life, 1993

The book's discussion of motor vehicles as an embodiment of working-class masculinity at the same time underscores the contradictory meanings of vehicles for working-class wives like Ida. She saw vehicles as an income generator and as a source of danger and then mobility in later life. Similarly, Ida's diaries complicate our understanding of postwar families and the baby boom. The Martin household would have appeared in official records as a nuclear family, but in reality it functioned as a series of overlapping hetero- and homosocial networks. Daughter Barbara's teenage years contained elements of the postwar ideal in the form of dating and schooling, but also continued to revolve around the Christian church, as had many female lives since the nineteenth century.

Ida's diaries also provide a lens into the evolution of communication mediums, particularly the effect of television on ordinary Canadian citizens in the postwar world. We also see Ida's diaries shift in content and volume, as she moved from recording the community around her to writing about local, national, and international affairs. And we detected the unfolding of an imagined English Canadian nationality over the course of the postwar period, as she recorded the adoption of the new flag in the 1960s, the patriation of the constitution in 1982, and the constitutional affairs of the 1980s and 1990s. And last, Ida's diaries are a textual representation of the changes and continuities associated with aging and widowhood in modern Canada. Ida's experience of growing old was in many ways reflective of centuries past, in terms of the gendered patterns of aging, and the centrality of the conjugal home for the care of the elderly. Moreover, it embodied the emergence of new short- and long-term-care institutions, and the ability to carve out one's own niche beyond the confines of marriage. These topics and themes say a great deal about how modernity unfolded in postwar Saint John, notably its limited effect on the social and cultural lives of many working-class residents of the city. This does not necessarily mean that working-class families in Saint John operated outside of the parameters of modern society. Rather, Ida Martin's diaries are an important reminder that working-class Canadians responded to modernity in a myriad of ways, including retaining nineteenth-century ideals and survival strategies in order to cope with the vagaries of modern life.

Our second objective in this book is to reflect on the value of diaries as historical sources. Personal diaries provide us access into the worlds of historical actors that often do not appear in official sources. They are particularly useful when written by under-represented groups in history, such as women and the working-class. They allow us to see bits of themselves preserved, not only in terms of what they said, but how they said it, and in what format. One of the shortcomings of this study is that it deals with the diaries of a single author. Nevertheless, these diaries reveal more than her life alone; they also provide insight into Ida Martin's family, community, and locality. So while these diaries may have been written by a "traditional" woman, they remain a unique window into the various lives and social contours of postwar Saint John.

We hope that future historians will be able to find multiple diaries written by working-class women and thus analyze them as a genre. Literary scholars have provided us with a valuable toolkit to use in interrogating these sources. However, most historians approach diaries with different perspectives and with different goals in mind. In that vein, we would like to conclude by providing tentative guidelines for historians who engage with diaries. Whenever possible, historians should avoid using diary entries merely as anecdotes or illustrations. While the critical analysis of primary sources is a staple of historical research and discourse, we are often guilty of mining diaries for snippets without considering the social context of the diarist and the nature of the diaries.[3] The assumption should not be made that personal diaries are expressions of the writers' innermost thoughts. We agree with Gail G. Campbell that "a diary is an edited version of a life."[4] It is edited by the author, by the format of the diary, and by the readership. Indeed, as we have shown, Ida at times went back to her diary entries years later and edited them.

It is also necessary to understand the conventions of diary writing. People have been writing in diaries for centuries, but they are not all written in the same way, by the same people, or for the same purposes. In this regard, historians need to be mindful of the class, gender, and/or ethnic dimensions of the diarist. We have characterized Ida's volumes as terse work diaries, but other forms also exist. For example, in the 1880s Maggie (Margaret) Loggie Valentine from New Brunswick kept a "log," or a "journal letter" of her various trips, including to Liverpool, England.[5] We must be aware of the different conventions of diary writing before we can use these sources effectively. Attention must also be paid to form as well as content, and consideration needs to be given to language, grammar, and handwriting, as well as the diary's format, as each is significant in assessing the source. Historians should be careful not be dismiss the seemingly mundane. Ida Martin's diaries are replete with everyday concerns and issues, which is why they are important. In this vein, researchers need to look for patterns and rhythms in diary writing in order to extrapolate the nuances in the entries. Historians should also expect the unexpected. Examining Ida Martin's diaries has opened up fields of inquiry that we would never have anticipated, such as the role of motor vehicles in the family economy, or a working-class wife's knowledge of her husband's workplace and homosocial behaviour and her views of working-class masculinity. Ultimately, we hope that this exploration of Ida Martin's diaries and her social worlds encourages others to interpret diaries and to pick up where we have left off and contribute to the emerging historical scholarship on diaries in new and imaginative ways – and, in the process, make diaries part of the "usual work" of historians.

Notes

ABBREVIATIONS

HIL-GOV: Harriet Irving Library Government Documents, University of New Brunswick.
HIL-SPECAR: Harriet Irving Library Archives and Special Collections, University of New Brunswick.
NBMARL: New Brunswick Museum, Archives, and Research Library.
PANB: Provincial Archives of New Brunswick.
LAC: Library and Archives Canada.
SJRL: Saint John Regional Library.

INTRODUCTION

1 Diane Tye, *Baking as Biography: A Life Story in Recipes* (Montreal and Kingston: McGill-Queen's University Press, 2010).
2 The authors have digitized all ten volumes of Ida Martin's diaries and keep the originals in a safety deposit box, bringing them out occasionally for students to peruse as part of class projects on using primary historical documents. The authors have arranged to eventually deposit the diaries in the Provincial Archives of New Brunswick in Fredericton.
3 Jim Barrett and Diane P. Koenker, "The Saga of History 492: The Transformation of Working-Class History in One Classroom," *Labour/Le Travail* 61 (Spring 2008): 183; Royden Loewen, *From the Inside Out: The Rural Worlds of Mennonite Diarists, 1863 to 1929* (Winnipeg: University of Manitoba Press, 1999), 20; and Bonnie Huskins and Michael Boudreau, "Irresponsibility, Obligation, and the 'Manly Modern': Tensions in Working-Class Masculinities in Postwar Saint John, New Brunswick," *Labour/Le Travail* 78 (Fall 2016): 165–96.
4 Bettina Bradbury, "The Home as Workplace," in *Labouring Lives: Work and Workers in Nineteenth-Century Ontario*, ed. Paul Craven (Toronto: University

of Toronto Press, 1995), 413–14. For one of the few analyses of a working-class diary in Canada, see Catherine Gidney, "The Dredger's Daughter: Courtship and Marriage in the Baptist Community of Welland Ontario, 1934–1944," *Labour/Le Travail* 54 (Fall 2004): 121–49. Diarist Sarah Jameson Craig is also interesting in that she was a poor rural woman who kept diaries in the late nineteenth and early twentieth centuries. Joanne Findon, *Seeking Eden: The Dreams and Migrations of Sarah Jameson Craig* (Montreal and Kingston: McGill-Queen's University Press, 2015).

5 Barrett and Koenker, "The Saga of History 492," 183; Mary-Jo Mayes, "Autobiography and Class Formation in Nineteenth-Century Europe: Methodological Considerations," *Social Science History* 16, no. 3 (Autumn 1992): 525; and David Vincent, *Bread, Knowledge and Freedom: A Study of Nineteenth-Century Working-Class Autobiography* (London and New York: Methuen, 1981).

6 Avra Kouffman, "'Why feignest thou Thyselfe to be another woman?': Constraints on the Construction of Subjectivity in Mary Rich's Diary," in *Women's Life-Writing: Finding Voice, Building Community*, ed. Linda S. Coleman (Bowling Green: Bowling Green University Popular Press, 1997), 12.

7 Jo Currie, Keith Mercer, and John G. Reid, eds, *Hector Maclean: The Writings of a Loyalist-Era Military Settler in Nova Scotia* (Kentville, Nova Scotia: Gaspereau Press, 2015); D. Murray Young and Gail G. Campbell, eds, *A Calendar of Life in a Narrow Valley: Jacobina Campbell's Diary, Taymouth, New Brunswick, 1825–1843* (Fredericton: Acadiensis Press, 2015); and Andrew C. Holman and Robert B. Kristofferson, eds, *More of a Man: Diaries of a Scottish Craftsman in Mid-Nineteenth-Century North America* (Toronto: University of Toronto Press, 2013).

8 Gail G. Campbell, *"I wish to keep a record": Nineteenth-Century New Brunswick Diarists and Their World* (Toronto: University of Toronto Press, 2017); Findon, *Seeking Eden*; and Robert M. Mennell, *Testimonies and Secrets: The Story of a Nova Scotia Family, 1844–1977* (Toronto: University of Toronto Press, 2013).

9 Lynne Marks, *Revivals and Roller Rinks: Religion, Leisure, and Identity in Late-Nineteenth-Century Small-Town Ontario* (Toronto: University of Toronto Press, 1996), 216.

10 Margaret Conrad, "Recording Angels: The Private Chronicles of Women from the Maritime Provinces of Canada, 1750–1950," in *The Neglected Majority: Essays in Canadian Women's History*, vol. 2, ed. Alison Prentice and Susan Mann Trofimenkoff (Toronto: McClelland and Stewart, 1985), 5.

11 Friars Genealogy, 1-3, MC 80/1361, PANB; Kathleen Mundee, "The Friars' Families on Ward's Creek," in *Ward's Creek and Area 1784–1984* (Sussex, Royal Printing, ca 1984), 83; and Grace Aiton, *The Story of Sussex and Vicinity* (Sussex, Kings County Historical Society, 1967), 32 and 35–6.

12 Certificate of Registration of Birth, Sussex, Kings County, RS 141 Alb, no. 80106, 1907, PANB; *Kings County Record*, 2 August 1907; Baptisms, Chalmers Presbyterian Church, Sussex, 2 June 1908, MC 1589, no. 313, PANB; Friars Family Bible, in authors' collection; Friars Genealogy, 24. "McGregor Brook" was in Studholm Parish, Kings County. It is now a dispersed community. Robert F. Fellows, *Community Place Names in New Brunswick* (Fredericton: Provincial Archives of New Brunswick, 1998), 152.

13 Friars Family Tree, Friars Family Bible, in authors' possession. See also Mike Mullen, "God Is Love. Church Secretary Barbara Huskins Says He's Proven That to Her Both at Home – and on the Job," *Evening Times Globe*, 17 April 1998.

14 Mullen, "God Is Love."

15 Ida's Guestbook, in authors' collection.

16 Poem to Ida, 1929, in authors' collection.

17 Ida's Guestbook, in authors' collection.

18 Ibid.

19 Neil Sutherland, *Growing Up: Childhood in English Canada from the Great War to the Age of Television* (Toronto: University of Toronto Press, 2002), 7.

20 Campbell, *"I wish to keep a record,"* 40.

21 Kathryn Carter, "Accounting for Time in Nineteenth-Century Manuscript Diaries and Photographs," *Life Writing* 12, no. 4 (2015): 424–6.

22 For works which view diaries as artifacts, see Catharine Anne Wilson, "The Farm Diary: An Intimate and Ongoing Relationship between Artifact and Keeper," *Agricultural History* 92, no. 2 (Spring 2018): 150–71, and Suzanne L. Bunkers, "'Faithful Friend': Nineteenth-Century Midwestern American Women's Unpublished Diaries," *Women's Studies International Forum* 10, no. 1 (1987): 7–17.

23 Kathryn Carter, *Diaries in English by Women in Canada, 1753–1995: An Annotated Bibliography* (Ottawa: Canadian Research Institute for the Advancement of Women, 1997), and Bonnie Huskins and Michael Boudreau, "'Daily Allowances': Literary Conventions and Daily Life in the Diaries of Ida Louise Martin (née Friars), Saint John, New Brunswick, 1945–1992," *Acadiensis* 34, no. 2 (Spring 2005): 91–2.

24 Findon, *Seeking Eden*, 14.

25 Mary Rubio and Elizabeth Waterston, eds, *The Selected Journals of L.M. Montgomery*, vol. 1: *1889–1910* (Toronto: University of Toronto Press, 1985); Rubio and Waterston, eds, *The Selected Journals of L.M. Montgomery*, vol. 2: *1910–1921* (Toronto: University of Toronto Press, 1987); Rubio and Waterston, eds, *The Selected Journals of L.M. Montgomery*, vol. 3: *1921–1929* (Toronto: University of Toronto Press, 1992); Rubio and Waterston, eds, *The Selected Journals of L.M. Montgomery*, vol. 4: *1929–1935* (Toronto: University of Toronto Press,

1998); and Rubio and Waterston, eds, *The Selected Journals of L.M. Montgomery*, vol. 5: *1935–1942* (Toronto: University of Toronto Press, 2004).

26 Campbell, *"I wish to keep a record."*

27 Joyce Ouellette, "Her Diaries Offer a Slice of Life," *Evening Times Globe* clipping in authors' collection.

28 Rubio and Waterston, eds, *Journals of L.M. Montgomery*, 5:xxi.

29 Helen M. Buss, "Canadian Women's Autobiography in English: An Introductory Guide for Researchers and Teachers," CRIAW *Papers* 24 (1991): 7–8.

30 Marilyn Ferris Motz, "Folk Expressions of Time and Place: Nineteenth-Century Midwestern Rural Diaries," *Journal of American Folklore* 100, no. 396 (April-June 1987): 132–3; Barbara Powell, "Discourse and Decorum: Women's Diaries in Nineteenth-Century Canada," in *Quilting a New Canon: Stitching Women's Worlds*, ed. Uma Parameswaren (Toronto: Sister Vision, 1996), 335 and 341; and Margo Culley, ed., *A Day at a Time: The Diary Literature of American Women from 1764 to the Present* (New York: Feminist Press at CUNY, 1985), 4. For an example of a spiritual diary, see "Eliza Ann Chipman 1807–1853," in *No Place Like Home: Diaries and Letters of Nova Scotia Women 1771–1938*, ed. Margaret Conrad, Toni Laidlaw, and Donna Smyth (Halifax: Formac Publishing, 1988), 81–96.

31 For example, see M.R.P. Foot, ed., *The Gladstone Diaries* (Oxford: Clarendon Press, 1968).

32 Culley in Gwendolyn Davies, "Gendered Responses: The Seccombe Diaries," in *Intimate Relations: Family and Community in Planter Nova Scotia 1759–1800*, ed. Margaret Conrad (Fredericton: Acadiensis Press, 1995), 134.

33 Kathryn Carter, "The Cultural Work of Diaries in Mid-Victorian Britain," *Victorian Review* 23, no. 2 (Winter 1997): 251–67, and Culley, *A Day at a Time*, 3–4.

34 Culley, *A Day at a Time*, 4 and 7.

35 Motz, "Folk Experiences of Time and Place," 131 and 133. For examples of this type of diary writing, see Laurel Thatcher Ulrich, *The Midwife's Tale: The Life of Martha Ballard Based on Her Diary, 1785–1812* (New York: Knopf, 1990), and Kathryn Carter, "'An Economy of Words': Emma Chadwick's Account Book Diary, 1859–60," *Acadiensis* 34, no. 1 (Autumn 1999): 43–56. Elizabeth Mancke has examined account books in "At the Counter of the General Store: Women and the Economy in Eighteenth-Century Horton, Nova Scotia," in Conrad, ed., *Intimate Relations*, 167–81.

36 "Lives Lived: Mary Catherine Redmond," *Globe and Mail*, 11 August 2015.

37 Gidney, "The Dredger's Daughter," 122.

38 Diane P. Koenker, "Scripting the Revolutionary Worker Autobiography: Archetypes, Models, Inventions, and Markets," *International Review of Social History* 49, no. 3 (December 2004): 372.

39 James B. Gardner and George Rollie Adams, eds, *Ordinary People and Every-day Life: Perspectives on the New Social History* (Nashville: American Association for State and Local History, 1983).

40 Danielle Fuller, *Writing the Everyday: Women's Textual Communities in Atlantic Canada* (Montreal and Kingston: McGill-Queen's University Press, 2004).

41 Joanne E. Cooper, "Shaping Meaning: Women's Diaries, Journals and Letters – the Old and the New," *Women's Studies International Forum* 10, no. 1 (1987), 91 and 96, and Joanne Ritchie, "'Cartographies of Silence': An Annotated Bibliography of English Language Diaries and Reminiscences of New Brunswick Women, 1783–1980," *CRIAW Papers* 3 (1997): 14.

42 Valerie Raoul, "Women and Diaries: Gender and Genre," *Mosaic* 22, no. 3 (1989): 61.

43 Rubio and Waterston, eds, *Journals of L.M. Montgomery*, 3:xxiii–xxiv.

44 Harriet Blodgett, "Preserving the Moment in the Diary of Margaret Fontaine," in *Inscribing the Daily: Critical Essays on Women's Diaries*, ed. Suzanne Bunkers and Cynthia A. Huff (Amherst: University of Massachusetts Press, 1996), 167, and Wilson, "The Farm Diary," 167.

45 Cooper, "Shaping Meaning," 95 and 97.

46 Conrad, "Recording Angels," 5.

47 Tanya Schaap, "'Girl Takes Drastic Step': Molly Bobak's W110278 – The Diary of a CWAC," in *Working Memory: Women and Work in World War II*, ed. Marlene Kadar and Jeanne Perreault (Waterloo, ON: Wilfrid Laurier University Press, 2015), 171–2.

48 Rubio and Waterson, eds, *Journals of L.M. Montgomery*, 5:xxi; Rubio and Waterston, eds, *Journals of L.M. Montgomery*, 1:xx; Rubio and Waterston, eds, *Journals of L.M. Montgomery*, 2:xi; and Rubio and Waterston, eds, *Journals of L.M. Montgomery*, 3:xviii.

49 Marlene A. Schiwy, "Taking Things Personally: Women, Journal-Writing, and Self-Creation," *NWSA Journal* 6, no. 2 (Summer 1994): 234 and 236.

50 Margaret E. Turner, "'I mean to try, as far as in me lies, to paint my life and deeds truthfully': Autobiographical Process in the L.M. Montgomery Journals," in *Harvesting Thistles: The Textual Garden of LM. Montgomery*, ed. Mary Henley Rubio (Guelph, ON: Canadian Children's Press, 1994), 98.

51 Gloria Bowles, "Going Back through My Journals: The Unsettled Self, 1961–1986," *NWSA Journal* 6, no. 2 (Summer 1994): 255 and 263; and Buss, "Canadian Women's Autobiography in English," 2.

52 Wilson, "The Farm Diary," 152.

53 Raoul, "Women and Diaries," 58.

54 Ibid.; Carter, "The Cultural Work of Diaries in Mid-Victorian Britain," 251–67; and Margo Culley, "Introduction," *A Day at a Time*, 3–4.

55 Conrad et al., *No Place Like Home*, 3–4. Gwendolyn Davies also notes that diaries allow women to "assert a voice of self-identity." See "'Old Maidism Itself: Spinsterhood in Eighteenth- and Nineteenth-Century Literary and Life-Writing Texts from Maritime Canada," in *Mapping the Margins: The Family and Social Discipline in Canada, 1700–1975*, ed. Nancy Christie and Michael Gauvreau (Montreal and Kingston: McGill-Queen's University Press, 2004), 237.

56 Joanne Ritchie, "'Cartographies of silence': An Annotated Bibliography of English Language Diaries and Reminiscences of New Brunswick Women, 1783–1980," CRIAW *Papers* 3 (1997): 14–16.

57 Conrad, "Recording Angels," 2. Rubio also argues that Montgomery's diaries are a "sample of what repressed, intelligent and silenced women suffered" under patriarchy. See Mary Rubio, "'A Dusting Off': An Anecdotal Account of Editing the L.M. Montgomery Journals," in *Working in Women's Archives: Researching Women's Private Literature and Archival Documents*, ed. Helen M. Buss and Marlene Kadar (Waterloo, ON: Wilfrid Laurier University Press, 2003), 62 and 74.

58 Turner, "I mean to try," 97.

59 Mary McDonald-Rissanen, *In the Interval of the Wave: Prince Edward Island Women's Nineteenth- and Early Twentieth-Century Life Writing* (Montreal and Kingston: McGill-Queen's University Press, 2014), xiii.

60 Raoul, "Women and Diaries," 58–9; and McDonald-Rissanen, *In the Interval of the Wave*, 7–9.

61 Culley as quoted in Gwendolyn Davies, "Gendered Responses: The Seccombe Diaries," in Conrad, ed., *Intimate Relations*, 134.

62 Wilson, "The Farm Diary," 152–3; Carter, "Accounting for Time," 421; Cooper, "Shaping Meaning," 95 and 99; Marilyn Ferris Motz, "Folk Expressions of Time and Place: Nineteenth-Century Midwestern Rural Diaries," *Journal of American Folklore* 100, no. 396 (April-June 1987): 131 and 133; and Carter, "An Economy of Words," 43–56.

63 Carter, "Accounting for Time," 421.

64 For a discussion of "family time" and "women's time," see John Gillis, "Making Time for Family: The Invention of Family Time(s) and the Reinvention of Family History," *Journal of Family History* 21, no. 1 (January 1996): 4–21; Margaret Conrad, "'Sundays Always Make Me Think of Home': Time and Place in Canadian Women's History," in *Rethinking Canada: The Promise of Women's History*, ed. Veronica Strong-Boag and Anita Clair Fellman (Toronto: Copp Clark Pitman, 1986), 67–81.

65 *The Standard Five Year Diary* (Cambridge, 1945).

66 Wilson, "The Farm Diary," 152–3.

67 Carter, "Accounting for Time," 418.

68 Wilson, "The Farm Diary," 158; and Carter "Accounting for Time," 420.

69 Wilson, "The Farm Diary," 152.

70 Ibid., 160.

71 Mancke, "At the Counter of the General Store," 177.

72 Wilson, "The Farm Diary," 155.

73 Huskins and Boudreau, "Daily Allowances," 46.

74 McDonald-Rissanen, *In the Interval of the Wave*, 213.

75 Motz, "Folk Expressions of Time and Place," 131; Cynthia Huff, "Textual Boundaries: Space in Nineteenth-Century Women's Manuscript Diaries," in Bunkers and Huff, *Inscribing the Daily*, 123.

76 "Mile Stones" in *The Standard Five Year Diary* (Cambridge, 1945).

77 Wilson, "The Farm Diary," 162.

78 Huff, "Textual Boundaries," in Bunkers and Huff, *Inscribing the Daily*, 125.

79 Wilson, "The Farm Diary," 162.

80 Martin Hewitt, "Diary, Autobiography, and the Practice of Life History," in *Life Writing and Victorian Culture*, ed. David Amigoni (Ashgate: Aldershot, 2006), 24; and Judy Nolte Lensink, "Expanding the Boundaries of Criticism: The Diary as Female Autobiography," *Women's Studies* 14 (1987): 44.

81 Rubio and Waterston, eds, *Journals of L.M. Montgomery*, 5:xxi.

82 Hewitt, "Diary, Autobiography, and the Practice of Life History," 33.

83 Conrad, "Recording Angels," 4.

84 Rubio and Waterston, eds, *Journals of L.M. Montgomery*, 5:xxi.

85 Ida Martin's Diary, 9 August 1959.

86 Huskins and Boudreau, "Daily Allowances," 89.

87 For example, "Allan started to renail the front of the house. But 2 face came and away they went till?," Ida Martin's Diary, 23 October 1952.

88 Ida Martin's Diary, 1 September, 4 September, and 21 September 1947. Also see 20 January 1967 and 1 March 1983.

89 Ida Martin's Diary, 26 December 1962.

90 Ida Martin's Diary, 29 April 1971.

91 Ida Martin's Diary, 3 June 1959.

92 Ouellette, "Her diaries offer a slice of life."

93 Ritchie, "Cartographies of Silence," 22. Also see Conrad, "Recording Angels," 4; Suzanne Bunkers and Cynthia Huff, "Issues in Studying Women's Diaries," in *Inscribing the Daily*, 11.

94 Wilson, "The Farm Diary," 153.

95 Rubio and Waterston, eds, *Journals of L.M. Montgomery*, 5:xxi. Also see Mary Rubio, "'A Dusting Off,'" in Buss and Kadar, *Working in Women's Archives*, 59.

96 Rebecca Hogan as quoted in Bunkers and Huff, "Issues in Studying Women's Diaries," in *Inscribing the Daily*, 5.

97 Wilson, "The Farm Diary," 153.

98 Hewitt, "Diary, Autobiography, and the Practice of Life History," 24.
99 Back pages of Ida Martin's Diary, 1981–85 volume.
100 Rubio and Waterston, eds, *Journals of L.M. Montgomery*, 2:xx.
101 Sutherland, *Growing Up*, 9–11.
102 Ida Martin's Diary, 26 January 1988. Also see Ritchie, "Cartographies of Silence," 20, and Motz, "Folk Expressions of Time and Place," 139.
103 Rubio and Waterston, eds, *Journals of L.M. Montgomery*, 4:xx; Rubio and Waterston, eds, *Journals of L.M. Montgomery*, 5:xxi; and Laura Higgins, "Snapshot Portraits: Finding L.M. Montgomery in Her 'Dear Den,'" in Rubio, *Harvesting Thistles*, 108.
104 Turner, "I mean to try," 94.
105 Rubio and Waterston, eds, *Journals of L.M. Montgomery*, 1:xxiv; 2:xx; 3:xxiii; and 5:xxii; Turner, "I mean to try," 96.
106 Culley, *A Day at a Time*, 14–16.
107 McDonald-Rissanen, *In the Interval of the Wave*, 83 and 97–9.
108 Raoul, "Women and Diaries," 62.
109 Ida Martin's Diary, 1 January 1967.
110 Ida Martin's Diary, 4 August 1959.
111 Ida Martin's Diary, 2 December 1981.
112 Ida Martin's Diary, 2 October 1948
113 Ida Martin's Diary, 27 November 1985 and 21 January 1963.
114 See Rubio and Waterston, eds, *Journals of L.M. Montgomery*, for details about her being troubled over Ewan and her sons and her own illness (4:xvi–xvii), bouts of depression (5:xiii) and "repulsion" at son Chester's relationship with women (5:xvi). Also see Elizabeth R. Epperly, "Approaching the Montgomery Manuscripts," in Rubio, *Harvesting Thistles*, 80–1.
115 For a discussion of the effects of old age on Montgomery's journals, see Rubio and Waterston, eds, *Journals of L.M. Montgomery*, 4:xvii and xxv, and 5:xxiii and xxvi.
116 Ruth Behar, *The Vulnerable Observer: Anthropology That Breaks Your Heart* (Boston: Beacon Press, 1996).
117 Ibid., 12.
118 Judith A. Cook and Mary Margaret Fonow, "Knowledge and Women's Interests: Issues of Epistomology and Method in Feminist Sociological Research," in *Feminist Research Methods*, ed. Joyce McCarl Nielson (Boulder, CO: Westview Press, 1990), 72.
119 Helen M. Buss, as quoted in *Working in Women's Archives*, ed. Helen M. Buss and Marlene Kadar (Waterloo, ON: Wilfrid Laurier University Press, 2001), 4.
120 Cook and Fonow, "Knowledge and Women's Interests," 76, and Jayati Lal, "Situating Locations: The Politics of Self, Identity, and 'Other' in Living and

Writing the Text," in *Feminist Dilemmas in Fieldwork*, ed. Diane L. Wolf (Boulder, CO: Westview Press, 1996), 207.

121 Suzanne L. Bunkers, "'Faithful Friend': Nineteenth-Century Women's Unpublished Diaries," *Women's Studies International Forum* 10, no. 1 (1987): 15.

122 Helen M. Buss, as quoted in Christl Verduyn, *Marian Engel's Notebooks: 'Ah, mon cahier, écoute* (Waterloo, ON: Wilfrid Laurier University Press, 1999), 5.

123 Hewitt, "Diary, Autobiography, and the Practice of Life History," 21 and 36.

124 Barbara Huskins, email correspondence to authors, 17 January 2004.

125 Susan Engel, as discussed in Jeanne Perreault and Marlene Kadar, "Introduction: Tracing the Autobiographical: Unlikely Documents, Unexpected Places," in *Tracing the Autobiographical*, ed. Marlene Kadar (Waterloo, ON: Wilfrid Laurier University Press, 2005), 6.

126 Carter, "The Cultural Work of Diaries in Mid-Victorian Britain," 251–67.

127 Bonnie Huskins and Michael Boudreau, "Negotiating the Personal: Working with the Diaries of Ida Martin," *Active History*, 25 September 2019, http://activehistory.ca/2019/09/negotiating-the-personal-working-with-the-diaries-of-ida-martin/.

128 Judy Nolte Lensink, "Expanding the Boundaries of Criticism: The Diary as Female Autobiography," *Women's Studies* 14 (1987): 48, and Wilson, "The Farm Diary," 161.

129 Lal, "Situating Locations," 193.

130 The Wolastoq Grand Council has launched a petition to change the name of the Saint John River back to "Wolastoq," its original Indigenous name. www.cbc.ca/news/Canada/new-brunswick/maliseet-river-naming-wolastoq-st-john-pronounciation-1.4150289 (accessed 26 October 2017).

131 John G. Reid, *Six Crucial Decades: Times of Change in the History of the Maritimes* (Halifax: Nimbus Publishing, 1987), 78–84.

132 T.W. Acheson, *Saint John: The Making of a Colonial Urban Community* (Toronto: University of Toronto Press, 1985), and Elizabeth W. McGahan, *The Port of Saint John*, vol. 1: *From Confederation to Nationalization 1867–1927* (Saint John: National Harbours Board, 1982).

133 McGahan, *The Port of Saint John*, 1:237.

134 Frederick William Wallace, *The Romance of a Great Port: The Story of Saint John New Brunswick* (Saint John: The Committee of the Transportation Festival Held on the Occasion of the Jubilee of His Majesty King George V, 1935), HIL-SPECAR; Bill Lovatt, "The Port of Saint John," *Atlantic Advocate* 53, no. 7 (March 1963): 19; Gerald Childs "Fight for the Super-Port: The Saint John Port Controversy," *Atlantic Advocate* 58, no. 7 (March 1968): 12; *National Harbours Board News Bulletin* (November 1961 and November 1962), HIL-GOV; supplement in *Telegraph Journal*, 11 July 2015, upon the announcement of a

$205 million modernization project for the Saint John port; and Alexander C. Pathy, *Waterfront Blues: Labour Strife at the Port of Montreal, 1960–1978* (Toronto: University of Toronto Press, 2004), 4.

135 Carmen Miller, "The 1940s: War and Rehabilitation," in *The Atlantic Provinces in Confederation*, ed. E.R. Forbes and D.A. Muise (Toronto: University of Toronto Press, 1993), 315 and 322, and Margaret Conrad and James Hiller, *Atlantic Canada: A Concise History* (Don Mills, ON: Oxford University Press, 2006), 179.

136 Tamara K. Hareven, *Family Time and Industrial Time: The Relationship between the Family and Work in a New England Industrial Community* (Cambridge: Cambridge University Press, 1982).

137 According to Ida Martin's National Selective Service certificate, dated 2 March 1943, in authors' possession, she was living at 213 Queen Street, Saint John. The population of Saint John grew from 70,927 to 78,337 between 1941 and 1951. Miller, "The 1940s: War and Rehabilitation," 311–16.

CHAPTER ONE

1 Bradbury, "The Home as Workplace," 413. For more on the working-class family economy see Mary Anne Poutanen, "Pigs, Cows, Boarders, and …: Brothels, Taverns, and the Household Economy in Nineteenth-Century Montreal," *Labour/Le Travail* 74 (2014): 276–83; Lara Campbell, *Respectable Citizens: Gender, Family, and Unemployment in Ontario's Great Depression* (Toronto: University of Toronto Press, 2009), 23–56; Bettina Bradbury, *Working Families: Age, Gender and Daily Survival in Industrializing Montreal* (Toronto: McClelland and Stewart, 1993); Suzanne Morton, *Ideal Surroundings: Domestic Life in a Working-Class Suburb in the 1920s* (Toronto: University of Toronto Press, 1995); Denyse Baillargeon, *Making Do: Women, Family and Home in Montreal during the Great Depression* (Waterloo, ON: Wilfrid Laurier University Press, 1999); Nancy M. Forestell, "The Miner's Wife: Working-Class Femininity in a Masculine Context, 1920–1950," in *Gendered Pasts: Historical Essays in Femininity and Masculinity in Canada*, ed. Kathryn MacPherson (Don Mills: Oxford University Press, 1999), 139–57; Derek Johnson, "Merchants, the State and the Household: Continuity and Change in a Twentieth-Century Fishing Village," *Acadiensis* 29, no. 1 (Autumn 1999): 57–75; Larry McCann, "Seasons of Labor: Family, Work, and Land in a Nineteenth-Century Nova Scotia Shipbuilding Community," *History of the Family* 4, no. 4 (1999): 485–528; Rusty Bittermann, "Farm Households and Wage Labour in the Northeastern Maritimes in the Early Nineteenth Century," in *Contested Countryside: Rural Workers and Modern Society in Atlantic Canada, 1800–1950*, ed. Daniel Samson (Fredericton: Acadiensis Press, 1994),

34–69; Steven Maynard "Between Farm and Factory: The Productive Household and the Capitalist Transformation of the Maritime Countryside,
Hopewell, Nova Scotia, 1869–1890," in *Contested Countryside: Rural Workers
and Modern Society in Atlantic Canada, 1800–1950*, ed. Daniel Samson (Fredericton: Acadiensis Press, 1994), 70–104; and Robert McIntosh, "The Family
Economy and Boy Labour in Sydney Mines, 1871–1901," *Nova Scotia Historical Review* 13, no. 2 (1993): 87–100. For a European perspective, see Louise A.
Tilly and Joan W. Scott, *Women, Work and Family* (London: Routledge, 1987).

2   For references on the role of informal economies in Canadian history, see
Rosemary E. Ommer and Nancy J. Turner, "Informal Rural Economies in
History," *Labour/Le Travail* 53 (2004): 127–57, and Catherine Anne Wilson,
"Reciprocal Work Bees and the Meaning of Neighborhood," *Canadian His-
torical Review* 82, no. 3 (September 2001): 431–64. For a concrete description
of the centrality of the informal economy in an eighteenth-century commu-
nity, see Ulrich, *A Midwife's Tale*. Also see Susan Porter Benson, "'What
Goes 'Round Comes Round': Secondhand Clothing, Furniture, and Tools
in Working-Class Lives in the Interwar United States," *Journal of Women's
History* 19, no. 1 (2007): 17–31.

3   Joy Parr, *Domestic Goods: The Material, the Moral, and the Economic in
the Postwar Years* (Toronto: University of Toronto Press, 1999), 78.

4   Conrad and Hiller, *Atlantic Canada*, 209.

5   Miller, "The 1940s: War and Rehabilitation," 315.

6   Conrad and Hiller, *Atlantic Canada*, 58–9.

7   "Public Welfare Services in New Brunswick," *The Report of a Survey Conducted by The Canadian Welfare Council at the Request of the Health Survey
Committee of the Provinces of New Brunswick in 1949*, 24. The 2016 census
indicates that New Brunswick is now at the bottom of the list of median
household incomes in Canada. http://www.cbc.ca/news/Canada/new-
brunswick/new-brunswick-lowest-median-income-1.4287073 (accessed
10 October 2017). By 1955, the per capita income of the Atlantic region was
33 per cent lower than the Canadian average. Conrad and Hiller, *Atlantic
Canada*, 57.

8   *Ninth Census of Canada – 1951, Volume III* (Ottawa: Queen's Printer, 1953),
142-1 and 142-2.

9   Ibid., 26-11, 46-1, 128-5, and 128-6.

10 Conrad and Hiller, *Atlantic Canada*, 59–60.

11 Greg Marquis, "Re-Imag[in]ing the Post-Industrial City: Contemporary
Saint John," paper presented at *Town and Country: Exploring Urban and
Rural Issues in New Brunswick*, St Thomas University, 23 June 2007; Greg
Marquis, "Multilevel Governance and Public Policy in Saint John, New
Brunswick," in *Sites of Governance: Multilevel Governance and Policy Making*

in Canada's Big Cities, ed. Bob Young and Martin Horak (Montreal and Kingston: McGill-Queen's University Press, 2012), 136–61; Greg Marquis, "Regime or Coalition? Power Relations and the Urban Agenda in Saint John, 1950–2000," *Journal of Enterprising Communities: People and Places in Global Economy* 3, no. 4 (2009): 355–68; and Greg Marquis, "Growth Fantasies: Setting the Urban Agenda in Saint John, New Brunswick, 1960–1976," *Acadiensis* 46, no. 1 (Winter/Spring 2017): 122–44.

12 "Saint John: An Industrial City in Transition," http://website.nbm–mnb.ca/transition/english/ (accessed 10 December 2017). This urban renewal plan was somewhat reminiscent of the major building projects that were undertaken in Saint John in the 1920s, including the Saint John Hospital, the Saint John Vocational Institute, and the New Brunswick Museum. Kirk Niergarth, *"The Dignity of Every Human Being": New Brunswick Artists and Canadian Culture between the Great Depression and the Cold War* (Toronto: University of Toronto Press, 2015), 109.

13 Muhammed Arif, "Saint John Regional Plan: Population," Province of New Brunswick Department of Municipal Affairs, 1977, 6, SJRL.

14 Conrad and Hiller, *Atlantic Canada*, 59.

15 Joan Sangster, *Earning Respect: The Lives of Working Women in Small-Town Ontario, 1920–1960* (Toronto: University of Toronto Press, 1995), 113.

16 See Ida Martin's Diaries for 1945–49, 1956–60, and 1961–65.

17 Cynthia Comacchio, *The Dominion of Youth: Adolescence and the Making of Modern Canada, 1920 to 1950* (Waterloo, ON: Wilfrid Laurier University Press, 2006), 11.

18 Sangster, *Earning Respect*, 113.

19 Betsy Beattie, *Obligation and Opportunity: Single Maritime Women in Boston, 1870–1930* (Montreal and Kingston: McGill-Queen's University Press, 2000).

20 "To Ida," 1929, in authors' collection.

21 Suzanne Sutton, *Westfield: A History Told by Residents* (Westfield: McMillan Lingley, 1997); see photo of telephone operators, 42.

22 According to AR's Employee Information Card for the International Longshoremen's Association Local 273, NBMARL, AR began to work regularly at the waterfront on 1 June 1943, although Ida's diaries do not make explicit reference to his work at the port until 28 August 1945: Ida Martin's Diaries, 28 August 1945. In the city directories, AR is reported as a longshoreman from 1955 to 1971: *McAlpine's and Might's Greater Saint John City Directory, 1941–76*, NBMARL. AR filed for a port pension in 1971: Ida Martin's Diaries, 13 April 1971.

23 Ida Martin's Diaries, 4 June 1946.

24 Ida Martin's Diaries, 10 December 1946 and 10 December 1947.

25 Ruth Roach Pierson, *"They're Still Women after All": The Second World War*

and Canadian Womanhood (Toronto: McClelland and Stewart, 1986), and *Ninth Census of Canada – 1951, Volume V* (Ottawa: Queen's Printer, 1953), 3-3 and 3-4.

26 Ida Martin's Diaries, 28 July 1946. "Thumbed way in from Westfield this Am"; 2 August 1946; "work on the 9:15 bus."

27 Ida Martin's Diaries, 21 July 1946.

28 Bradbury "The Home as Workplace," 415, and Baillargeron, *Making Do*, 99.

29 Ida Martin's Diaries, 8 December 1962: "Mr. Beck brot me a dress to fix"; 21 February 1963: "sewed for Mr Beck all afternoon"; 22 February 1963: "fixed drapes"; 13 September 1963: "sewed 5 things for Becks"; 25 September 1963: "sewing for Becks all day."

30 Bradbury, "The Home as Workplace," 448 and 452.

31 Ida Martin's Diaries, 28 September 1959–17 December 1959.

32 *Public Welfare Services in New Brunswick*, 20–2.

33 Ibid., 42.

34 Scrapbook 93 1947a), 51, SJRL.

35 Conrad and Hiller, *Atlantic Canada*, 292–3.

36 L. Richard Lund, "'Fishing for Stamps': The Origins and Development of Unemployment Insurance for Canada's Commercial Fisheries, 1941–71," *Journal of the Canadian Historical Association* 6 (1995): 181.

37 *Public Welfare Services in New Brunswick*, 131–2.

38 References to filing for UI or going to UI office: Ida Martin's Diaries, 19 May 19 1952; 4 June 1952; 21 May 1953; 24 June 24 1953; 15 July 15 1953; 28 October 1953; 29 April 1954; 6 May 1954; 9 May 1955; 9 May 1956; 14 April 1960; 19 April 1961; 11 December 1963; 21 March 1972; 13 December 1972; 11 January 1973; 10 December 1973; L. Richard Lund, "Fishing for Stamps," 181.

39 Johnson, "Merchants, the State and the Household," 57–75.

40 Ommer and Turner, "Informal Rural Economies in History," 22.

41 *Health Care in New Brunswick, 1784–1984* (New Brunswick Department of Health, 1984).

42 For a discussion of old-age security, see James Struthers, "Building a Culture of Retirement: Class, Politics, and Pensions in Post–World War II Ontario," *Journal of The Canadian Historical Association* 8 (1997): 259.

43 Ida Martin's Diaries, 21 January 1947: "1st compensation cheque"; 4 February 1947: "working for first time since hurt"; 28 June 1952: "compensation cheque."

44 Alan Derickson, "Health Security for All? Social Unionism and Universal Health Insurance, 1935–1958," *Journal of American History* 80, no. 4 (March 1994): 1354–5.

45 The authors have in their collection ILA benefit cards that cover the months of 15 March 1954 to 14 March 1955, 15 March 1955 to 14 March 1956, and 15 March 1956 to 14 March 1957.

46 Correspondence from D.W. Quinn, Manager-Secretary of The Shipping Federation of Canada – I.L.A. Maritime Records Bureau, to Mrs. Ida L. Martin, 1 March 1985; correspondence from Dwyer to Martin, 14 April 1987: this letter detailed that "Any surviving spouse of a retired member who deceased after December 31, 1984 will be covered for 60% of the retired member's pension," retroactive from January 1987, in authors' collection.

47 Correspondence from D.M. Dwyer, Manager-Chairman, I.L.A. Trust Funds, re: annual board meeting of Board of Trustees of the Shipping Federation of Canada – I.L.A. Trust Funds, 26–7 April 1989, in authors' collection.

48 Correspondence from D.M. Dwyer, Manager-Chairman, I.L.A. Trust Funds, re: annual board meeting of Board of Trustees of the Shipping Federation of Canada – I.L.A. Trust Funds, 24–5 April 1990. For other increases in the pension, see correspondence from Clark Administrative Consultants, re: annual board meeting of Board of Trustees of the Shipping Federation of Canada-I.L.A. Trust Funds, 16 February and 10–11 July 1995; correspondence from Clark Administrative Consultants, memo to retired pensioners, 11 October 1996; correspondence from Shirley Corkum, Administrator of ILA Pension, Clark Administrative Consultants Ltd., 7 August 1996; correspondence from Clark Administrative Consultants, re: annual board meeting of Board of Trustees of the Shipping Federation of Canada – I.L.A. Trust Funds, 21 February and 29 April 1997, in authors' collection.

49 For loan of $1,420: see Promissory Note issued on behalf of Central Mortgage and Housing Corporation to Mr. and Mrs. Ida Martin, 25 November 1980, Account No. 10-971-869; for loan of $2,555, see Promissory Note from CMHC to Martins, 25 November 1980, Account No. 10-971-851, in authors' collection. Ida also mentions going "to see about CMHC grant" in her diaries, 24–5 November 1980.

50 Correspondence from Debbie Currie, clerk, CMHC to Mr. and Mrs. AR Martin, 22 December 1983, and correspondence from L. Holman, Manager of the Saint John Local Office of the CMHC, to Mrs. Ida Martin, 28 November 1986, in authors' collection.

51 Invoice No. 7301 from Eastern Insulation Co. Ltd, Saint John, 31 January 1981, for insulation, total $2,177 (on the back of this receipt is the phone number of the CHIP and Ida has written "ask for Grant forms for insulation"); Invoice No. 7332 from Eastern Insulation Co. Ltd, Saint John, Feb 26, 1981, for aluminum storm and screen windows, total $1,745; Invoice No. 81-82 from Joseph Dugay and Son Ltd., Saint John, 22 January 1981, for asphalt gravel roof, in authors' collection. Ida also mentions the insulation and roofing in her diaries: 12 November 1980; 15 December 1980; 16 December 1980, 18–19 December 1980; 22 December 1980; and 21 January 1981. Also see John Bacher, "W.C. Clark and the Politics of Canadian Housing Policy," in *Social*

Welfare Policy in Canada: Historical Readings, ed. Raymond B. Blake and Jeff Keshen (Toronto: Copp Clark, 1995), 280–8.

52 Ida Martin's Diaries, 15 July 1970, 28 September 1977.

53 Ida Martin's Diaries, 15 July 1970, 22 September 1970.

54 Bradbury, "The Home as Workplace," 427.

55 Larry McCann, "Living a Double Life: Town and Country in the Industrial-ization of the Maritimes," in *Geographical Perspectives on the Maritime Provinces*, ed. Douglas Day (Halifax: St Mary's University, 1988), 93–113. Ida Martin's Diaries, "lobstering": 2 November 1952, 11 May 1954; "clamming": 27 March 1953; "hunting": 15 October 1953, and 8 October 1956. Berrying was an important part of domestic work. See Forestall, "The Miner's Wife," 151.

56 Bradbury, *Working Families*, and Forestell "The Miner's Wife," 148–50.

57 Meg Luxton, *More Than a Labour of Love: Three Generations of Women's Work in the Home* (Toronto: Women's Press, 1980), 70, and Bradbury, "The Home as Workplace," 417 and 460.

58 Bradbury, "The Home as Workplace," 459 and Forestall, "The Miner's Wife," 146.

59 Bradbury, "The Home as Workplace," 415.

60 "Got AR's license": Ida Martin's Diaries 21 May 1947; 19 January 1949: "payment on truck"; 4 April 1951: "stood in line for truck license"; 13 June 1963: "paid ILA dues"; 29 January 1968: "over to pay ILA dues and Truckers dues." Also see Luxton, *More Than a Labour of Love*, 173, and Forestall, "The Miner's Wife," 150.

61 Metropolitan Life Insurance Company Weekly Premium Receipt Book, Office Address 61 Union Street, Saint John, NB, Agency Number 630, Premium Payer Ida Martin, 213 Queen Street, West Saint John, NB, in authors' collection.

62 Parr, *Domestic Goods*, 113.

63 For a discussion of AR's drinking, see Huskins and Boudreau, "Daily Allowances," 100. For more on these strategies see chapter 5, "Managing and Stretching Wages: The Work of Wives," in Bradbury, *Working Families*, 152–81.

64 The balance would have been more, but Ida took out a sizable withdrawal of over $10,000 in 1974 – The Bank of Nova Scotia passbook, Branch 10314, West Saint John N.B., in authors' collection.

65 See section on "poverty city" in Marquis, "Multilevel Governance and Public Policy in Saint John, New Brunswick," 13–16.

66 Only 540 of these dwellings had owners who had a first mortgage. *Ninth Census of Canada – 1951, Volume III*, 62-1, 66-1, and 70-1.

67 Bradbury, "The Home as Workplace," 422.

68 David Goss, *Saint John Curiosities* (Halifax: Nimbus Publishing, 2008), 196.

69 Parr, *Domestic Goods*, 112.

70 Agreement to purchase 213 Queen Street, signed by AR Martin and Ida N. Martin, 25 November 1948, office of Clinton B. D'Arcy, real estate and fire insurance broker; Assignment of Lease No. 144842 between Reta Pyke and AR R. Martin and Ida L. Martin, 18 February 1949; written receipt from Reta Pike for $41 for "Final Payment and Interest on Queen St. Property," 20 March 1956; Discharge of Mortgage with Clinton B. D'Arcy, 277167, 25 September 1959; Statement of Adjustments between The City of Saint John and AR and Ida L. Martin, 213 Queen Street, West, 29 December 1980; Draft of Indenture between The City and Saint John and AR R. Martin, 10 November 1980; Schedule "A" to a Deed between The City of Saint John and AR R. and Ida L. Martin, in authors' collection.

71 Luxton, *More Than a Labour of Love*, 173 and Forestell, "The Miner's Wife," 151.

72 Ida Martin's Diaries, 21–30 November 1951; 17 December 1951; and 7 June 1952.

73 Ida Martin's Diaries, 4, 7, 15 January 1956; 15 February 1956; 12–14 November 1956; 16 November 1956; 11 December 1956; 16 March 1957; and 3 April 1957. On 8 January 1959, Ida secured Len Byrne a place with Dolly Evans. On 2 June 1959, she sent "Earl R." to the Salvation Army.

74 Ida Martin's Diaries, 13 June 1955: "started to work at London life"; 11 August 1961: "last day of work at London Life."

75 *McAlpine's Greater Saint John Directory*, 1942–46; *Might's Greater Saint John City Directory*, 1947–58, 1960, NBMARL.

76 Ida Martin's Diaries, 29 January 1959.

77 Ida Martin's Diaries: 28 May 1959; 28 January 1960; 22 February 1960; 20 June 1962; 15 August 1963; 7 March 1963; and 31 August 1964.

78 *Might's Greater Saint John and Lancaster City Directory*, 1964, NBMARL.

79 Ida Martin's Diaries, 24 July 1966: "In flat for first time."

80 Traci Friars and Heather Stilwell, "Ida Louise Martin July 18, 1901 – October 11, 2004," funeral eulogy, 13 October 2004, in authors' collection.

81 Traci Friars and Heather Stilwell, "Ida Louise Martin," in authors' collection.

82 Ida Martin's Diaries, 18 July 1956 and 12 November 1978.

83 Ida Martin's Diaries, 27 February 1961 and 11 November 1966.

84 Ida Martin's Diaries, 16 October 1951.

85 Ida Martin's Diaries, 26 June 1962.

86 Ida Martin's Diaries, 1 July 1947. Also, "Mildred's kids": 18 January 1952.

87 Bradbury, "The Home as Workplace," 423.

88 Ida Martin's Diaries, 7 February 1946 and 24 May 1947.

89 Ida Martin's Diaries, 12, 14, 15 October 1946.

90 Ida Martin's Diaries, 27 October 1965.

91 Ida Martin's Diaries, 12 January 1966 and 11 January 1967.

92   Ida Martin's Diaries, 23 October 1963; 26 November 1963; 7 December 1963;
      28 July 1963; 20 April 1964; 19 May 1965; 31 December 1966; 17 March 1969; 23
      May 1969; and 3 September 1969.
93   Ida Martin's Diaries, 15 November 1955; 19 November 1955; and 5 January 1956.
94   Ida Martin's Diaries, 9 January 1971.
95   Ida spent many days at Pat and Arthur's, often staying the night. On 26 Sep-
      tember, Patsy went to the hospital for blood tests. On 15 August 1977, Ida
      went to Pat's where she "washed dishes for 4 days." Arthur doing income tax:
      16 April 1952; 7 April 1953; 27 April 1955; 26 April 1956; 15 April 1971; 19 May
      1972; and 6 April 1977. In 1988, Ida's daughter Barbara did her taxes:
      15 March 1988.
96   Gold Cross Contract Issued to Allan Robert Martin, 213 Queen St. West by
      Memorial Gardens Association (Canada) Limited, Contract No. G-940; Deed
      in Ocean View Memorial Gardens to AR R. Martin and his wife Ida L. Mar-
      tin, Spaces 2–3, Lot 207D, Garden Christus, Deed #2920; letter from George
      Stevens, Manager, Ocean View Memorial Gardens Limited, Saint John, 12
      August 1961; Protection Agreement No. G-940 from Memorial Gardens Asso-
      ciation Limited, 12 August 1961; Gold Cross Certificate No. 39554, Deed No.
      2920, Memorial Gardens Association (Canada) Limited; collection of re-
      ceipts acknowledging payment from AR Martin to Ocean View Memorial
      Gardens Limited, 22 Germain Street, Saint John. The first receipt No. 5883
      dated 12 August 1961 is a down payment of $200.85. The rest are for $10–$20
      instalments and date from 18 September 1961 to 22 April 1966; typed letter
      from Ida L. Martin to Memorial Gardens Association Ltd., Saint John, 4 July
      1966 (original draft of letter is in Barbara's handwriting); letter from Mrs.
      J.N. Fowler, Executive Assistant, Memorial Gardens Association Limited,
      Toronto, 8 July 1966, in authors' collection.
97   Ida Martin's Diaries, 11 September 1948 and 30 March 1951.
98   Ida Martin's Diaries, 10 February 1956, "gave him collection of $66" and 4
      March 1966: "gang boys" brought $68.
99   Ida Martin's Diaries, 17 December 1979.
100 Ida Martin's Diaries, 8 November 1973; 20 December 1973; 11 February 1974;
      and 11 July 1983.
101 Ida Martin's Diaries, 9 November 1980, 9–10 December 1980; 21 May 1981;
      and 1 June 1981.
102 Parr, *Domestic Goods*, 78.
103 Ibid., 240.
104 Ida Martin's Diaries, 24 December 1957.
105 Ida Martin's Diaries, 31 December 1974.
106 Ida Martin's Diaries, 26 March 1977.
107 Ida Martin's Diaries, 2 February 1976.

108 *Ninth Census of Canada – 1951, Volume III*, 99-4 and 99-5, and Parr, *Domestic Goods*, 219.

109 Ida Martin's Diaries, 2 February 1965: "Butch in to take the wringer roller."

110 Ida Martin's Diaries, 27 November 1968 and 22 February 1974.

111 Parr, *Domestic Goods*, 240.

112 *Ninth Census of Canada – 1951, Volume V*, 3-3 and 3-4.

113 Cheryl MacDonald, "Washday: The Weekly Ritual," *The Beaver* 81, no. 4 (August/September 2001), 16 and 21, and Baillargeon, *Making Do*, 127–30.

114 In Luxton's study of the women of Flin Flon, women over forty "ironed everything." Luxton, *More Than a Labour of Love*, 156.

115 Ibid., 155.

116 Baillargeon, *Making Do*, 203.

117 Ibid., 130–2; Luxton, *More Than a Labour of Love*, 119; and Gidney, "The Dredger's Daughter," 143–5.

118 Barbara Huskins email correspondence to authors, 26 January 2004.

119 Baillargeon, *Making Do*, 445.

120 MacDonald "Washday," 16 and 21, and Baillgeron, *Making Do*, 127–30. For a description of the nineteenth-century laundry process, see Christina Bates, "Blue Monday: A Day in the Life of a Washerwoman, 1841 being "A Description of the Tools of Her Trade, and How She Used Them," *Canadian Collector* (July/August 1985): 44–8.

121 Ida Martin's Diaries, 7 April 1972.

122 Gidney, "The Dredger's Daughter," 145.

CHAPTER TWO

1 Christopher Dummit, *The Manly Modern: Masculinity in Postwar Canada* (Vancouver: UBC Press, 2007).

2 For the "masculine strength" of miners, see Nancy M. Forestell, "'And I Feel Like I'm Dying from Mining for Gold': Disability, Gender, and the Mining Community, 1920–1950," *Labor: Studies in Working-Class History of the Americas* 3, no. 3 (2006): 78. For a discussion of male breadwinners, see Bettina Bradbury, *Working Families: Age, Gender, and Daily Survival in Industrializing Montreal* (Toronto: McClelland and Stewart, 1993). For literature on males' recreational culture see Craig Heron, *Lunch-Bucket Lives: Remaking the Workers' City* (Toronto: Between the Lines, 2015), and Mark Rosenfeld, "'It Was a Hard Life': Class and Gender in the Work and Family Rhythms of a Railway Town, 1920–1950," in *Constructing Modern Canada: Readings in Post-Confederation History*, ed. Chad Gaffield (Toronto: Copp Clark Longman, 1994), 329–69. For studies of the masculine culture of drinking, see Craig Heron, "The Boys and Their Booze: Masculinities and Public Drinking

in Working-Class Hamilton, 1890–1946," *Canadian Historical Review* 86
(September 2005): 411–52; Craig Heron, "Boys Will Be Boys: Working-Class
Masculinities in the Age of Mass Production," *International Labor and
Working-Class History* 69 (Spring 2006): 6–34; and Paul Michel Taillon
"'What We Want Is Good, Sober Men': Masculinity, Respectability, and Tem-
perance in the Railroad Brotherhoods, c. 1870–1910," *Journal of Social History*
36 (Winter 2002): 319–38. For a lively analysis of the relationship between
working-class masculinity and sport, notably lob-ball, see Thomas W.
Dunk, *It's a Working Man's Town: Male Working-Class Culture* (Montreal and
Kingston: McGill-Queen's University Press, 2003), 65–100. For more explicit
examinations of male homosocial culture, see Adele Perry, "'Poor Creatures
Are We without Our Wives': White Men and Homosocial Culture," *On the
Edge of Empire* (Toronto: University of Toronto Press, 2001), 20–47 and
208–15; Robert Harney, "Men without Women: Italian Migrants in Canada,
1885–1930," in *A Nation of Immigrants: Women, Workers, and Communities in
Canadian History, 1840s–1960s*, ed. Franca Iacovetta (Toronto: University of
Toronto Press, 1998), 206–30; and Nancy M. Forestell, "Bachelors, Boarding-
Houses, and Blind Pigs: Gender Construction in a Multi-Ethnic Mining
Community, 1909–1920," in ibid., 251–90. For discussions of the relationship
between masculinity and organized labour in the Canadian context, see
Todd McCallum, "'Not a Sex Question?' The One Big Union and the Politics
of Radical Manhood," *Labour/Le Travail* 42 (Fall 1998): 15–54; Mark Leier,
"Portrait of a Labour Spy: The Case of Robert Raglan Gosden, 1882–1961,"
Labour/Le Travail 42 (Fall 1998): 55–84; and Gillian Creese, *Contracting
Masculinity: Gender, Class and Race in a White-Collar Union, 1944–1994* (Don
Mills, ON: Oxford University Press, 1999). For American studies, see Gregory
Wood, "'The Paralysis of the Labor Movement': Masculinity and Unions
in 1920s Detroit," *Michigan Historical Review* 30 (2004): 59–91; and Francis
Shor, "'Virile Syndicalism' in Comparative Perspective: A Gender Analysis
of the IWW in the United States and Australia," *International Labor and
Working-Class History* 56 (Fall 1999): 65–77.
3 Forestell, "And I Feel Like I'm Dying from Mining for Gold," 93.
4 Peter Cole, "Quakertown Blues: Philadelphia's Longshoremen and the Decline of the IWW," *Left History* 8, no. 2 (2003): 39–70; Colin J. Davis, "'Launch
Out into the Deep and Let Down Your Nets': Father John Corridan, S.J., and
New York Longshoremen in the Post–World War II Era," *Catholic History Review* 86, no. 1 (January 2000): 66–85; Colin J. Davis, "New York City and London Dockworkers: A Comparative Perspective of Rank-and-File Movements
in the Post–Second World War Era," *Labour History Review* 65, no. 3 (2000):
295–316; Howard Kimeldorf, "World War II and the Deradicalization of
American Labor: The ILWU as a Deviant Case," *Labor History* 33, no. 2 (1992):

248–78; and Bruce Nelson, "Unions and the Popular Front: The West Coast Waterfront in the 1930s," *International Labor and Working-Class History* 30 (Fall 1986): 59–78.

5 Marc Levinson, *The Box: How the Shipping Container Made the World Smaller and the World Economy Bigger* (Princeton, NJ: Princeton University Press, 2006); John Bellamy Foster, "Two Ages of Waterfront Labour," *Labour/Le Travail* 26 (Fall 1990): 155–63; Pathy, *Waterfront Blues*; William Finlay, *Work on the Waterfront: Worker Power and Technological Change in a West Coast Port* (Philadelphia: Temple University Press, 1988); Bryan O'Neill, *Work and Technological Change: Case Studies of Longshoremen and Postal Workers in St. John's* (St John's: NAFE-TEN DAYS Committee, 1981); Francis Bairstow and Jane von Eicken, eds, *The Dynamics of Change : Labour Relations on the Montreal Waterfront* (Montreal: Industrial Relations Centre, McGill University, 1970); Joseph P. Goldberg, "Containerization as a Force for Change on the Waterfront," *Monthly Labor Review* 91, no. 1 (1968): 8–13; International Labour Conference, *Social Repercussions of New Methods of Cargo Handling (Docks)*, 58th Session (Geneva: International Labour Office, 1972); and Archibald A. Evans, *Technical and Social Changes in the World's Ports* (Geneva: International Labour Office, 1969).

6 Andrew Parnaby, *Citizen Docker: Making a New Deal on the Vancouver Waterfront, 1919–1939* (Toronto: University of Toronto Press, 2008); Andrew Parnaby, "'The best men that ever worked the lumber': Aboriginal Longshoremen on Burrard Inlet, BC, 1863–1939," *Canadian Historical Review* 87 (March 2006): 53–78; Calvin Winslow, ed., *Waterfront Workers: New Perspectives on Race and Class* (Urbana: University of Illinois Press, 1998); Cole, "Quakertown Blues"; Colin J. Davis, "'Shape or Fight'?: New York's Black Longshoremen, 1945–1961," *International Labor and Working-Class History* 62 (Fall 2002): 143–63; Arnold R. Hirsch, "On the Waterfront: Race, Class and Politics in Post-Reconstruction New Orleans," *Journal of Urban History* 21, no. 4 (May 1995): 511–17; Eric Arneson, "Learning the Lessons of Solidarity: Work Rules and Race Relations on the New Orleans Waterfront, 1880–1901," *Labour's Heritage* 1, no. 1 (January 1989): 26–45; and Harvey Schwartz, "A Union Combats Racism: The ILWW's Japanese-American 'Stockton' Incident of 1945," *Southern California Quarterly* 62, no. 2 (1980): 161–76.

7 Employee Information Card, ILA Local 273 Collection, NBMARL. Ida's first diary reference to longshoring is 28 August 1945. According to *McAlpine's* and *Might's Greater Saint John City Directories*, AR was listed as a longshoreman from 1955 to 1971, NBMARL.

8 Mike Landry, "Ties That Bind: The Family Legacy of Longshoremen," *Telegraph-Journal*, 5 October 2016.

9 Goss, *Saint John Curiosities*, 162.

10 Robert H. Babcock, "Saint John Longshoremen during the Rise of Canada's Winter Port, 1895–1922," *Labour/Le Travail* 25 (Spring 1990): 8 and 43; Bonnie Huskins and Michael Boudreau, "'Getting By' in Postwar Saint John: Working-Class Families and New Brunswick's Informal Economy," in *Exploring the Dimensions of Self-Sufficiency for New Brunswick*, ed. Michael Boudreau, Peter G. Toner, and Tony Tremblay (Fredericton: New Brunswick and Atlantic Studies Research and Development Centre, 2009), 77–99.

11 International Labour Organization, Inland Transport Committee, *Decasualization of Dock Labour*, Third Session (Geneva: International Labour Office, 1949), 2–3.

12 Edgar T. Dosman, *Labour Management Relations on the Saint John Waterfront: ILA Local 273 and the Maritime Employers Association*, University of Toronto/York University Joint Program in Transportation, Transportation Paper No. 6 (Canada: National Harbours Board, CMTA and Transport Canada, 1980), 12, HIL-GOV; Evans, *Technical and Social Changes in the World's Ports*, 64; Charles P. Larrowe, *Shape-Up and Hiring Hall: A Comparison of Hiring Methods and Labor Relations on the New York and Seattle Waterfronts* (Westport, CT: Greenwood Press, 1955), 53.

13 Gerald Mars, "Longshore Drinking, Economic Security and Union Politics in Newfoundland," in *Constructive Drinking: Perspectives on Drink from Anthropology*, ed. Mary Douglas (London and New York: Routledge, 2003), 193.

14 Ida Martin's Diaries, 15 December 1952; 12 November 1953; and 10 February 1959.

15 Longshoremen would also obtain their information from bulletin boards at various piers or by checking the newspapers: Larrowe, *Shape-Up and Hiring Hall*, 69.

16 Ibid., 53, and Ida Martin's Diaries, 14 February 1969. On 5 February 1951, a "Frenchman" (an Acadian?) took AR's place on the *Empress of Britain*.

17 Larrowe, *Shape-Up and Hiring Hall*, 52–3, and Patti Breen, *Along the Shore: Saint John Longshoremen 1849 to 1999* (Saint John: New Brunswick Consortium of Writers, 1999), 41.

18 Ida Martin's Diaries, 6 January 1969 and 9 April 1969.

19 The retention of the "shape up" was largely due to the ILA, which saw it as a way to restrict the entry of newcomers and control the workforce: Larrowe, *Shape-Up and Hiring Hall*, 74–5; Winslow, "Introduction," *Waterfront Workers*, 6–7; and Dosman, *Labour Management Relations on the Saint John Waterfront*, 19–20.

20 Ida Martin's Diaries, Cold, 31 January 1951; 13 February 1967; and rain, 29 December 1966.

21 Swan Wooster Engineering Company Ltd, *Saint John Port Development Study*, 128.

22 Ida Martin's Diaries, "AR's license": 21 May 1947; "payment on truck": 19 January 1949; "stood in line for truck license": 4 April 1951; "paid ILA dues": 13 June 1963; "paid ILA and truckers dues": 29 January 1968.

23 Ida Martin's Diaries: 3 February 1959; 18 December 1972; and 4 January 1980.

24 In the minutes of ILA Local 273, a Saint John dock worker defended his outburst on the waterfront by asserting that "he was mad because the Business Agent told him he was Hungry in front of the other men" and "tol[d] him he wanted all the work on the Water-front." The Business Agent seems to have insinuated that the longshoreman was hungry because he was not a good provider, which was an affront to the worker's masculinity: ILA Local 273, Executive Board Minutes, 7 September 1971, 2-F3-39, F28, NBMARL.

25 Deborah Stiles, "Martin Butler, Masculinity, and the North American Sole Leather Tanning Industry: 1871–1889," *Labour/Le Travail* 42 (Fall 1998): 85–114 and Deborah Stiles, "The Gender and Class Dimensions of a Rural Childhood: Martin Butler in New Brunswick, 1857–1871," *Acadiensis* 33, no. 1 (Autumn 2003): 82.

26 Barbara Gilliland, "Fred Haslam's Swimming Exploits and Other Mischief Surprise Daughter," in *West Side Stories: People, History and Local Lore from West Saint John*, ed. David Goss (Halifax: Nimbus Publishing, 2004), 31–4.

27 Babcock, "Saint John Longshoremen during the Rise of Canada's Winter Port," 22, and O'Neill, *Work and Technological Change*, 27.

28 Barbara Huskins, email correspondence to authors, 18 May 2006.

29 Heron, "Boys Will Be Boys," 7.

30 Ida Martin's Diaries, 19 February 1954; Babcock, "Saint John Longshoremen during the Rise of Canada's Winter Port," 19–20.

31 As quoted in Taillon, "'What We Want Is Good, Sober Men,'" 320–1.

32 Rosenfeld, "It Was a Hard Life," 343–5; Heron, "Boys Will Be Boys," 66–7; and Heron, "The Boys and Their Booze," 411.

33 Greg Marquis, "'A Reluctant Concession to Modernity': Alcohol and Modernization in the Maritimes," *Acadiensis* 32, no. 2 (Spring 2003): 44–5. Also see Greg Marquis, "Civilized Drinking: Alcohol and Society in New Brunswick, 1945–1975," *Journal of the Canadian Historical Association* 2 (2000): 173–203. In St John's, Newfoundland, for example, longshoremen did most of their drinking in taverns, where they would discuss workplace issues, notably challenges loading or unloading particular boats or grievances with management or co-workers. Mars, "Longshore Drinking, Economic Security and Union Politics in Newfoundland," 196–7.

34 Ida Martin's Diaries, 10 March 1955; 18 February 1955; and 10 September 1958. Ida used question marks as literary devices to indicate that AR had been drinking. Huskins and Boudreau, "Daily Allowances."

35 Mars, "Longshore Drinking, Economic Security and Union Politics in New-
    foundland," 192.
36 Ida Martin's Diaries, 19 October 1959; 16 May 1958; and 9 September 1960.
37 Marquis, "A Reluctant Concession to Modernity," 46 and 48–9.
38 Rosenfeld, "It Was a Hard Life," 345.
39 Huskins and Boudreau, "Daily Allowances," 97.
40 Ibid., 100.
41 Rosenfeld, "It Was a Hard Life," 345.
42 Heron, "Boys Will Be Boys," 41.
43 Huskins and Boudreau, "Daily Allowances," 100.
44 Ibid.
45 Heron, "Boys Will Be Boys," 68.
46 Ida Martin's Diaries, 13 May 1964; 20 May 1964; 12 September 1964; 12 Janu-
    ary 1965; and 9 August 1965.
47 Babcock, "Saint John Longshoremen during the Rise of Canada's Winter
    Port, 1895–1922," 16–32, and History of Saint John Labor Unions (Saint John:
    Saint John Trades and Labor Council and Subordinate Unions, 1929), 15–46,
    HIL-GOV.
48 Ida Martin's Diaries, 11 March 1968 and 9 March 1970.
49 "Saint John … On the Move: 'A City in Transition,'" Atlantic Advocate 62
    (February 1972): 20. For a photograph of the automobile exports parked at
    the port, see National Harbours Board Bulletin 16 (March 1965), HIL-GOV.
50 S.E. Truman, Unemployment Insurance Commission, to Economics and Re-
    search Branch, Department of Labour, Ottawa, 15 February 1965, in Labour
    Canada, Strike and Lockout Files, RG 27, Vol. 3106, LAC.
51 Truman to Economics and Research Branch, Department of Labour, Ottawa,
    15 February 1965, in Labour Canada RG 27, Vol. 3106, LAC; Evening Times
    Globe 12–13, 15 February 1965, and 1 March 1965; Telegraph Journal, 15 Febru-
    ary 1965; Sudbury Star, 15 February 1965; and Telegraph Journal 13 February
    1965 in Labour Canada, Strike and Lockout Files, RG 27, Vol. 3106 (LAC);
    Labour Gazette 65, no. 4 (April 1965): 389, HIL-GOV.
52 Dosman, Labour Management Relations on the Saint John Waterfront, 10
    and 44.
53 Ryan Stairs, "The Making of a Labour Activist: James W. Orr, Saint John,
    New Brunswick, 1936–2009" (MA thesis, University of New Brunswick, 2014),
    49–52. John Bellamy Foster, "On the Waterfront: Longshoring in Canada," in
    On the Job: Confronting the Labour Process in Canada, ed. Craig Heron and
    Robert Story (Montreal and Kingston: McGill-Queen's University Press,
    1986), 296; and Dosman, Labour Management Relations on the Saint John
    Waterfront, 22. The bwf was a "'flexible and interchangeable' work force,

devoid of any gang structure" and not subject to the same work allocation rules as other longshoremen. Foster, "On the Waterfront," 295.

54 George Vair, *The Struggle against Wage Controls: The Saint John Story, 1975–1976* (St John's: The Canadian Committee on Labour History, 2006); Raymond Léger, "October 14, 1976 – The Saint John General Strike," http://www.wfhathewaylabourexhibitcentre.ca/labour-history/october-14-1976-the-saint-john-general-strike/ (accessed 12 December 2017).

55 Pathy, *Waterfront Blues*, 4; Breen, *Along the Shore*, 40; and Dosman, *Labour Management Relations on the Saint John Waterfront*, 3.

56 *Evening Times Globe*, 11 February 1970. For a discussion of this centralized computer dispatch system, see Foster, "On the Waterfront," 281.

57 Ian McKay, "Socialist Vision and the Realm of Freedom: An Open Letter to Colin McKay," in *For a Working-Class Culture in Canada: A Selection of Colin McKay's Writings on Sociology and Political Economy, 1897–1939* (St John's: Canadian Committee on Labour History, 1996), 502.

58 Taillon, "What We Want Is Good, Sober Men," and Wood "The Paralysis of the Labor Movement," 70.

59 Shor, "'Virile Syndicalism' in Comparative Perspective," 66.

60 Taillon, "What We Want Is Good, Sober Men," 330.

61 Babcock, "Saint John's Longshoremen during the Rise of Canada's Winter Port," 23.

62 *By-Laws of Local No. 273 General Longshore Workers of Saint John New Brunswick Adopted and Effective May 1, 1939*, F85-1 F20, NBMARL.

63 ILA Local 273, Executive Board Minutes, 27 January 1970, 2-F1-6, NBMARL.

64 ILA Local 273, Executive Board Minutes, 27 January 1970, NBMARL.

65 Larrowe, *Shape-Up and Hiring Hall*, 19–41. Colin J. Davis "'All I Got's a Hook': New York Longshoremen and the 1948 Dock Strike," in Winslow, *Waterfront Workers*, 131–54. Labour priests often drew attention to this corruption: see Davis, "Launch Out into the Deep and Let Down Your Nets."

66 Peter S. McInnis, *Harnessing Labour Confrontation: Shaping the Postwar Settlement in Canada, 1943–1950* (Toronto: University of Toronto Press, 2002), 6.

67 ILA Local 273, Executive Board Minutes, 27 January 1970, ILA Box 2-F1-6, NBMARL.

68 Stairs, "The Making of a Labour Activist," 51. Also see Stairs's biography of Jimmy Orr at the Frank and Ella Hatheway Labour Exhibit Centre website: http://www.wfhathewaylabourexhibitcentre.ca/labour-history/lives-lived-jimmy-orr/ (accessed 12 December 2017).

69 Babcock, "Saint John's Longshoremen during the Rise of Canada's Winter Port," 45.

70 Dunk, *It's a Working Man's Town*, 97.

71 Forestell, "And I Feel Like I'm Dying from Mining for Gold," 80.

72 Babcock, "Saint John Longshoremen during the Rise of Canada's Winter Port," 18.
73 Ida Martin's Diaries, 29 January 1952 and 6 January 1969.
74 Breen, *Along the Shore*, 32–3.
75 Ida Martin's Diaries, 14 March 1953.
76 Barbara Huskins, email correspondence to authors, 18 May 2006. For another description of the unloading of grain, see Breen, *Along the Shore*, 34.
77 *Evening Times Globe*, 14 January 1957.
78 International Labour Conference, *Partial Revision of the Conventions concerning the Protection against Accidents of Workers Employed in Loading or Unloading Ships*, Sixteenth Session (Geneva: International Labour Office, 1932); Breen, *Along the Shore*, 39; and Dosman, *Labour Management Relations on the Saint John Waterfront*, 56.
79 Forestell, "'And I Feel Like I'm Dying from Mining for Gold,'" 81.
80 Ida Martin's Diaries, 14 January 1960; 7 November 1951; 3 November 1955; 29 January 1960; 25 March 1960; and 14 March 1969.
81 Ida Martin's Diaries, 12 March 1953; 28 November 1959; 14 February 1960; 26 February 1960; 10 January, 13 January, and 16 January 1952. See obituary and funeral notice for Kenneth Middleton in *Evening Times Globe* 14 January 1952; Middleton also appears in the records of Brenan's Funeral Home, MC 793, PANB. For newspaper stories on the deaths of Edward LeBreton, Addison L. Maxwell, James E. LeClair, and Irvine E. Moore, see *Evening Times Globe* 12 March 1953, 30 November 1959, 15 February 1960, 26 February 1960. Also see information for Irvine E. Moore in Brenan's Funeral Home records, PANB. We are indebted to Harold Wright for sharing his research on these longshoremen. For information on the ILA Local 273 monument, see http://wfhathewaylabourexhibitcentre.ca/photo-galleries (accessed 12 December 2017), and David Frank and Nicole Lang, *Labour Landmarks in New Brunswick / Lieux historiques ouvriers au Nouveau-Brunswick* (St John's: Canadian Committee on Labour History, 2010).
82 Ida Martin's Diaries, 7 January 1947; "back at work": 4 February 1947.
83 Ida Martin's Diaries, 29 February 1947.
84 Ida Martin's Diaries, 18 September 1952; 29–30 December 1955; and "back at work": 26 January 1956.
85 Ida Martin's Diaries, 29 February 1960; 28 December 1961; and 5 April 1969.
86 Breen, *Along the Shore*, 37–9.
87 Barbara Huskins, email correspondence to authors, 18 May 2005.
88 Ida Martin's Diaries, 19 December 1961 and 27 December 1965.
89 Heron, "Boys Will Be Boys," 7, and Wood, "The Paralysis of the Labor Movement," 91.
90 Barbara Huskins, email correspondence to authors, 18 May 2006.

91 Forestell, "And I Feel Like I'm Dying from Mining for Gold," 87.

92 Evans, *Technical and Social Changes in the World's Ports*, 183.

93 Craig Heron and Steve Penfold, *The Workers' Festival: A History of Labour Day in Canada* (Toronto: University of Toronto Press, 2005), 91–105; Wood, *Technical and Social Changes in the World's Ports*, 97; and Forestell, "And I Feel Like I'm Dying from Mining for Gold," 77–8.

94 Heron and Penfold, *The Workers' Festival*, 96.

95 *Ship … Via Saint John New Brunswick … The Port That Puts Performance First!* (Ottawa: National Harbours Board, n.d., HIL-GOV.

96 Stairs, "The Making of a Labour Activist," 58.

97 Bill Lovatt, "The Port of Saint John," *Atlantic Advocate* 53, no. 7 (March 1963): 17, and Breen, *Along the Shore*, 40 and 44.

98 For some of the new tools and technologies, see Breen, *Along the Shore*, 46–7; Pathy, *Waterfront Blues*, 15; and Foster, "On the Waterfront," 291–92.

99 Breen, *Along the Shore*, 23.

100 Greg Marquis, "Rethinking the Militant 70s: Labour-Business Cooperation in Saint John, New Brunswick," paper presented at the Canadian Historical Association, University of Western Ontario, 30 May – 1 June 2005, 14.

101 Special Supplement of *Telegraph Journal* and *Evening Times Globe*, 16 February 1970.

102 Ida Martin's Diaries, 13 April 1971.

103 Heron, "Boys Will Be Boys," 7.

CHAPTER THREE

1 Ben Bradley, *British Columbia by the Road: Car Culture and the Making of a Modern Landscape* (Vancouver: UBC Press, 2017), 8; emphasis in original.

2 David Charters, "It's a Guy Thing: The Canadian Experience of Women in Canadian Sports Car Competitions," *Sport History Review* 37 (2006): 90.

3 Jennifer Elizabeth Berkley "Women at the Motor Wheel: Gender and Car Culture in the USA, 1920–1930" (PhD thesis, Claremont Graduate School, 1996), 5.

4 Ibid.

5 Tamara Gene Myers, *Youth Squad: Policing Children in the Twentieth Century* (Montreal and Kingston: McGill-Queen's University Press, 2019), 136.

6 Doug Owram, *Born at the Right Time: A History of the Baby-Boom Generation* (Toronto: University of Toronto Press, 1996), 70–1, and Myers, *Youth Squad*, 142.

7 Statistics Canada, *Historical Statistics of New Brunswick*, MC80/1078, 191, PANB. Our sincere thanks to Ryan Stairs at PANB for locating these statistics.

8 James J. Flink, *The Car Culture* (Cambridge, MA: MIT Press, 1975), 155.

9 Ida Martin's Diaries, 6 May 1972.
10 Ida Martin's Diaries, 23 January 1961; 18 May 1962; and 17 July 1974.
11 Virginia Scharff, *Taking the Wheel: Women and the Coming of the Motor Age* (New York: Free Press, 1991), 175.
12 Bradley, BC *by the Road*, 3.
13 Ida Martin's Diaries, 29 May 1968; 15 June 1968; and 6 July 1968.
14 Ida Martin's Diaries, 21 April 1974.
15 Flink, *The Car Culture*, 143–4, and Catherine Gudis, *Buyways: Bill Boards, Automobiles, and the American Landscape* (New York: Routledge, 2004), 44.
16 Ida Martin's Diaries, 11 January 1966; 28 April 1972; 28 May 1976; and 12 August 1982.
17 Ida Martin's Diaries, 5 May 1971.
18 *McAlpine's Greater Saint John City Directory 1941–1943*, NBMARL. No employment was listed for AR in the directories between 1944 and 1946.
19 Ida Martin's Diaries, 27 September 1946; 28 May 1947; and 11 September 1951.
20 Ida Martin's Diaries, 27 April 1959; 7 November 1967; 11 November 1970; 1–2 May 1946; and 4 November 1974.
21 Ida Martin's Diaries, 8 August 1960 and 7 August 1967.
22 "50 Years in the Making, RE and JE Friars' Limited," pamphlet (Saint John: RE and JE Friars, 1995), in authors' collection.
23 Scharff, *Taking the Wheel*, 10–13.
24 Ronald Kline and Trevor Pinch, "Users as Agents of Technological Change: The Social Construction of the Automobile in the Rural United States," *Technology and Culture* 37, no. 4 (October 1996): 778–9.
25 Lydia Simmons, "Not from the Back Seat," in *The Automobile and American Culture*, ed. David L. Lewis and Laurence Goldstein (Ann Arbor: University of Michigan Press, 1983), 154.
26 John Steele Gordon, "Engine of Liberation: What You Owe Your Car," *American Heritage* 47, no. 7 (November 1996): 4.
27 Sasha Mullally, "'Daisy,' 'Dodgie' and 'Lady Jane Grey Dart': L.M. Montgomery and the Automobile," in *L.M. Montgomery and Canadian Culture*, ed. Irene Gammel and Elizabeth Epperly (Toronto: University of Toronto Press, 1999), 121–6.
28 Scharff, *Taking the Wheel*, 13.
29 Ibid., 26–30, and Berkeley, "Women at the Motor Wheel," 57.
30 Berkeley, "Women at the Motor Wheel," 17–19.
31 Scharff, *Taking the Wheel*, 136, 142, and 170.
32 Ibid, 52.
33 Dummit, *The Manly Modern*, 127–9.
34 Scharff, *Taking the Wheel*, 119.
35 Ida Martin's Diaries, 20 February 1971.

36 Simmons, "Not from the Back Seat," 154.
37 Ida Martin's Diaries, 2 October 1948.
38 Ida Martin's Diaries, 2 November 1957; 16 November 1951; 29 May 1946; 24 March 1948; and 31 July 1959.
39 Ida Martin's Diaries, 3 February 1954 and 6 October 1960.
40 Dummitt, *The Manly Modern*, 132.
41 Ida Martin's Diaries, 10 December 1973, and "back at work": 6 May 1974.
42 Ida Martin's Diaries, 10 December 1973; 6 May 1974; and 2 October 1974.
43 Archibald A. Wood, *Technical and Social Changes in the World's Ports* (Geneva: International Labour Office, 1969), 117.
44 Ida Martin's Diaries, 1 October 1975; 11 November 1975; 18 December 1975; and 20 December 1976.
45 RS133 Container 38076, D8a Motor Vehicle Branch Records, PANB.
46 Scharff, *Taking the Wheel*, 33
47 Andrew Wernick, *Promotional Culture: Advertising, Ideology, and Symbolic Expression* (London: Sage, 1991), 73.
48 Ida Martin's Diaries, 6 May 1986.
49 Ida Martin's Diaries, 31 July–7 August 1982.
50 Scharff, *Taking the Wheel*, 172.
51 Bradley, *BC by the Road*, 3.

CHAPTER FOUR

1 Magda Fahrni, *Household Politics: Montreal Families and Postwar Reconstruction* (Toronto: University of Toronto Press, 2005), 15. Some of the key works that deal with these themes are: Valerie J. Korinek, *Roughing It in the Suburbs: Reading Chatelaine Magazine in the Fifties and Sixties* (Toronto: University of Toronto Press, 2000); L.B. Kuffert, *A Great Duty: Canadian Responses to Modern Life and Mass Culture, 1939–1967* (Montreal and Kingston: McGill-Queen's University Press, 2003); Peter McInnis, *Harnessing Labour Confrontation: Shaping the Postwar Settlement in Canada, 1943–1950* (Toronto: University of Toronto Press, 2002); Suzanne Morton, *Wisdom, Justice, and Charity: Canadian Social Welfare through the Life of Jane B. Wisdom, 1884–1975* (Toronto: University of Toronto Press, 2014); and Parr, *Domestic Goods*.
2 Cameron Lynne Macdonald and Karen V. Hansen, "Sociability and Gendered Spheres: Visiting Patterns in Nineteenth-Century New England," *Social Science History* 25, no. 4 (Winter 2001): 536. Although this article deals with the nineteenth century, we suggest that the pattern of sociability identified here can also be applied to the postwar period.
3 Ibid., 536.
4 Owram, *Born at the Right Time*, 4.

5   Isabel Campbell, "Exemplary Canadians? How Two Canadian Women Remember Their Roles in a Cold War Military Family," *Journal of the Canadian Historical Association* New Series 27, no. 1 (2016): 63.

6   Marquis, "A Reluctant Concession to Modernity," 38.

7   Ida Martin's Diaries, 18 January 1946; 5 March 1946; 27 April 1946; 4 July 1946; and 9 August 1946. The Maritime Farmers radio program was popular in the Maritimes in the postwar period.

8   Goss, *Saint John Curiosities*, 192–3.

9   Paul Rutherford, *When Television Was Young: Primetime Canada, 1952–1967* (Toronto: University of Toronto Press, 1990), 149.

10 Ida Martin's Diaries, 24 January 1947; 28 September 1946; 4, 19 October 1946; and Goss, *Saint John Curiosities*, 159.

11 Ida Martin's Diaries, 12 November 1951: "anniversary"; at other times they went with friends and family but only on an occasional basis. "Al and Barb to *Gone with the Wind*": 27 August 1954; "Went to Coronet picture with Mrs. McFarlane": 11 June 1953; "To Capitol with Eileen": 20 October 1957; "To Capitol with Vera and Murray": 25 October 1957, 16 July 1955.

12 Campbell, *Respectable Citizens*, 153.

13 Ibid., 155 and 157.

14 Ida Martin's Diaries, 10–25 August 1945.

15 Ida Martin's Diaries: 16 August 1946; 27–31 December 1947; 27 December 1948; 3 January 1949; and 6–10 April 1961.

16 Ida Martin's Diaries, 20 and 28 July 1946.

17 John Webster Grant, *The Church in the Canadian Era* (Burlington: Welch Publishing, 1988), chapters 8 and 9.

18 Catherine Gidney, *A Long Eclipse: The Liberal Protestant Establishment and the Canadian University, 1920–1970* (Montreal and Kingston: McGill-Queen's University Press, 2004), xvii; Tina Block, "'Families That Pray Together, Stay Together': Religion, Gender, and Family in Postwar Victoria, British Columbia," *BC Studies* 145 (Spring 2005): 31–54; and Marguerite Van Die, ed. *Religion and Public Life in Canada: Historical and Comparative Perspectives* (Toronto: University of Toronto Press, 2001).

19 Grant, *The Church in the Canadian Era*, 216.

20 For examples of this approach, see David Hall, ed., *Lived Religion: Toward a History of Practice* (Princeton, NJ: Princeton University Press, 1997), and Margurerite Van Die, *Religion, Family, and Community in Victorian Canada: The Colbys of Carrollcroft* (Montreal and Kingston: McGill-Queen's University Press, 2007).

21 Block, "Families That Pray Together, Stay Together," 34.

22 Gidney, "The Dredger's Daughter," 124.

23 In the Official Notice of Marriage, Sussex, 1895, RS 141B7, no. 001668, PANB,

the officiating clergyman is listed as J.S. Sutherland, who was ordained in Chalmers Presbyterian Church in 1892; see Chalmers Presbyterian Church, MC 1589, PANB. When Ida's brother Aubrey died unexpectedly in 1914, his funeral was held at their home in Millstream, officiated by Rev. Thomas Mitchell, also from Chalmers Presbyterian Church; see obituary for Aubrey A. Friars, newspaper clipping in authors' collection. Rev. Thomas Mitchell was at Chalmers Presbyterian Church from 1911 to 1916; see Grace Aiton, *History of St. Paul's Church, Sussex, N.B.* (Sackville: privately published, 1949), 44, HIL-SPECAR. In the church's record of Aubrey's death, he and his parents are identified as Presbyterians; see Deaths, Chalmers Presbyterian Church, 22 September 1914, No. 28, MC1589, PANB. For references to the interment of Simon Peter and Louisa Maud Friars at Kirk Hill, see John R. Elliott, *Gone but Not Forgotten – Vol 2. Sussex Parish Kings County Cemeteries* (St. John: privately printed, 1992), 186, MC 80/1722, PANB, and obituary for S. Peter Friars in *Kings County Record*, 31 October 1946, 5. Aubrey A. Friars was also buried in Kirk Hill; obituary in authors' collection; Leonard T. Friars and Ora E. Friars in Elliott, *Gone but Not Forgotten*, 186, 206.

24 Baptisms, Chalmers Presbyterian Church, Sussex, 2 June 1908, MC 1589, no. 313, PANB; Certificate of Baptism, 2 June 1908, in authors' collection. The baptism certificate is signed by Rev. Frank Baird, who was inducted in 1901 and remained at Chalmers for ten years; see Aiton, *History of St. Paul's Church, Sussex, N.B.*, 43–4. See also Official Notice of Marriage, Studholm, Kings County, RS 141B7, no. 5463, 1932, PANB; *Kings County Record* 17 November 1932, 5, and "Our Wedding Day" program in authors' collection.

25 Rev. Andrew Donald, who organized a Presbyterian circuit in Kings County in 1844, went on to be a founder of the Free Church Synod in Canada. He was also elected moderator of the Presbyterian Church of Canada; see Aiton, *The History of St. Paul's Church in Sussex N.B.*, 29, 32. Rev. Frank Baird of Chalmers Presbyterian Church also became a moderator in the early twentieth century; see Aiton, *The Story of Sussex and Vicinity*, 92–97.

26 Mullen, "God Is Love."

27 Harry A. Renfree, *Heritage and Horizon: The Baptist Story in Canada* (Mississauga, ON, Canadian Baptist Federation, 1988), 238, and G.A. Rawlyk, *Champions of the Truth: Fundamentalism, Modernism, and the Maritime Baptists* (Montreal and Kingston: McGill-Queen's University Press, 1990), 73.

28 Barry Mack, "Of Canadian Presbyterians and Guardian Angels," in *Amazing Grace: Evangelicalism in Australia, Canada and the United States*, ed. George A. Rawlyk and Mark A. Noll (Montreal and Kingston: McGill-Queen's University Press, 1994), 287.

29 Hannah M. Lane, "Tribalism, Proselytism, and Pluralism: Protestants, Family, and Denominational Identity in Mid-Nineteenth-Century St.

NOTES TO PAGES 82–4   161

Stephen, New Brunswick," in *Households of Faith: Family, Gender, and Community in Canada, 1760–1969*, ed. Nancy Christie (Montreal and Kingston: McGill-Queen's University Press, 2002), 103.

30 Official Notice of Marriage, Sussex, 1895, RS 141B7, no. 001668, PANB.

31 Aiton, *History of St. Paul's Church, Sussex, N.B.*, 36 and 41.

32 Obituary for "Mrs. Peter Friars," *Kings County Record*, 6 April 1939, 4.

33 Lane, "Tribalism, Proselytism, and Pluralism," 104 and 122.

34 Rawlyk, *Champions of the Truth*, 41–2.

35 This union of the sacred and the secular was perhaps best encapsulated in the Social Gospel. Michael Boudreau, "'There is … no pernicious dualism between sacred and secular': Nova Scotia Baptists and the Social Gospel, 1880–1914," *Nova Scotia Historical Review* 16, no. 1 (1996): 109–31.

36 Ida Martin's Diaries, 3 June 1946; 9 July 1946; 3 February 1947; 10 September 1956; 2 June 1958; "devotional at Women's Missionary Society": 3 October 1977; and 9 July 1985.

37 Ida Martin's Diaries, 5–8 September 1978.

38 Ida Martin's Diaries, 8 January 1979: "made a Dominion Life member"; Baptist Missionary Dominion Life Membership card, December 1978; Baptist Missionary Dominion Life Membership pamphlet, in authors' collection.

39 Marks, *Revivals and Roller Rinks*, 52. For a recent study of how Anglican women in Newfoundland combined faith and work to forge an identity, see Bonnie Morgan, *Ordinary Saints: Women, Work, and Faith in Newfoundland* (Montreal and Kingston: McGill-Queen's University Press, 2019).

40 Ida Martin's Diaries, 28 May 1957 and 21 June 1957.

41 Ida Martin's Diaries, 12 June 1977 and 24 February 1980.

42 Ida Martin's Diaries, 21 March 1981 and 26 June 1982.

43 Ida Martin's Diaries, "6 came forward": 21 March 1981; "Roll call 3 went up front": 23 September 1979; "To my own church" and "3 RCs made decision": 14 October 1979; "5 baptized": 13 January 1980; "5 made their commitment": 30 November 1980; "7 baptized": 28 December 1980; "6 baptized couple renewed vows": 31 May 1981; "10 baptized": 11 May 1982; "10 made decision": 21 February 1984; "6 people accepted Christ": 17 February 1985; "a lot of teens made decisions": 20 February 1985; and "20 baptized": 7 April 1985.

44 Ida Martin's Diaries, 20 January 1985.

45 Ida Martin's Diaries, 18 and 25 February 1962: "Sterling baptized" and "Sterling made deacon": 25 January 1966.

46 Ida Martin's Diaries, 11 June 1966.

47 Ida Martin's Diaries, "Took BL to Church": 28 July 1963 and "BL to baby band": 5 June 1965.

48 Ida Martin's Diaries, 3 February 1980.

49 Ida Martin's Diaries: 2–5 and 8–12 July 1957.

50 "Our Baby Band: United Baptist Women's Missionary Union of the Maritimes Provinces," pamphlet, in authors' collection.

51 Ida Martin's Diaries, "missionary meeting": 5 December 1977: "lunch for closing of Mission Band": 24 April 1946; "Carleton Mission Band concert": 6 March 1946, and 15 May 1958. H. Miriam Ross, "Sharing a Vision: Maritime Baptist women educate for Missions, 1870–1920," in *Changing Roles of Women within the Christian Church in Canada*, ed. Elizabeth Gillian, Muir and Marilyn Fardy Whiteley (Toronto: University of Toronto Press, 1995), 77–98.

52 Ida Martin's Diaries, 11 December 1958: "box for shut-ins"; 22 December 1960; 21 December 1961; 23 December 1963; 23 December 1964; 23 December 1965, 22 December 1966; "shopping for poor boxes for church families": 29 November 1965; "box for missionary in India": 22 December 1966; 18 December 1967 and 2 March 1967: "grocery shopping for benevolent fund."

53 Ida Martin's Diaries, 23–24 February 1981 and 3 November 1970.

54 Ida Martin's Diaries, 7 June 1985.

55 Ida Martin's Diaries, 8 October 1946 and 10 October 1946.

56 Ida Martin's Diaries, 28 May 1946; 6 June 1946; 6 June 1947. "Still cooking for baby band": 14 June 1966; "party": 25 September 1968; "party": 18 June 1969 and 16 June 1970.

57 Ida Martin's Diaries, 16 February 1956.

58 Ida Martin's Diaries, "sent missionary parcel to India": 30 December 1981; "missionary meeting": 12 April 1982; and "brought 5 women home": 4 March 1968.

59 Ida Martin's Diaries, 15 April 1962 and 12 December 1978.

60 Ida Martin's Diaries, "joined WCTU in evening": 8 March 1946; and "meeting": 13 March 1946.

61 Ida Martin's Diaries, "president": 25 September 1947.

62 Ida Martin's Diaries, "At Mrs. Todds tonight": 17 May 1946; "Mrs. Henderson's": 14 June 1946; "Mrs. Hargroves": 13 September 1946; "Mrs. Henderson's": 14 June 1946; "Mrs. Hargroves": 13 September 1946; and "Mrs. Fullertons": 11 October 1946.

63 Ida Martin's Diaries, 3 February 1946.

64 Marquis, "A Reluctant Concession to Modernity," 33.

65 Marks, *Revivals and Roller Rinks*, 215.

66 Ida Martin's Diaries, 2 May 1946.

67 Block, "'Families That Pray Together, Stay Together,'" 45–54.

68 Ida Martin's Diaries, 15, 25 November 1962; 9 December 1962; and 30 January 1977.

69 Grant, *The Church in the Canadian Era*, 178.

70 Ida Martin's Diaries, 29 May 1982, and Certificate of Baptism, 29 May 1982, Full Gospel Assembly, Saint John, in authors' collection.

71 Ida Martin's Diaries, 13 August 1979; 8 January 1979; and "healing at Calvary":
    1 April 1973.
72 Ida Martin's Diaries, "many make decision for Christ at Calvary": 12 August
    1973; and "Calvary 20 made decision": 18 February 1979.
73 Ida Martin's Diaries, 26 January 1975; 3 February 1978; and 7 April 1974.
74 Ida Martin's Diaries, Home and School Association: 16 May 1946. Faye
    Somers, *Saint John Vocational School: In Retrospect* (Saint John: Dream
    Catcher Publishing, 2001), 52.
75 Traci Friars and Heather Stilwell, "Ida Louise Martin," in authors' collection.
76 Ida Martin's Diaries, 16 June 1947 and 20 February 1948.
77 Ida Martin's Diaries, "music lessons started": 20 September 1946; "Barbs and
    Anne to see Bud Abbot": 26 January 1946; and "Roller skating ... skinned
    face": 17 September 1946.
78 Owram, *Born at the Right Time*, 43. It is important to note, however, that
    Cynthia Comacchio has argued that by the 1920s "Canadian adolescents were
    spending much of their leisure time ... apart from their families and out of
    the home." Comacchio, *The Dominion of Youth*, 161–2.
79 Ida Martin's Diaries, "Ann's birthday party": 7 February 1946; "Elaine's birth-
    day": 16 March 1946; and "music in morning," "Elva's party in afternoon": 9
    February 1946; and 19 February 1947.
80 Ida Martin's Diaries, "high school graduation": 27 June 1954; and "Vocational
    School": 8 September 1954; "graduation from Voc": 30 June 1955.
81 Comacchio, *The Dominion of Youth*, 161–88 and Ida Martin's Diaries, 31 May
    1958.
82 Mary Louise Adams, *The Trouble with Normal: Postwar Youth and the Making
    of Heterosexuality* (Toronto: University of Toronto Press, 1997), 98–100.
83 Ida Martin's Diaries, 29 April 1958 and 31 May 1957.
84 Ida Martin's Diaries, 28 June 1956.
85 Ida Martin's Diaries, 9 December 1959, and 13, 15 January 1960.
86 Sterling Huskins, "Ida – A Woman above Rubies," eulogy for Ida Martin, in
    authors' collection.
87 Ida Martin's Diaries, 30 June 1961, and "linen shower": 21 June 1961.
88 Ida Martin's Diaries, "display gifts": 13 June 1961.
89 Susan Vincent, "Preserving Domesticity: Reading Tupperware in Women's
    Changing Domestic, Social and Economic Roles," CRSA/RCSA 40, no. 2
    (2003): 179–81.
90 Ida Martin's Diaries, "Barb and Sterling moved from 145 to 213 Queen
    Street": 28 June 1966.
91 James G. Snell, *The Citizen's Wage: The State and the Elderly in Canada, 1900–
    1951* (Toronto: University of Toronto Press, 1996), 20 and 24.
92 Sterling Huskins, "Ida – A Woman above Rubies."

93 Ida Martin's Diaries, 8 March 1977.
94 Mark Novak, *Aging and Society: A Canadian Perspective*, 2nd ed. (Scarborough, ON: Nelson Canada, 1993), 369.
95 Ida Martin's Diaries, 19 June 1971 and 14–24 August 1971.

CHAPTER FIVE

1 Gerald Friesen, *Citizens and Nation: An Essay on History, Communications and Canada* (Toronto: University of Toronto Press, 2000), 224.
2 Korinek, *Roughing It in the Suburbs*, especially chapter 9.
3 Friesen, *Citizens and Nation*, 5.
4 Ida Martin's Diaries, "Jim wounded": marginalia 1945–49 volume; "Jim back home": 8 March 1946; "George discharged": 6 April 1946; "Jim to Halifax, then Saint John": 7 September 1945; "Jim discharged": 7, 13, 15 September 1945; "socials": 25 September 1945, 17 October 1945, 19 December 1947; and "war bonds": 19 September 1951.
5 David Harvey, *The Condition of Postmodernity* (Cambridge, MA: Blackwell, 1990), 61.
6 Conrad and Hiller, *Atlantic Canada*, 383 and 395.
7 Owram, *Born at the Right Time*, 90.
8 Ida Martin's Diaries, "visiting others to watch TV at Robertsons": 29 March 1954, 29 August 1954; "at Scotts": 11 January 1954, 22 October 1954, 31 October 1954, 5 November 1954, 4 December 1954; "at Vera's": 30 October 1954; "at Charlie's": 13 November 1954; and "at Faye's": 5 January 1955, 16 January 1955.
9 Ida Martin's Diaries, "TV furniture table": 9 March 1962; and "TV lamp": 12 November 1955.
10 Ida Martin's Diaries, "bought TV": 5 November 1955; "linked up": 7 November 1955; and "finished payments": 9 April 1956.
11 Owram, *Born at the Right Time*, 89.
12 Ida Martin's Diaries, "new black and white sets": 10 August 1965 and 31 December 1970.
13 Ida Martin's Diaries, "Eileen's colour TV": 29 July 1969; "bought colour TV": 30 November 1972; "good reception": 30 December 1972; and "cable": 20 September 1978.
14 Ida Martin's Diaries, 6 January 1956; 24 September 1965; and 20 July 1973.
15 Owram, *Born at the Right Time*, 96.
16 Ida Martin's Diaries, "Ed Sullivan": 21 May 1967; "Bonanza": 28 January 1968; and "Carol Burnett": 25 March 1978.
17 Ida Martin's Diaries, "Tommy Hunter": 14 January 1985.
18 Rutherford, *When Television Was Young*, 208.

19 Ida Martin's Diaries, "Don Messer": 31 August 1958; 19 August 1960; 10 April 1986; and Rutherford, *When Television Was Young*, 205.

20 Ida Martin's Diaries, "Moncton fellow": 31 January 1958; "Grey Cup": 23 November 1980; "NHL": 18 April 1959; 19 May 1974; 11 May 1976; 5, 29 April 1986; and 3, 16, 20 May 1986.

21 Rutherford, *When Television Was Young*, 164.

22 Friesen, *Citizens and Nation*, 191.

23 Ida Martin's Diaries, "space race": 1 September 1960; 29 August 1965; 20 February 1962; 21 July 1969; 23 July 1969; 1 April 1970; 21 April 1970; 31 January 1971; 6 February 1971; 31 July 1971; 16 April 1972; 22 April 1972; 22 June 1973; 10 April 1981; and 11 April 1981.

24 Bonnie Wagner, "A Form of Insanity: The Impact of Television on Saskatchewan in the 1950s and 1960s," *Prairie Forum* 32, no. 2 (Fall 2007): 386.

25 Ida Martin's Diaries, 4 October 1965; 2 September 1972; 26 March 1979; and back pages of diary 1981–85.

26 Ida Martin's Diaries, 4 April 1968; 20 January 1961; 22 November 1963, 5–6 June 1968; 20 January 1969; 8 August 1974; 28 October 1980; and back pages of diary 1981–85.

27 See the special collection of articles, "Women's Exercise of Political Power: Building Leaderships in Atlantic Canada," in *Atlantis: A Women's Studies Journal* 27, no. 2 (2003): 72–143. Also see Jane Arscott and Linda Trimble, eds, "The Atlantic Provinces," in *In the Presence of Women: Representation in Canadian Governments* (Toronto: Harcourt, Brace, 1997), 254–337. For the involvement of women in municipal politics see Judith Fingard and Janet Guildford, eds, *Mothers of the Municipality: Women, Work, and Social Policy in Post-1945 Halifax* (Toronto: University of Toronto Press, 2005).

28 On the campaign for suffrage and political rights, see Arscott and Trimble, "Atlantic Provinces"; Catherine Cleverdon, *The Woman Suffrage Movement in Canada* (Toronto: University of Toronto Press, 1974); Carol Lee Bacchi, *Liberation Deferred? The Ideas of the English-Canadian Suffragists, 1877–1918* (Toronto: University of Toronto Press, 1983); E.R. Forbes, "The Ideas of Carol Bacchi and the Suffragists of Halifax," *Challenging the Regional Stereotype: Essays on the Twentieth Century Maritimes* (Fredericton: Acadiensis Press, 1989), 90–9; Gail G. Campbell, "The Most Restrictive Franchise in British North America? A Case Study," *Canadian Historical Review* 71, no. 2 (1990): 159–88; and Elsbeth Tulloch, *We, the Undersigned* (Moncton: New Brunswick Advisory Council on the Status of Women, 1985). On informal political activism, see Gail G. Campbell, "Disenfranchised but Not Quiescent: Women Petitioners in New Brunswick in the Mid-Nineteenth-Century," *Acadiensis* 43, no. 2 (Spring 1989): 22–54; Rusty Bittermann, "Women and the Escheat

Movement: The Politics of Everyday Life on Prince Edward Island," in *Separate Spheres: Women's Worlds in the Nineteenth-Century Maritimes*, ed. Janet Guildford and Suzanne Morton (Fredericton: Acadiensis Press, 1994), 23–38; Forbes, "Battles in Another War: Edith Archibald and the Halifax Feminist Movement," *Challenging the Regional Stereotype*, 67–89; and excerpts from Elizabeth W. McGahan, ed., *Whispers from the Past: Selections from the Writings of New Brunswick Women* (Fredericton: Fiddlehead Poetry Books and Goose Lane Editions, 1986). For an anthology that explores the various ways in which women in Atlantic Canada engaged with the state, see Suzanne Morton and Janet Guildford, eds, *Making Up the State: Women in Twentieth-Century Atlantic Canada* (Fredericton: Acadiensis Press, 2010).

29 Don Desserud, "Women in New Brunswick Politics: Waiting for the Third Wave," in Arscott and Trimble, eds, *In the Presence of Women*, 257.
30 Ida Martin's Diaries, 30 October 1972.
31 Ida Martin's Diaries, 22 May 1979 and 19 February 1980.
32 Ida Martin's Diaries, 1 July 1984.
33 Ida Martins Diaries, 25 July 1984 and 21 November 1988.
34 A.S.C. Hampton, "'I Don't Think Canadians Are Going to Sit Still and Let It Happen': The New Brunswick Ad Hoc Committee on the Constitution and Citizens' Response to the Meech Lake Accord" (MA thesis, University of New Brunswick, 2008), 1–2.
35 Ibid., 163.
36 Friesen, *Citizens and Nation*, 222–3.
37 David Thelen, *Becoming Citizens in the Age of Television: How Americans Challenged the Media and Seized Political Initiative during the Iran-Contra Debate* (Chicago: University of Chicago Press, 1996), 8.
38 We have not been able to locate these letters. Sonja Boon has also studied letter-writing campaigns by women in Newfoundland. Sonja Boon, "'I Am Very Badly in Need of Help': Promises and Promissory Notes in Women's Letters to J.R. Smallwood," in *Creating This Place: Women, Family, and Class in St. John's, 1900–1950*, ed. Linda Cullum and Marilyn Porter (Montreal and Kingston: McGill-Queen's University Press, 2014), 221–41.
39 W. Russell Neuman, Marion R. Just, and Ann N. Crigler, *Common Knowledge: News and the Construction of Political Meaning* (Chicago: University of Chicago Press, 1992), 77.
40 Marilyn Ferris Motz, "The Private Alibi: Literacy and Community in the Diaries of Two Nineteenth-Century American Women," in *Inscribing the Daily: Critical Essays on Women's Diaries*, ed. Suzanne Bunkers and Cynthia A. Huff (Amherst: University of Massachusetts, 1996), 144.
41 Paul Delaney, as quoted in Anna Walters, "Self Image and Style: A Discussion Based on Estelle Jelinek's 'The Tradition of Women's Autobiography from

Antiquity to the Present,'" *Women's Studies International Forum* 10, no. 1 (1987): 87.

42 Conrad, "Recording Angels," 2.

43 Campbell, "*I wish to keep a record,*" 265–83.

44 Ida Martin's Diaries, "coronation": 11 June 1953; and "Princess Anne": 14 November 1973.

45 Ida Martin's Diaries, 6 November 1951; 29 July 1959; and 17 June 1983.

46 William Cross and Ian Stewart, "Ethnicity and Accommodation in the New Brunswick Political System," *Journal of Canadian Studies* 36, no. 4 (Winter 2001–2002): 33 and 44.

47 Cross and Stewart, "Ethnicity and Accommodation in the New Brunswick Political System," 43, and Margaret R. Conrad and James K. Hiller, *Atlantic Canada: A History*, 2nd ed. (Don Mills, ON: Oxford University Press, 2010), 225.

48 Ida Martin's Diaries, 23 October 1978.

49 Ida Martin's Diaries, 26 September 1975. For discussion of the Bricklin car, see Conrad and Hiller, *Atlantic Canada*, 198.

50 Ida Martin's Diaries, 13 April 1985.

51 Ida Martin's Diaries, 30 July 1962; 31 October 1966; and 4 January 1974.

52 Ida Martin's Diaries, "Harbour Bridge": 11 June 1967, 17 August 1968: "Mactaquac": 11 September 1966; and "Legere": 24 November 1988.

53 Ida Martin's Diaries, "Vincent": 28 May 1973, 9 May 1976, 5 May 1983; "Friars": 12 May 1980; and "Haslem": 12 May 1980.

54 For more on women's political activism, notably in the Cold War era, see Brian T. Thorn, *From Left to Right: Maternalism and Women's Political Activism in Postwar Canada* (Vancouver: UBC Press, 2016).

55 Motz, "The Private Alibi," 191.

CHAPTER SIX

1 Suzanne Morton, *Ideal Surroundings*, 54.

2 Deborah van den Hoonard, "Identity Foreclosure: Women's Experiences of Widowhood as Expressed in Autobiographical Accounts," *Ageing and Society* 17, no. 5 (September 1997): 549fn3 and 533–5.

3 Anne Martin Matthews, "Support Systems of Widows in Canada," in *Widows: North America, Volume 2*, ed. Helena Znaniecka Lopata (Durham, NC: Duke University Press, 1987), 225.

4 Bettina Bradbury, *Wife to Widow: Lives, Laws, and Politics in Nineteenth-Century Montreal* (Vancouver: UBC Press, 2011), 206.

5 Ida Martin's Diaries, 13 January 1986.

6 Pat Chambers, *Older Widows and the Life Course: Multiple Narratives of Hidden Lives* (Aldershot: Ashgate Publishing, 2005), 6–7.

7 Bradbury, *Working Families*, 184.

8 Matthews, "Support Systems of Widows in Canada," 249.

9 Anne Martin Matthews, *Widowhood in Later Life* (Toronto and Vancouver: Butterworths, 1991), 79.

10 Scotiabank passbook 10314 West Saint John, NB Account No 896527, Sept. 11, 1984 – July 6 1990, in authors' collection.

11 Bradbury, *Wife to Widow*, 23.

12 Ida Martin's Diaries, 2 August 1984; 2 November 1984; and 5 November 1985.

13 Novak, *Aging and Society*, 61.

14 Snell, *The Citizen's Wage*, 9.

15 Scotiabank passbook 10314 West Saint John, NB Account No 896527, July 5, 1996 – Dec 22 1997, in authors' collection. Her account total ranged between $3,000 and $5,000.

16 Matthews, "Support Systems of Widows in Canada," 236, and Ellen M. Gee and Meredith M. Kimball, *Women and Aging* (Toronto: Butterworths, 1987), 59–60.

17 Gee and Kimball, *Women and Aging*, 54. This trend was also evident in the 1960s. A 1965 report by the Dominion Bureau of Statistics found that the average income of elderly women was less than one-half that of elderly men. Moreover, 56 per cent of widowed or single elderly women not in families had annual incomes below $1,000.00. James Struthers, "Grizzled Old Men and Lonely Widows: Constructing the Single Elderly as a Social Problem in Canada's Welfare State, 1945–1967," in *Mapping the Margins: The Family and Social Discipline in Canada, 1700–1975*, ed. Nancy Christie and Michael Gauvreau (Montreal and Kingston: McGill-Queen's University Press, 2004), 367–8.

18 Bradbury, *Wife to Widow*, 202.

19 Ida Martin's Diaries, 14, 16, 18–19, 25, 27 February 1985, and 10–11 March 1985.

20 van den Hoonard, *The Widowed Self*, 27.

21 Correspondence from Dr Darrell C. Pond to Ida Martin, Hillcrest United Baptist Church, Saint John, 11 February 1986, in authors' collection.

22 Ida Martin's Diaries, March and April 1977.

23 Ida Martin's Diaries, 28 June – 27 July 1976 and 31 May – 2 June 1977.

24 Ida Martin's Diaries, "Vera's": 31 May – 1 June 1976; "Flo's": 3 September 1976; 23 February 1977; and "Muriel's": 12–29 January 1976.

25 Snell, *The Citizen's Wage*, 20.

26 Ida Martin's Diaries, "heart spell": 21 February 1979; "to doctor": 7 May 1979; "cardiogram": 8, 11 May 1979; "pains": 27 September 1979; "sick": 29 Oct 1979 and 1–2 November 1979; "a real stress in the chest": 3 November 1979; and "couldn't get breath": 29–30 December 1979.

27 Ida Martin's Diaries, 7–8 May 1979.
28 Ida Martin's Diaries, 27 September 1979; 29 October 1979; and 1–3 November, 29–30 December 1979.
29 Ida Martin's Diaries, 3–4 July; 6–12 July; 12–16 September; 3, 10 November 1981; 21, 25 June; and 18 July 1982.
30 Snell, *The Citizen's Wage*, 7–8.
31 Ida Martin's Diaries, 27 August 1981; 11 July 1982; and 15 September 1982.
32 Ida Martin's Diaries, 7, 11, and 29 October 1983.
33 Ida Martin's Diaries, 5 March 1984.
34 Ida Martin's Diaries, 21 March 1985.
35 Ida Martin's Diaries, 15, 27 February, 11, 17, 21, 26 March, 16 May, and 5 October 1985.
36 Ida Martin's Diaries, 14–15 October 1985.
37 Correspondence from Ida to niece Janet née Friars, ca. October 1985, in authors' collection.
38 William F. Forbes et al., *Institutionalization of the Elderly in Canada* (Toronto: Butterworths, 1987), 11.
39 Friars eulogy, *Kings County Record*, 31 October 1946; guest register for viewing of Peter S. Friars, 29 October 1946, Brennan's Funeral Home, 111 Paradise Row, Saint John, in authors' collection; and Elliott, *Gone but Not Forgotten*, 206.
40 Novak, *Aging and Society*, 9.
41 Helena Znaniecka Lopata, *Current Widowhood: Myths and Realities* (Thousand Oaks, CA: Sage, 1996), 189 and 193; van den Hoonard, *The Widowed Self*, 52; and Snell, *The Citizen's Wage*, 25.
42 Matthews, *Widowhood in Later Life*, 80–1.
43 Correspondence from Ida to niece Janet née Friars, ca. October 1985, in authors' collection.
44 Ida Martin's Diaries, 21 January 1986.
45 Correspondence from W.S. Reid Chedore of Mosher Chedore Barristers and Solicitors, Saint John, to Mr. and Mrs. Sterling Huskins, 6 June 1989, re: Sale of 213 Queen St. West, including Statement of Adjustments, in authors' collection. Ida had granted the deed to the property at 213 Queen Street to Sterling and Barbara as "joint tenants" on 22 October 1986: Registry Office County of Saint John, Deed to 213 Queen Street conveyed to Sterling Dale Huskins and Barbara Ida Huskins, as joint tenants, 22 October 1986, registered as 337057 in book 1209 on 16 April 1987; also includes Affidavit from Ida Martin that she has "personal knowledge of the matters herein deposed to" and that she has no spouse; in authors' collection.
46 Ida Martin's Diaries, 21 November 1986.

47   Matthews, "Support Systems of Widows in Canada," 242; Matthews, *Widowhood in Later Life*, 82; van den Hoonard, *The Widowed Self*, 133; and Bradbury, *Wife to Widow*, 360.

48   For discussion of special care homes, see Forbes et al., *Institutionalization of the Elderly in Canada*, 21.

49   Correspondence from Richard A. Steeves, Assistant Executive Director of Hillcrest Village Inc. to Ida Martin, 7 March 1995, in authors' collection. First entry in Scotiabank passbook noting rent for Hillcrest Village of $300 was 3 December 1985, then monthly; $315 by 10 April 1987; $325 by 8 April 1988; $335 by 4 April 1989; $340 by 2 May 1990: Scotiabank passbook 10314 West Saint John, NB Account No 896527, 11 September 1984–6 1990, in authors' collection. Rent at Hillcrest Village: 2 December 1994: $280; 3 April 1995: $285: Scotiabank passbook 10314 West Saint John, NB Account No 896527, 7 November 1994–3 July 1996, in authors' collection.

50   Susan A McDaniel, "Untangling Love and Domination: Challenges of Home Care for the Elderly in Reconstructing Canada," *Journal of Canadian Studies* 34, no. 2 (Summer 1999): 192.

51   Scotiabank passbook 10314 West Saint John, NB Account No 896527, 7 November 7 1994–3 July 1996, in authors' collection; Scotiabank passbook 10314 West Saint John, NB Account No 896527, 27 March 1999 – 26 May 2000, in authors' collection.

52   Ida Martin's Guest book, in authors' collection.

53   Katie Pickles, "Locating Widows in Mid-Nineteenth Century Pictou County, Nova Scotia," *Journal of Historical Geography* 30, no. 1 (2004): 70.

54   Chambers, *Older Widows and the Life Course*, 31, and van den Hoonard, *The Widowed Self*, 101.

55   Lopata, *Current Widowhood*, 208, and van den Hoonard, *The Widowed Self*, 124, 127–8.

56   Ida Martin's Diaries, 16 February 1989, 1, 22 February 1990; and 24 April 1990.

57   Ida Martin's Diaries, 28 December 1986; 25 August 1987; and 13 July 1989.

58   van den Hoonard, *The Widowed Self*, 133 and Novak, *Aging and Society*, 277.

59   van den Hoonard, *The Widowed Self*, 146.

60   Ida Martin's Diaries 28 January 1989; 6 February 1989; 29 August 1989; and 19 January 1990, 4 March 1990.

61   Matthews, "Support Systems of Widows in Canada," 239; Gee and Kimball, *Women and Aging*, 40.

62   Novak, *Aging and Society*, 361.

63   Ora: newspaper clipping of obituary, in authors' collection; Len: authors' photo of gravestone, in authors' collection; and Elliott, *Gone but Not Forgotten*, 186.

64 Ida Martin's Diaries: 4, 13, 23, 26, 30 June 1978; 5, 7, 10–11, 25, 28 July 1978; 12 August 1978; 23 September 1978; 2, 10 October 1978; and 17, 30 April 1979.

65 Ida Martin's Diaries, 24 October 1983, 4 December 1983; 15–16, 18, 20 January 1984; 11, 13, 16 February 1984; and 5 April 1984; Elliott, *Gone but Not Forgotten*, 99; newspaper clipping of obituary, in authors' collection.

66 Ida Martin's Diaries, 27 June 1985.

67 Ida Martin's Diaries, 4–5 May 1985.

68 Carter, *Diaries in English by Women in Canada, 1753–1995*, 21, and Carter, "The Cultural Work of Diaries in Mid-Victorian Britain."

69 Engel, as discussed in Perreault and Kadar, *Tracing the Autobiographical* 6.

70 Findon, *Seeking Eden*, 15, and Wilson, "The Farm Diary," 166.

71 Ida Martin's Diaries, 20 June 1986.

CONCLUSION

1 Ida Martin's Guest Book, 14 October 2004.

2 Patricia Smart, *Writing Herself into Being: Quebec Women's Autobiographical Writings from Marie de l'Incarnation to Nelly Arcan* (Montreal and Kingston: McGill-Queen's University Press, 2017), 10.

3 An excellent example of examining the social context of a diarist is Daniel Sampson, "'Damn TORYISM say I': Dissent, Print Culture, and Anti-Confederation Thought in James Barry's Diary," *Acadiensis* 46, no. 1 (Winter/ Spring 2017): 177–90.

4 Campbell, *"I wish to keep a record,"* 56.

5 Ibid., 29. Other diary formats are also discussed by Campbell in *"I wish to keep a record."*

Index